AN
INTRODUCTION
TO
ONLINE
SEARCHING

Recent Titles in
Contributions in Librarianship and Information Science
Series Editor: Paul Wasserman

AN INTRODUCTION TO ONLINE SEARCHING

Tze-chung Li

Contributions in Librarianship and Information Science, Number 50

Greenwood Press
Westport, Connecticut • London, England

Library of Congress Cataloging in Publication Data

Li, Tze-chung, 1927-
  An introduction to online searching.

  (Contributions in librarianship and information
science, ISSN 0084-9243 ; no. 50)
  Bibliography: p.
  Includes index.
  1. On-line bibliographic searching. 2. Machine-
readable bibliographic data. 3. Information retrieval.
I. Title. II. Series.
Z699.L473 1985   025.5′24   84-6686
ISBN 0-313-24274-7 (lib. bdg.)

Library of Congress Catalog Card Number: 84-6686
ISBN: 0-313-24274-7
ISSN: 0084-9243

First published in 1985

Greenwood Press
A division of Congressional Information Service, Inc.
88 Post Road West
Westport, Connecticut 06881

Printed in the United States of America

10 9 8 7 6 5 4 3

Copyright Acknowledgments

Grateful acknowledgement is given for permission to reprint the following:

Extracts from Albert Krishmar, "Command language ease of use." 5 Online Review (1981) 227-28.

Extracts from Arlene Somerville's article, "The Pre-search Reference Interview"
published in the February 1982 issue of DATABASE magazine and citation to
articles.

BRS Aid Page for the Education Resources Information Center, BRS, Bryn Mawr,
Pa.

Sample entry from the THESAURUS OF ERIC DESCRIPTORS and listing of
words under the term "safety." Reprinted with the permission of Oryx Press,
2214 N. Central Ave., Phoenix, AZ 85004.

Keyboard layout of Texas Instrument printer terminal. Courtesy of Texas Instruments.

Search results and the first page of the ERIC blue sheet. Reproduced with permission of DIALOG* Information Services, Inc. *Service mark Reg. U.S. Pat. and Trademark Office.

DePaul University Library Computer Index Search Service-Request Form, with the permission of DePaul University Libraries and Computer Search Logbook.

Search examples from Predicasts are used with permission.

Copyright material from the Tandy Corporation used with permission.

Search examples from Information Access Company databases used with permission.

Search examples from INSPEC database used with permission.

ABI/INFORM abstracts reproduced with permission of Data/Courier Inc.

Material from Congressional Information Service used with permission.

Excerpts from sample searches on Dow Jones News/Retrieval ® used with permission.

Screens from CompuServe used with permission.

Search examples from databases from The Source used with permission.

In Memory of My Father,
Ken-hsiang Li, Esq.

Contents

Preface

This book intends to familiarize readers with online searching, stressing bibliographic searching basics. The study consists of two parts. In Part one, readers are introduced to the development of online searching, selected reference sources of which a beginner should be aware, and features of online searching and thesauri. Also in this part, types of databases, database vendors, and library management of online searching services are briefly discussed. Part two, the heart of the book, is devoted to searching basics including three manuals for DIALOG, SDC, and BRS systems with some exposure to DIALOG's Knowledge Index and BRS/After Dark services. Readers are also introduced to CompuServe, The Source, and Dow Jones searching basics and to the use of microcomputers for searching and downloading.

All major vendors have their own searching manuals as well as simplified versions for training beginners. The manuals are compiled in such a way as to reflect a vendor's particular preference and emphasis. It is not easy for a beginner to comprehend the various systems by using manuals which differ in their format, arrangement, and approaches. The three manuals in Part two are compiled and arranged in as consistent a format and approach as possible to facilitate using and comparing the three systems. The step-by-step approach, from simple searching to searching variations to non-subject searching, should be easily understood by readers. Also discussed are searching features and basics of CompuServe, The Source, and Dow Jones services.

The book features searching basics of major vendors of bibliographic services and information utilities. It is of particular use to those who have little or no experience in online searching. Experience in classroom teaching suggests that a reader should be able to grasp the basic searching skills of the three systems after having read the chapters on the searching basics, and having had, with pre-searching preparations, three to four hours of hands-on practice.

One of the problems in using the DIALOG, SDC, and BRS systems is the diversity in searching protocols, commands, and print format options. Even single systems lack standard and consistency in the fields of unit records and print format options. The last chapter presents the problems of diversity in searching and the need for standardization.

I am very grateful to Pauline Angione, Ann Hullihan, and Jean Caldwell and Diane J. Hoffman for the time and effort they expended to read the chapters of basic searching on SDC, DIALOG, and BRS, respectively, and for the valuable suggestions and comments they made. Of course, all the mistakes, if any, in those chapters are mine. Thanks are due to William Brace and Margaret Bush for their review and comments on parts of the work and to Mary R. Sive, Acquisitions Editor at Greenwood Press, for her valuable suggestions on the format and structure of the book. I am also indebted to the students who took or are currently taking my course in Online Searching. Their questions and class discussions contributed greatly to the refinement of the manuals. I wish to express my gratitude to Rosary College Graduate School of Library and Information Science for allowing me to use its facilities and for the free use of connect time, to Joan Bauer and Marge Scanlan for typing a portion of the manuscript, and to Sr. Florus Castle and my daughter, Rose, for their assistance in proofreading.

Grateful acknowledgement is made to the following vendors, producers and publishers, for their permission to cite and to reproduce illustrations from various sources: Bibliographic Retrieval Services, Congressional Information Service, CompuServe, DIALOG Information Services, Dow Jones News/Retrieval, Information Access Company, Data Courier, DePaul University, INSPEC, Online, Online Review, Oryx Press, Predicasts, Radio Shack, System Development Corporation, The Source, and Texas Instruments.

Abbreviations

Note: This list does not include database commands and codes for searching.

AACR2	*Anglo-American Cataloging Rules.* 2nd edition
ACCT	Accounting System (database)
ACS	American Chemical Society
AGRICOLA	AGRICultural On-Line Access (database)
AIM	*Abridged Index Medicus*
ALA	American Library Association
AMI	Advertising and Marketing Intelligence (database)
AMIS	Account Management of Information System
ARIST	*Annual Review of Information Science and Technology*
ARPA	Advanced Research Projects Agency
ASCII	American Standard Code for Information Interchange
BALLOTS	Bibliographic Automation of Large Library Operations Using a Time-Sharing System
BIOSIS	BioSciences Information Service (database)
BKS	Books file in RLIN
BLAISE	British Library Automated Information Service

BPS	Bits per second
BRS	Bibliographic Retrieval Services
BT	Broader term
BULL	BRS/Bulletin (database)
CA	*Chemical Abstracts*
CAB	Commonwealth Agriculture Bureau (database)
CAIN	CAtaloging and INdexing System of the National Agricultural Library (database)
CALS	Computer-Assisted Literature Searching
CASSI	Chemical Abstracts Service Source Index (database)
CBPI	Canadian Business Periodicals Index (database)
CDI	Comprehensive Dissertation Index (database)—now Dissertation Abstracts Online
CHEMNAME	CA Chemical Name Dictionary (database)
CHEMSIS	CHEM Singly Indexed Substances (database)
CIJE	*Current Index to Journals in Education*
CIN	Chemical Industry Notes (database)
CLASS	California Library Authority for Systems and Services (now Cooperative Library Agency for Systems and Services)
CROS	BRS/CROS (database)
CNI	Canadian Newspaper Index (database)
COHD	Copyright Office History Document
COHM	Copyright Office History Monograph
CPS	Characters per second
CR	Carriage Return
CRDS	Chemical Reactions Documentation Service (database)
CRT	Cathode-ray tube
DBI	Data Base Index (database)
DIMDI	Deutsches Institut fer Medizinische Dokumentation und Information
EDP	Electronic data processing
ERIC	Educational Resources Information Center (database)
ESA	European Space Agency
GPO	Government Printing Office
IAC	Information Access Company

ID	Identification
INKA	Information System Karlaruche
INSP	INSPEC (database). See below.
INSPEC	INformation Service in Physics, Electrotechnology and Control (database)
In-WATS	Inward Wide Area Telephone Service
IRCS	International Research Communication Service
IRS	Information Retrieval Services
ISBN	International Standard Book Number
ISI	Institute for Scientific Information
ISO	International Organization for Standardization
ISSN	International Standard Serial Number
LRI	Legal Resource Index (database)
MARC	MAchine Readable Catalogue Project
MDC	Mead Data Central
MEDLARS	Medical Literature Analysis and Retrieval System
MEDLINE	MEDLARS On-Line (database)
METRO	Metropolitan Reference and Research Agency
MI	Magazine Index (database)
MRDF	Machine-readable data files
NAARS	National Automated Accounting Research System (database)
NASA	National Aeronautics and Space Administration
NCJRS	National Criminal Justice Reference Service (database)
NLM	National Library of Medicine
MNI	National Newspaper Index (database)
NT	Narrower term
NTIS	National Technical Information Service (database)
NUC	*National Union Catalog*
NYTIS	The *New York Times* Information Service
OBAR	Ohio Bar
OCLC	Online Computer Library Center
ONTAP	ONline Training And Practice
ORBIT	On-Line Retrieval of Bibliographic Information Timeshared
PAIS	Public Affairs Information Service (database)
PREM	Pre-Med (database)

PsycINFO	Psychological Abstracts Information Service (database)
PTS	Predicasts Terminal System
RAM	Random access memory
RASD	Reference and Adult Service Division
RECON	REmote CONsole
RIE	*Resources in Education*
RLIN	Research Libraries Information Network
RT	Related term
SCORPIO	Subject-Content-Oriented Retriever for Processing Information On-Line
SDC	System Development Corporation
SDI	Selective Dissemination of Information
SN	Scope note
SRIF	School Practices Information File (database)
SSCI	Social Sciences Citation Index (database)
STAIRS	STorage And Information Retrieval System
TI	Trade and Industry Index (database)
TWX	Teletypewriter Exchange Service
UF	Used for
UNISIST	United Nations Information System in Science and Technology
USPSD	United States Political Science Documents (database)
VDT	Visual display terminal
WPI/WPIL	World Patents Index/World Patents Index latest, (database)

Part One

1

Introduction

The term "online searching" refers to the use of a computer to retrieve information online from databases.[1] A database contains machine-readable records for the purpose of information storage and retrieval. A distinction may be made between databases and data banks. Databases are bibliographical. A typical one consists of citations with or without abstracts. Data banks are non-bibliographical. They allow the user to directly retrieve data without using a primary source for further information. The difference between data banks and databases becomes, however, less distinct in practice.

Information in the databases may be retrieved in either batch or online mode. The batch mode, also known as serial or sequential, is the predecessor of online. Data are collected and processed in a particular group or batch. The input data must be sorted and organized serially or sequentially or in some logical order before they can be processed. In contrast, the online mode features direct-access processing with a keyboard connected to the central processor and without the use of media such as punched cards. It is conducted as if the user conversed with the computer. Each takes a turn in conversation. The online processing, therefore, also called conversational or interactive.

Online systems are best suited to applications in which the computer is used to maintain large files of information and to retrieve information interactively from those files in a short period of time through a terminal. Hock elaborates four advantages of online over batch systems:[2] (1) The cost of online retrospective searches in most cases is significantly less than batch searches, (2) The turnaround time of online is shorter than batch, (3) The interactive capability is only available online, (4) The number of online databases has been increasing rapidly.

Online information retrieval services were available to the public around 1970, but the use of the computer to process bibliographical information was initiated much earlier. The *Chemical Abstracts* generates about 400,000 abstracts annually from 12,000 scientific and technical periodicals published in 106 countries, patents issued by 26 countries, and monographs, reports, and proceedings printed elsewhere in the world. For fast dissemination, the Chemical Abstracts Service began a low-cost, computer alert service, *Chemical Titles*, listing the titles of new papers appearing in 650 periodicals.[3] The listing of titles of papers in a periodical often appears before the papers are published. Since 1962, *Chemical Titles* has been issued simultaneously in print and on magnetic tape for computer searching.

In the field of medical sciences, MEDLARS (Medical Literature Analysis and Retrieval System), a computer-based system, began its operation in 1964 with the publication of the first computer-produced *Index Medicus*. For specific information needs that cannot be met by using *Index Medicus*, the user may request a MEDLARS demand search.[4]

In 1968, the State University of New York Biomedical Communication Network began its online service, which is considered to be the first online database vendor.[5] Earlier, in 1967, a study was reported on user reactions to RECON (REmote CONsole), the first large-scale online system, designed by the Lockheed Missiles and Space Company for the National Aeronautics and Space Administration. RECON was later developed by Lockheed to be commercially available in DIALOG.

In 1970, the System Development Corporation initiated for the National Library of Medicine an experiment called AIM-TWX (*Abridged Index Medicus* via the Teletypewriter Exchange Network). AIM-TWX contains bibliographical information for over 100 periodicals in clinical medicine stored in a large, time-shared computer run by SDC. AIM-TWX can be accessed via TWX terminals or teletype terminals connected to the telephone network in about 350 medical libraries throughout the United States and in some foreign countries. With the success of AIM-TWX, MEDLARS went online in October 1971 as MEDLINE (MEDLARS On-Line), with an initial database of over 100,000 citations of all the articles in the top 239 medical journals indexed for MEDLARS since January 1, 1969.[6]

The number of databases has grown rapidly in recent years. The 1982 edition of *Computer-Readable Data Bases*, noted in the next chapter, contains some 290 databases that were not listed in the 1979 edition, reflecting an increase of 55 percent in three years. The 1982 fall issue of *Directory of Online Databases*, also noted in the next chapter, lists over 1,300 databases, up 40 percent from its previous year. The H. W. Wilson Company has developed its retrieval system called the Wilsonline with eight of its indexes available online at present for testing: *Applied Science and Technology Index, Biological and Agricultural Index, Business Periodicals Index, Book Review Digest, Cumulative Book Index, Index to Legal Periodicals, Readers' Guide to Periodical Literature,* and *Social Sciences Index*. A unique feature is multifile searching, that is, databases can be merged into a single file for searching.[7]

Practically any type of information can be stored and searched online. Some yellow pages are accessible via telephones. Users may search with a terminal over 470,000 manufacturing firms compiled from a variety of sources, including 4,800 U.S. telephone directories. A computer-based cattle auction system has been developed by the Texas Agricultural Experiment Station and the Texas Agricultural Extension Service at Texas A & M University.[8] Auctions can be conducted through remote control. In anticipation of increased use of on-line services, Travelhost Communications, Inc., is establishing hotel-room terminals through which a hotel guest may have access to an electronic mail system and to such other information as restaurant guides, computer games, and stock market quotations.[9]

Demands for database services have also increased. It is estimated that there may have been 100,000 people in the country who had used database services in 1970.[10] In 1975 alone, there were 700,000 online retrospective searches performed in the United States and Canada.[11] International Resource Development, a market research firm in Norwalk, Connecticut, predicts that revenues to suppliers and distributors of online databases will reach more than $5.5 billion by 1991.[12]

In the late 1970s and early 1980s, users of online services were primarily from the commercial, university, and federal government sectors.[13] No public libraries and only an insignificant number of junior colleges were using online services. In 1984, online services are available in all sectors of the library world. A survey of attitudes toward automated information retrieval services among members of the Reference and Adult Services Division (RASD), and the American Library Association (ALA), reports that most of them think that academic-research libraries should provide online retrieval services and that most other types of libraries except school and smaller public libraries should also offer such services.[14]

The availability of online retrieval service and its fast growth are due to three technical developments: (1) large-capacity computers with disk storage for time-sharing at a low cost, (2) software for machine-readable databases and interactive capability, and (3) telecommunication to link the terminals of users in many locations with a single computer. Telecommunication is a process by which messages are being sent and received by terminals via a communication channel.[15] The link of the computer through telecommunications is perhaps the most important factor causing the rapid development of online retrieval services.

A computer's speed, storage capacity, greater accuracy, and complex processing make it an ideal tool for information storage and retrieval. An average online search can be completed in fifteen minutes or less over the terminal by an experienced searcher. The operation may involve various strategies from a substantial number of records in different databases. This kind of search can never be performed in minutes manually. All major systems allow the user to search through numerous citations to find out whether or not there are items on the topic and, if so, how many there are and to see some samples. More significantly, the computer's time-sharing capacity permits numerous searchers to have simultaneous access to the database. It is physically impossible for numerous searchers to use one printed product at the same time. In some databases, items are entered before their publication in print sources. The Commerce Business Daily database, for instance, can be searched before the printed version becomes available.

The computer is used to do searching not just for its speed and time-sharing capacity but more importantly for its mechanism for retrieving information. The computer's query language enables the user to communicate with the computer. The user is interactively engaged in direct conversation with the computer. The user receives feedback from which to modify or restructure the strategy, change directions, and refine questions as the search proceeds.[16]

Because of the computer's speed and variety of searching features, online searches are considered less expensive than the manual ones and are, therefore, cost-effective. At the University of Florida, the library saved agricultural researchers alone 172.75 hours per week or 8,983 man-hours per year by making available the National Agricultural Library's CAIN (CAtaloging and INdexing, now AGRICOLA—AGRICultural On-Line Access) online database.[17] At Lockheed, online searches were compared with manual searches by the library staff. The result was that an online search, completed in 45 minutes with an offline print, cost $47.00, while the manual search required 22 hours plus typing, for an average cost of $250.00.[18] At the library of the National Oceanic and Atmosphere Administration's Environmental Research Laboratories in Boulder, Colorado, 160 man-hours were spent on the manual search to retrieve 622 citations on six topics, whereas online searching took only 15 hours to find 2,234 citations on the same six topics.[19] Searching online for titles in the ordering process at Waukegan Public Library was reported to have a substantial saving in staff time.[20]

The Marriott Library, University of Utah, estimated online search and personnel cost at $42.50 for preparing an annual bibliography of Utah geology against $61.04 for the manual search for the same purpose.[21] At Purdue University, online services produced considerable cost benefit because of the value of time saved and the value of that information to the work of the end user.[22] In law, the use of online database services has proven to significantly save time and money.[23]

The manual search must be conducted in a place where indexes and catalogs are located. In online searches, there is no such geographical limitation. Through the use of the terminal via communication networks, the user can have access to millions of records in hundreds of databases that might not be locally available in their printed forms. Houghton and Convey state flatly that geographical location as barriers to the transfer of information is eliminated through online access.[24] Access to the Copyright Card Catalog used to be limited by its geographical location. On October 1, 1982, the catalog was made available online. Registrations and other documents from 1978 onward are now accessible online through COHM (Copyright Office History Monograph) and COHD (Copyright Office History Document), part of the Library of Congress SCORPIO System (Subject-Content-Oriented Retriever for Processing Information Online). Online databases are not merely supplementary tools to existing printed products; they are actually expanding the source materials that are otherwise unavailable.[25] As Wanger and others point out, the most important and perhaps most socially significant benefit of online services is that online capability permits users to establish a literature searching service within their organization.[26]

The manual search is monodimensional by nature. The search is conducted by consulting the printed index and locating the desired entry from the subject headings, one at a time. For instance, the search of PAIS (Public Affairs Information Service) for items on the effect of unemployment in the auto industry on the wages and salaries of automobile workers will find that PAIS provides three significant subject headings, namely, "industry," "unemployment," and "wages and salaries." The user can only search the topics one at a time and from a single point of approach. It is not certain which documents retrieved from three distinct subjects have all subjects in common. On the other hand, online searches available in many systems retrieve materials in a multidimensional approach.[27] The computer matches the subject terms that have been assigned to documents and retrieves only those documents in which a match occurs.[28] The multidimensional approach is possible by using the logical capabilities of the computer, which will be discussed in chapter three.

It may be noted that both OCLC and RLIN are databases that can be accessed online. OCLC (Online Computer Library Center, formerly Ohio College Library Center) was founded in 1967 by the Ohio College Association.[29] The development of OCLC aims at increasing availability of library resources for use of member libraries and reducing per-unit costs. OCLC consists of six sub-systems: (1) Cataloging bibliographic information; (2) Serials Control for check-in, union listing, claiming, and binding; (3) Interlibrary Loan, enabling libraries to request loans from other libraries; (4) Acquisitions for acquisitions and fund status information; (5) Circulation Control planned for loan processing; and (6) Information Retrieval and Subject Access. The information contained in OCLC can be searched by author, title, author-title, and other methods, such as ISBN (International Standard Book Number) and the Library of Congress printed card number. At present, only the first four sub-systems are in operation. Despite the availability of sub-systems, OCLC's principal function has been cataloging, and the emphasis in most libraries is on the use of the system as a cataloging support device.

RLIN (Research Libraries Information Network), formerly called BALLOTS (Bibliographic Automation of Large Library Operations Using a Time-Sharing System), began as a project of automated cataloging at the Stanford University Libraries in 1972. The RLIN database of more than 4 million records composes five subsystems: acquisitions, cataloging, message, print, and tables.[30] In 1981, the RLIN database was reorganized as RLIN II. RLIN II serves four major purposes: (1) bibliographic citations of monographs on the topic, (2) verification, (3) union catalog, and (4) interlibrary loan.[31] One of its features, which is lacking in OCLC, is that all the records in the BKS (books) file are searchable by subject. RLIN II is considered basically a database for cataloging.[32]

In both OCLC and RLIN II, there are limitations in searching. Subject searching is not available in OCLC. Neither system has the capability of coordinating a search. They are primarily cataloging support databases. As such, OCLC and RLIN will not be included for discussion in this book.

NOTES

1. Cf. Donald T. Hawkins and Carolyn P. Brown, "What Is an Online Search? 4 *Online* (1980) 12.

2. Randolph E. Hock, "Providing Access to Externally Available Bibliographic Databases in an Academic Library," 36 *College and Research Libraries* (1975) 210.

3. Cale B. Baker, "Chemical Abstracts Service," 4 *Encyclopedia of Library and Information Science* (1970) 479-80, 491.

4. U.S. Department of HEW, Public Health Service, National Institute of Health, *National Library of Medicine Guide to MEDLARS Service* (Washington, D.C.: Superintendent of Documents, 1970) p. 7.

5. Donna R. Dolan and Michael C. Kremin, "The Quality Control of Search Analysis," 3 *Online* (1979) 8.

6. 58 *Bulletin of the Medical Library Association* (1970) 611-12; 60 *Bulletin of the Medical Library Association* (1972) 336.

7. Martin Kesselman, "Online Update," 58 *Wilson Library Bulletin* (1983) 286-87.

8. 13 *Information Hotline* (1981) 2.

9. 2 *Library Systems Network* (1982) 88.

10. Martha E. Williams, "Data Bases—A History of Developments and Trends from 1966 through 1975," 28 *Journal of the American Society for Information Science* (1977) 71-78.

11. Martha E. Williams, "Criteria for Evaluation and Selection of Data Bases and Data Base Service," 66 *Special Libraries* (1975) 562.

12. 55 *Wilson Library Bulletin* (1981) 652-53.

13. Judith Wanger et al., *Impact of On-line Retrieval Services: A Survey of Users, 1974-1975* (Santa Monica, Calif.: System Development Corporation, 1976) pp. 19-23; Roger K. Summit, "The Challenge Continues," 12 *Chronolog* (1981) 1.

14. Danuta A. Nitechi, "Attitudes towards Automated Information Retrieval Services among RASD Members," 16 *RQ* (1976) 141.

15. Brigitte L. Kenney, "Basics of Telecommunications" in *Telecommunications and Libraries: A Primer for Librarians and Information Managers* (White Plains, N.Y.: Knowledge Industry, 1981) p. 23.

16. Lawrence H. Berul, "Document Retieval," 4 *Annual Review of Information Science and Technology* (1969) 208-9.

17. Ryan E. Hoover, "Patron Appraisal of Computer-Aided Online Bibliographic Retrieval Services," 9 *Journal of Library Automation* (1976) 346-347.

18. Ibid.

19. Ibid.

20. Tina Roose, "Online Database Searching in Smaller Public Libraries," 108 *Library Journal* (1983) 1770.

21. Ryan E. Hoover, "Patron Appraisal," p. 337.

22. Katherine N. Markee, "Economics of Online Retrieval," 5 *Online Review* (1981) 439-44.

23. Francis H. Musselman, "A Boon to Legal Research Computers," 1 *Legal Economics* (1976) 33.

24. Bernard Houghton and John Convey, *On-line Information Retrieval Systems* (Hamden, Conn.: Linnet Books, 1977) p. 44.

25. Ibid.

26. Judith Wanger, *Impact of On-line Retrieval Services,* pp. 208-9.

27. I. A. Warheit, "The Use of Computers in Information Retrieval" in Wesley Simonton, ed., *Information Retrieval Today*, papers presented at the Institute conducted by the Library School and the Center for Continuation Study, University of Minnesota, September 19-22, 1962 University of Minnesota, 1963) p. 64.

28. Allen Kent and Thomas J. Garvin, *The On-Line Revolution in Libraries* (New York: Marcel Dekker, 1978) pp. 5-18.

29. "A Primer on OCLC for all Libraries," 7 *American Libraries* (1976) 258-75; for a brief description of OCLC, see *Bringing Information to People* (Dublin, Ohio: OCLC, 1981).

30. David R. McDonald and Robert Hurowitz, "Research Libraries—Automation and Cooperation," 2 *Perspectives in Computing* (1942) 4-11.

31. Sharon Cline Farmer, "RLIN as a Reference Tool," 6 *Online* (1982) 17.

32. Marydee Ojala, "Using RLIN as a Reference Tool: BALLOTS Revisited," 6 *Online* (1982) 26.

2

Reference Sources On Online Searching

Literature about online searching began to appear in the mid-1960s with rapid growth between 1970 and 1975 and a dramatic increase from 1976 onward. Hall identified 720 titles in the first decade, 1965-1976; and in the next four years, from 1976 to late 1979, about 1,040 titles were listed in Hall's update. Journal articles constitute a large portion of this literature. Over 60 percent were journal articles published between 1976 and 1979.[1] According to Hawkins, articles on online information retrieval were published in some 190 journals, of which 19 were considered productive.[2]

No journal was devoted entirely to online searching until 1977 when *Online: The Management of Online Information Systems* and *Online Review: The International Journal of Online Information Systems* began their publication and, a year later, were joined by *Database: The Magazine of Database and Review*, an *Online* companion. Two monthly newsletters on current information of databases were published in 1983: *Database Update* (April, 1983-   ) by DB Newsletter Associates and *Data Base Alert* (April, 1983-   ) of Knowledge Industry Publications. A subscriber to *Database Update* receives free the publisher's *Guide to Online Databases*. In each issue, a column called Media Scan lists works on online databases. *Data Base Alert* is available for separate subscription or as part of a package deal of the Data

Base User Service. The service provides its subscribers with *Data Base Alert, Database Directory*, ACCESS for online searching on current information, and CALL, the publisher's toll-free hotline for personal assistance and additional information. Readers may also find useful *Information Today: The Newspaper for Users and Producers of Electronic Information Services.* After its premiere issue in November 1983, *Information Today* began publication as a monthly in January 1984. This chapter reviews briefly some major reference sources on online searching services.

GUIDES[3]

Carol H. Fenichel and Thomas H. Hogan, *Online Searching: A Primer*, Marlton, N.J.: Learned Information, 1981, 152p.

J. L. Hall, *On-line Information Retrieval Sourcebook*, London: Aslib, 1977, 267p.

W. M. Henry et al., *Online Searching: An Introduction*, Boston: Butterworths, 1980, 109p.

Ryan E. Hoover, *The Library and Information Manager's Guide to Online Services*, White Plains, N.Y.: Knowledge Industry, 1980, 270p.

Ryan E. Hoover, *Online Search Strategies*, White Plains, N.Y.: Knowledge Industry, 1982, 345p.

Charles T. Meadow and Pauline A. Cochrane, *Basics of Online Searching*, New York: John Wiley, 1981, 245p.

Hall consists of three parts: Part one, "Commentary," deals with the concept of online retrieval and covers online databases, systems, searching, user, cost, training, and some technical aspects of online searching. Part two, "Data Bases and Systems," includes a directory of online databases, a directory of online systems and installation, and a brief description of four systems—BLAISE, DIALOG, ORBIT, and STAIRS—and their use. "Historical Perspective Bibliography and Indexes" constitutes part three. The bibliography stresses publications between 1974 and 1977, listing some 400 items.

The 1980 book edited by Hoover is a collection of twelve articles, which may be grouped into four parts: (1) an overview of online information retrieval and future prospects; (2) directory information, including chapters on types of databases and on producers and vendors of bibliographic online services; (3) management of online service, such as online user groups; and (4) online searching, a brief introduction to the technical aspects of searching with examples of simple searching modes in DIALOG, ORBIT, and BRS. But no explanation of the function of commands is given. The book would have been more useful if the use of controlled vocabulary and the free-text searching, the different results, and the search and default search modes were introduced. Bibliographical references follow each chapter, and at the end are included a selected bibliography and a glossary of online terms.

Fenichel and Hogan's book consists of twelve chapters. The first four provide an overall view of the online industry and three types of organizations, namely, online vendors, database producers, and users. Chapter five deals with searching. The next five chapters discuss equipment, the reference process, costs and charging policies, management aspects, and training. In the last two chapters, non-bibliographic databases and prospects for the future are briefly mentioned. The book also includes a glossary, a bibliography, and five appendixes: (1) selected large databases, (2) selected vendors, (3) professional associations, (4) selected consultants, brokers, networks, and (5) selected terminal manufacturers.

As compared with Hoover, Fenichel and Hogan's book features separate chapters on terminal equipment and non-bibliographic databases and is strong in directory information, but the book is much more concise than the former. In some aspects, clarity is sacrificed for brevity. Examples in DIALOG searching, for instance, are too brief to be comprehended by a beginner. Another flaw is that works cited in the text are often not listed in the references.

Meadow and Cochrane, and Henry are two books that stress the concept, principles, and techniques of online searching. The book by Meadow and Cochrane consists of twelve chapters with a substantial portion as appendixes. The first four chapters present the concept of searching, elements of interactive searching, the pre-search interview, and the terminals and networks. The remaining chapters deal with search mechanics and search strategy of the DIALOG, ORBIT, and BRS systems. Aspects of searching procedures are well presented with illustrations. Of particular usefulness to searching are three chapters: chapter seven on basic commands with a clear explanation of the use of Boolean logic; chapter eight on text searching, fraction of word searching, and the use of logical operators, such as (W) in DIALOG and ADJ in BRS; and chapter nine on beginning and ending a search. A beginner will find useful the tips on using terminals and the explanation of key functions of terminal switches. Since the book stresses searching basics, little effort has been made to explain the management aspects of online service.

Meadow and Cochrane's book is not intended as a substitute for search manuals. As indicated in its preface, the purpose of the book is "to teach principles, not the detailed mechanics of any particular search system." Within this context, the book is well presented. Its appendixes constitute 40 percent of the book. Two of the three appendixes are simple reproductions of DIALOG's publications.

Henry et al. has a similar purpose but differs from Meadow and Cochrane in that the book discusses the management aspects of online service and training of online searching, and it covers European database vendors, such as BLAISE and Euronet. The book gives a general review of online searching and discusses equipment, data structure, search facilities, search techniques, role of intermediary, data management, and education and training. Like Meadow and Cochrane, Henry includes a large body of appendixes, such as a checklist for search preparation and search strategy—a useful guide for beginners—and six vendors—BLAISE, ESA-IRS, Infoline, Lockheed, SDC, and Euronet. For each vendor, except Euronet, the authors provide searchable fields, databases, and a summary of commands. The brochure of the Euronet Launch Team of the Commission of the European Communities is reproduced as one of the appendixes.

An experienced searcher may refer to Hoover's other book

(1982), a collection of ten articles on search strategies in various disciplines, such as government, bioscience, social and behavioral sciences, patents, law, health sciences, and news. Each article describes fairly well the coverage and features of databases in the discipline, followed by search examples. The book also contains "Directory of Selected Data Base Producers and Online Service" and a short bibliography of some seventy items.

BIBLIOGRAPHIES

Some of the guides just mentioned contain valuable bibliographies. Current bibliographies were published as part of Byerly (see Dictionaries) and in *Library Journal*[4] and in *Online Searching Technique and Management*.[5] The following are bibliographies on online searching published as monographs:

J. L. Hall, *On-line Information Retrieval, 1965-1976*, London: Aslib, 1977, 125p.

J. L. Hall and A. Dewe, *Online Information Retrieval, 1976-1979: An International Bibliography*, London: Aslib, 1980, 250p.

Donald T. Hawkins, *Online Information Retrieval Bibliography, 1965-1979*, New York: Learned Information, 1980, 174p. Updated by *Online Review*.

Hall (1977) is both a directory and a bibliography. It consists of four parts: databases, systems/installation, bibliography, and indexes. The bibliography is an unannotated listing of 720 items published from 1965 to the summer of 1976. Hall and Dewe (1980) is a continuation of the former. It includes bibliographies only, being an annotated listing of 890 items with a supplement, without annotations, of about 150 items published between July 1979 and late 1979. Three indexes are given: (1) a personal author index, (2) a report number index, and (3) a general index to subject/topic terms and other entries.

Hawkins, first published in 1977 as a supplement to the first issue of *Online Review*, lists 1,784 items grouped into seven categories: (1) books, reviews, conferences; (2) descriptions of online systems, databases, and services; (3) man-machine studies, the user interface and attitudes, system design and evaluation; (4) profile development, searching techniques, indexing; (5) usage studies, economics, promotion and impact, management; (6) user education and training; and (7) general, miscellaneous. It ends with a permuted title index and an author index. The bibliography is updated annually in *Online Review*. The latest was published in 1983.[6]

BIBLIOGRAPHICAL REVIEWS

One of the important bibliographical reviews is the *Annual Review of Information Science and Technology* (ARIST). The annual, a project since 1966 of the American Documentation Institute, now the American Society for Information Science, gives wide coverage to the communication process, "providing ideas, trends, and references to the literature of the information science field" (purpose). Its first review of databases was published in 1969.[7] *Database*, noted earlier, is devoted to reviewing databases, a must for in-depth reviews of online retrieval services. Both *Online* and *Online Review* have published reviews of databases frequently.

In 1981, the Outstanding Reference Sources Committee of RASD, ALA, was replaced by a new standing committee, the Reference Sources Committee, with responsibility to review both print and non-print sources. As a result, reviews of databases were published for the first time in volume 20, number 4 of *RQ* in 1981.[8] *Reference Service Review* began to publish a new column of "Reference Data Bases" in 1982. Also a new column on databases has appeared since the February 1983 issue of *Library Journal*.

DICTIONARIES

Greg Byerly, *Online Searching: A Dictionary and Bibliographic Guide*, Littleton, Colo.: Libraries Unlimited, 1983, 288p.

The book contains over 1,200 terms in the dictionary and 722 annotated journal articles in the bibliography. The terms are primarily those used in three commercial search services, that is, BRS, DIALOG, and SDC. Its inclusion of terms is substantial. There are, however, omissions, such as Control D, FILE (DIALOG command), UP and DOWN (SDC commands), and

BRS/After Dark, just to name a few. Journal articles are grouped into two parts. Part one consists of 32 sections providing a general overview of online searching. Part two in 13 sections by disciplines is for the experienced searcher. The bibliography also includes "Sources of Additional Information" listing 27 books, directories, bibliographies, proceedings, annuals, and journals, some with annotations.

DIRECTORIES

Marvin C. Gechman's listing of databases released in 1972[9] is perhaps the first directory of its kind. Other directories of databases were compiled by John H. Schneider[10] and Roger Christian.[11] Since 1977, *Online Review* has published, as its regular feature, a directory of databases. All these directories were published as parts of larger works. Below are some of the directories published as monographs or monographic serials:

Directory of Online Databases, Santa Monica, Calif.: Cuadra Associates, 1979– , quarterly.
Directory of Online Information Resources, 10th ed., Rockville, Md.: CGS Press, 1982, 150p.
James L. Hall and Marjorie J. Brown, *Online Bibliographic Databases: An International Directory*, 2d ed., London: Aslib, 1981, 213p.
John Schmittroth, Jr., and Doris Morris Maxfield, *Online Database Search Services Directory*, 1st ed., Detroit: Gale Research, 1983, 572p. (part one of two parts).
Martha E. Williams, *Computer-Readable Data Bases: A Directory and Data Sourcebook*, White Plains, N.Y.: Knowledge Industry, 1982, 1472p.

Directory of Online Databases, updated quarterly with a complete reissue every six months, is the most current directory. For each database, descriptions include the name of the database producer, the online service organization(s) through which it is available, the type and amount of information contained in the database, correspondence with printed products, geographical and chronological coverage, and frequency of updating. Both bibliographic and non-bibliographic databases are included.

Directory of Online Information Resources, updated three times a year, provides in three columns concise information on databases. The first column lists database names, with cross-references interfiled. A brief note on the subject content of the file, its correspondence with printed indexes, and producers for each database are given in the second column. The third column gives coverage, file size, unit record, and supplier(s).

Hall and Brown's *Online Bibliographic Databases* includes 189 bibliographic databases produced throughout the world. For each database, information includes database name or acronym, supplier, printed version, subject field, file details, online service supplier(s), typical access charge(s), and documentation available. The section of online file details includes time span, total citation, update, and typical update and indicates whether the database contains abstracts and keywords. One feature of the directory is its introduction to databases with statistical profiles of the online database repertory, such as the growth in total number of references available online, knowledge fields covered by online databases, and provenance of database suppliers.

Computer-Readable Data Bases, first published in a loose-leaf format in 1976 under the title, *Computer-Readable Bibliograhic Data Bases,* lists more than 700 databases both bibliographic and non-bibliographic as reflected by the current title which dropped the word "bibliographic." Data entries contain eight major groups of information: (1) basic information, (2) producer/distributor/-generator of information, (3) availability and charges for acquisition of database tape (or other media), (4) subject matter and scope of data in database, (5) subject analysis/indexing data, (6) data elements, (7) database services offered, and (8) user aids available. It has four indexes: producer, processor, name/acronym/synonym, and subject.

Different from directories mentioned before, the work by Schmittroth and Maxfield covers only search services available to outside users by "public, academic, and special libraries, private information firms, and other organizations in the United States and Canada" (introduction). This is part one of two parts listing 634 institutions that offer online database search services. Descriptions for each entry include organization name, address, telephone number, staff, key contact, number of staff, search activity, online systems accessed, subject area, search frequency, fee policy, search personnel, and search procedure. Since information was collected from questionnaires that were not all returned, its coverage is far from complete. Part two, scheduled for publication in summer 1984, is expected to have a substantially large number of entries. There are six indexes: (1) Organizations, (2) Organizations by Online Systems Accessed, (3) Organizations by Databases Searched, including a "Cross-Index of Database Names and Acronyms," (4) Organizations by Subject Areas Searched, (5) Search Personnel, and (6) Geographic.

In addition, there are directories that, though not devoted exclusively to databases and database services, contain substantial information on them. Two directories may be mentioned.

Information Industry Market Place: An International Directory of Information Products and Services [IIMP], New York: Bowker, 1981– .

Anthony T. Kruzas and John Schmittroth, Jr., *Encyclopedia of Information Systems and Services*, 4th ed., Detroit: Gale Research, 1981, 973p.

IIMP, also published under the title *Information Trade Directory* outside North and South America by Learned Information, lists information products and services grouped into seven major sections, and eighteen sub-sections. The major sections include, for example, information production, information distribution, information retailing, association, and government agencies. Descriptions vary but in general include subject coverage, currency, access method, and scope of services. Its first sub-section, "Information Publishers," lists publisher, subject coverage, training and user aids, machine-readable database, and print products.

Kruzas and Schmittroth is a guide to 2,030 information systems and services of over 50 countries, arranged by parent organization in a single alphabet. It includes "computer-readable data bases, data base producer and publishers, online vendors and time-sharing companies, telecommunication networks, video/ teletext systems, information retrieval software . . . " (title page). Compared with its third edition, the number of listings is less, yet it includes nearly 700 new operations. Each organization is listed in up to seventeen categories of information, including name, founding date, head of unit, staff, related organizations, description of system or service, scope and/or subject matter, input sources, holdings and storage media, and publications. For information systems and services of a particular category, such as "computer-readable data bases," reference must be made to indexes. There are twenty-two indexes of which eighteen are related to the categories. Other non-category indexes are combined index to organizations, systems, and services; personal name index; geographic index; and subject index. The combined index is particularly useful for locating information on sub-divisions of parent organizations.

HANDBOOKS

Bill Katz and Anne Clifford, *Reference and Online Service Handbook: Guidelines, Policies, and Procedures for Libraries*, New York: Neal-Schuman, 1982, 581p.

This is a collection of guidelines, policies, and procedures in the day-to-day operations of reference services from fifty-three academic libraries, thirty-three public libraries, and some special libraries. Authors are devoted to reference service primarily with very little coverage of online services. According to the authors, there is a lack of formal online policy. Online statements in the book are mostly made up of directories, memorandums, and other forms from a combination of forty academic, public, and special libraries. A twelve-page manual for online services from the University of Houston is printed at the end of the book.

MANUALS

Manuals for use of products and systems are made available by the vendors and producers. Vendors' manuals are intended for general discussion and familiarity with the systems as a whole and are not for a particular database. As features of databases vary, the user should consult, in addition to manuals, the description of each database which is, in general, published separately from manuals. Manuals prepared by BRS, DIALOG, and SDC will be discussed in part two of this book. Listed below are two manuals for the major vendors.

Ching-chih Chen and Sussana Schweizer, *Online Bibliographic*

Searching: A Learning Manual, New York: Neal-Schuman, 1981, 227p.

Roger C. Palmer, *Online Reference and Information Retrieval,* Littleton, Colo.: Libraries Unlimited, 1983, 149p.

Chen is "a beginner's guide to the skills necessary for the retrieval of information from computerized bibliographic files, with special emphasis on techniques of online information searching" (preface).[12] It consists of seven chapters dealing with the concept, searching techniques, vendors, and management. Each chapter lists references for further reading. All three major vendors, that is, DIALOG, SDC's ORBIT, and BRS are introduced, but the searching technique is demonstrated using DIALOG primarily. The DIALOG searching technique is presented in some detail in chapters two, four, and five, with an appendix, "Answers to Online Exercises of DIALOG Lab Workbook." Some aspects are well treated, such as the difference between the use of controlled vocabularies and searching of terms limited by /DE and /DF in DIALOG. The use of examples of a simple search, followed by explanation of functions of different commands in DIALOG, is a good approach. The book also gives a concise comparison of features of the three systems.

Palmer is designed as a text for online searching with a good portion of it on searching basics. It consists of three parts. Part one is an overview dealing with databases and inverted files. The structure of inverted files, and the process of retrieving information are well presented. Nearly half of the book is devoted to part two, an introduction to basic searching in SDC, DIALOG, and BRS, with class and/or lab assignments for each chapter. Stress is placed on SDC. The part would have been more useful if detailed searching basics, particularly in the DIALOG and BRS systems, were included. Part three briefly discusses the client interview, the term project, and trends and issues in online searching.

USER AIDS

Most database producers provide user aids. According to Un-ruh, as of 1979, 62 percent of for-profit databases, 37 percent of the non-profit databases, and 31 percent of the government databases provide search aids (materials indicating database coverage, editorial policy, search hints, and so forth).[13] Most of the databases now have search aids, though the degree of their treatment varies. A listing of user aids included in the *Guide to DIALOG Searching* mentioned in part two of this book, though limited in number, is a useful tool for finding search aids. The user aid listed here is a convenient, quick reference to search features of databases in DIALOG, SDC, and BRS.

Sharon Cline Farmer, *Quick-Search: Cross-System Database Search Guides*, San Jose, Calif.: California Library Authority for Systems and Services, 1980, loose-leaf.

Quick-Search consists of charts for selective databases—one chart for each database. The guide, designed for use by an experienced searcher, provides ready reference to the input formats of the most commonly used fields across each system offering access to that file (preface). Each chart lists subject approach and other access points of BRS, DIALOG, and SDC systems in three columns.

NOTES

1. J. L. Hall and A. Dewe, *Online Information Retrieval 1976-1979: An International Bibliography* (London: Aslib, 1980) pp. 8, 12.

2. Donald T. Hawkins, "Bibliometrics of the Online Information Retrieval Literature," 2 *Online Review* (1978) 345-59.

3. *See also* Tze-chung Li, "Recent Books on Online Database Searching: A Review," 8 *Journal of Library and Information Science* (1982) 245-51.

4. Carol Tenopir, "Databases: Catching Up and Keeping Up," 108 *Library Journal* (1983) 180-82.

5. Emelie J. Shroder, "Online Reference Service: How to Begin" and RASD-MARS Committee on Measurement and Evaluation of Service, comp., "The Evaluation of Information Retrieval Services: A Selected Bibliography" in James J. Maloney, ed., *Online Searching Technique and Management* (Chicago, Ill.: American Library Association, 1983) pp. 181-91.

6. Donald T. Hawkins, "Online Information Retrieval Bibliography," 7 *Online Review* (1983) 127-87.

7. Lawrence H. Berul, "Document Retrieval," 4 *Annual Review of Information Science and Technology* (&1969) 203-77.

8. Janet Sheets and Deborah C. Masters, "The RASD Outstanding Reference Source Committee: Retrospect and Prospect," 20 *RQ* (1981) 360.

9. Marvin C. Gechman, "Machine-Readable Bibliographic Data Bases," 7 *Annual Review of Information Science and Technology* (1972) 327-78.

10. John H. Schneider et al., *Survey of Commerically Available Computer-Readable Bibliographic Data Bases* (Washington, D.C.: American Society for Information Science, 1973) p. 181.

11. Roger W. Christian, *The Electronic Library: Bibliographic Data Bases, 1975-1976* (White Plains, N.Y.: Knowledge Industry, 1975) pp. 90-118.

12. *See also* Tze-chung Li, "Recent Books."

13. Betty Unruh, "Database User Aids and Materials—A Study," 5 *Online Review* (1981) 12.

3

The Free-Text Searching and the Thesaurus

The conventional approach for information on a topic is to search the index terms or subject headings. A subject heading is characterized by its uniformity and specificity. For the sake of specificity, subject headings once chosen must be adhered to, and an item should be entered under the most specific subject headings. Choosing a particular term or phrase as a subject heading suggests the following:

1. Not every term or phrase is used as a subject heading, only the term or phrase that best expresses the subject of a work is chosen.

2. Accordingly, the term or phrase that is chosen disregards the author's choice of term or phrase.

3. Synonyms or near synonyms of the chosen term or phrase are not used. In *Sears List of Subject Headings*, the word "disarmament" is chosen over seven other words or phrases, such as "armament," "arms control," and "atomic weapons and disarmament." Again, "audio-visual materials" is preferred as a subject heading to "multi-media materials" and "nonprint materials."

4. Only the spelling of the chosen term is used, such as "color," if it is a chosen term, not "colour."

5. Either the singular or the plural, or in some cases both, of the chosen is used.

To insure specificity, subject headings may be subdivided by variant aspects. In the *Library of Congress Subject Headings*, topic, place, period, and form are used for sub-divisions. The relationship of chosen terms or phrases to their variant spelling, synonyms or near synonyms, or related terms or phrases is indicated by either scope notes or cross-references. Scope notes are used to specify the range of subject headings. In cross-references, *see* references refer to terms used, whereas *see also* references link different yet related subject headings and indicate a hierarchical structure among terms.

But the use of subject headings requires knowledge of the chosen terms. The searcher must use the correct term and spelling. As indicated, color cannot be replaced by colour. Not everyone can use the subject headings with ease.

A different approach is the natural language or free-text searching, that is, any term in the text can be searched as a subject. In free-text searching, terms searched as subjects need not be uniform; neither do they call for specificity. The searcher can use any term from the text as a search clue. There are, however, problems.

First, the term or terms retrieved do not necessarily relate to the content of a document. The free-text searching will miss documents whose contents are described by terms other than those searched, such as synonyms, related terms, and abbreviations. Second, it may retrieve irrelevant documents described by the terms, which may not be meant for their subject contents. Third, searching for a broad term, such as "vehicle," may not retrieve its specific terms, such as "automobile" and "truck."

The most serious drawback of free-text searching is the difficulty of coordinating terms to retrieve documents described by such terms. In free-text searching, the single-term approach is most specific in retrieving documents that contain the term. If a document's topic is represented by more than one term, the search of multiterms does pose a problem. The searcher has to scan a large number of documents retrieved separately from each term and then find documents on the topic represented by different terms.

The development of the uniterm system provided a mechanism by which to coordinate multiple terms, thus facilitating the otherwise cumbersome searching. The uniterm system features inverted file arrangement and post-coordinating capability.[1]

The inverted file is different from the conventional approach such as the library card catalog in which each document is assigned index terms. Instead of having one card per document, the uniterm system uses one term as a subject heading per card, which records a number of documents within the subject. It has two identifications: (1) descriptor identification, that is, subject heading, and (2) document identification, that is, document identified by, for instance, a number. In the uniterm system, the card is divided into ten columns, indicated by the last digit 0 through 9. As the documents are indexed, instead of filing each card per document behind a subject heading, the number of documents is recorded in the appropriate column on the card. The number of documents is entered on as many uniterm cards as is desired.

Documents are recorded by their numbers under each subject. For example, the searcher finds under the subject "automobile" are listed documents 20, 310, 11, 117, and others. The searcher may also find out how many documents there are dealing with the topic "import of automobiles from Japan" by scanning through the numbers of documents listed under three terms, namely, "automobile," "import," and "Japan." Assuming document 117 is listed under all three terms, it is the one looked for. The coordination of different terms to generate the topic "import of automobiles from Japan" is another feature of the uniterm system.

In coordinating, the searcher compares terms, coordinates or combines them, and generates new terms. Indexing may be either pre-coordinate or post-coordinate. In a pre-coordinating index, terms are compared and combined at the time of indexing. It is predetermined and is used in the conventional subject headings. For the topic "libraries in Cook County, Illinois" the *Library of Congress Subject Headings* assigns it the subject heading "Libraries-Illinois-Cook County." The subject heading is pre-coordinated. It may achieve the purpose of directness and specificity, yet its main problem lies in its inflexibility in the degree of coordination.

In a post-coordinating index, terms can be compared and combined to create a desired search mode. If has two obvious advantages. First, the order of terms is insignificant. Second, combination of terms is flexible; it can result in any desired search subjects. In the example, "Libraries-Illinois-Cook County," the terms "libraries," "Illinois," and "Cook County" can be searched and combined in any one of the following sequences:

Libraries-Cook County-Illinois
Libraries-Illinois-Cook County
Illinois-Libraries-Cook County
Illinois-Cook County-Libraries
Cook County-Illinois-Libraries
Cook County-Libraries-Illinois

In addition, terms can be combined with any other terms to generate another subject. For instance, combine the term "libraries" with the term "special" to generate the subject "special libraries."

Coordinate indexing is logical, not grammatical. The combination of terms will have the same result regardless of the order of the combined terms. Tauber considers a uniterm index prima facie a better reference tool than a standard index.[2]

The major difficulty of the uniterm system is, however, that its use is extremely time-consuming and economically unfeasible. In the earlier example, three terms were searched. It is difficult to scan through a large number of documents that contain the three terms, and the degree of difficulty increases in proportion to the growth of the size of the file. The uniterm system, though an ingenious device, is not practical for manual searching. With the introduction of the computer, it becomes practically feasible to coordinate in unmatchable speed a large number of documents.

For computer searching, documents are arranged in the same

concept as the uniterm system. They are entered in an inverted file recorded by their numbers under each word or term. Here is an illustration:

Words/Terms	Automobiles	Import	Japan
	197770	197760	200780
	196780	196777	197770
	192737 ──	192938	──192737
Documents	191118	192888	191110
	187907	└─192737───	189003
	—	—	187978
	—	—	186770
	—		185670
	—		
	147680		—
			—

The computer searches the documents by comparing and combining the terms under which the documents are recorded. In the illustration, the document number 192737 appears under three terms. It is the document that deals with three terms, namely, "import," "automobiles," and "Japan." In comparing and combining terms, three Boolean logical operators are used: OR, AND, and NOT.

1. OR: broadens; makes the result larger, that is, it retrieves documents in which any of the search terms appear. For instance, the user desires information on both cataloging and classification as shown in the figure. The shaded area represents the information searched for.

Cataloging 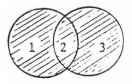 Classification

2. AND: narrows; makes the result smaller, that is, it retrieves documents in which all search terms appear. As the figure shows, the user desires information on cataloging and classification, but not cataloging or classification alone.

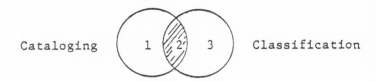

3. NOT: removes some unwanted elements, that is, it removes documents in which certain search terms appear. The user desires information on cataloging only; thus it is necessary to remove information on classification and information on both cataloging and classification.

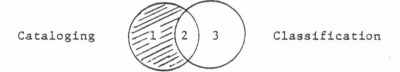

Retrieving information from different parts can be done by using logical operators as follows:

For part 1, cataloging NOT classification;

For part 2, cataloging AND classification;

For part 3, classification NOT cataloging;

For parts 1 and 3, (cataloging OR classification) NOT (cataloging AND classification) *or* cataloging NOT classification OR classification NOT cataloging

The use of parentheses is to specify the order of execution. Logical operators in parentheses are executed first.

The capability of coordinating any terms in the text is a most important feature of online searching. It must be noted, however, that the coordinate capability is not available in all online searching services. Services, such as The Source and CompuServe, which will be mentioned in part two, use the menu search, that is, streamlined display of pre-determined menu items for the user to choose. It is easy to use because the user simply follows the displayed instructions to take a next step, yet the menu approach involves repeated steps and lacks the flexibility and volatility of coordinate capability in free-text searching.

The coordinate search is based on probability. The more that is searched the more relevant items will be recalled. The relevancy and precision depend, however, on the nature of the search question. An open-end search question can hardly be 100 percent effective in recall and precision.[3] Recall is the ratio between relevant documents retrieved and the total of relevant documents in the file.[4] Precision is the ratio between relevant documents retrieved and the total number of documents actually retrieved.[5] Assuming the total number of relevant documents is 100, the total number of documents retrieved is 80, and the relevant number of documents retrieved is 60, the ratio for recall and precision is as follows:

recall = 60/100 = 60%

precision = 60/80 = 75%

Precision is in general sacrificed by large recall. Markey and others report that free-text searching has higher recall (93%) than controlled vocabulary (76%) but lower precision (71%) than the controlled vocabulary strategy (95%).[6] In a conservative estimate, Wessell considers that 60 percent recall of documents is about the best that can be achieved, and of the 60 percent recall, anywhere between 20 and 80 percent of the documents retrieved are totally irrelevant to the search request.[7] For the topic "import of automobiles from Japan" the searcher has to search not only the terms "import," "automobiles," and "Japan," but also their related terms and synonyms, such as "export," "Exportation," "exported," "exporting," "exports," "import," "imported," "importing," "importation," "automobile," "auto," "Japan," "Japanese," and many others to make sure that no documents on the topic will be missed. But the more serious problem is that terms coordinated do not necessarily relate, to the document contents. A document on import of drugs in automobiles from Japan may be retrieved, since all three terms—import, automobiles, and Japan—are represented in the document. Despite the computer's speed, the basic problem of natural language or free-text searing remains unsolved, namely, lack of consistency and uniformity, and lack of control of synonyms and related terms as well. For relevancy of retrieval, the control of vocabularies as subjects for searching becomes a necessity, thus resulting in the development of thesauri.

A thesaurus is a listing, in hierarchical structure, of controlled terms representing relationships among the terms. The UNISIST (United Nations Information System in Science and Technology) defines a thesaurus as a terminological control device used in translating from the natural language of document indexers or users into a more constrained "system language" and a controlled and dynamic vocabulary of semantically and generically related terms which covers a specific domain of knowledge.[8] Controlled vocabularies in a thesaurus are generally called descriptors. A descriptor is a term or short phrase used to characterize a document; it consists of two parts: (1) a label, or a term or phrase, specifying a particular concept, and (2) a definition explaining the meaning and scope of the label.[9]

Thesauri vary in their arrangement and structure. *Management Contents Data Base Thesaurus*[10] consists of four listings: (1) alphabetical listing of controlled vocabularies of 1,200 single words, multiword terms, and some acronyms, (2) a listing of numbers assigned to individual terms, (3) subject listing, a classified listing of index terms under twenty general categories, and (4) journal listing. Predicasts's *PTS Thesauri*[11] is composed of two parts: The first part is a dictionary, listing product names, geographic names, country names, event names, and measures names in alphabetical order. Thesauri terms listed in the dictionary are of two kinds: (1) proper thesauri terms, that is, indexable terms, which are searchable, and (2) cross-reference terms or non-indexable terms, which can be searched by using appropriate thesauri codes only. The second part is codes, which consists of product codes (PC), geographic codes (GC), event codes (EC), quick codes (QC) for U.S. and international statistics, and measures codes (MC).

The *Thesaurus of ERIC Descriptors*[12] is one of the finest thesauri.[13] Descriptors are arranged in an alphabetical order and represent a hierarchical relationship among them. An example is reproduced here.

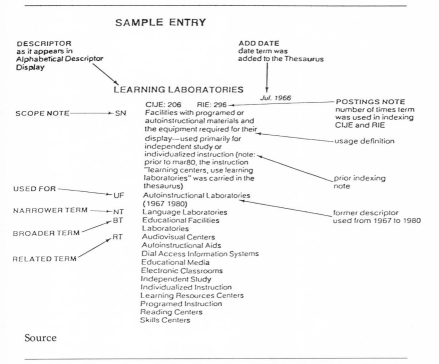

SAMPLE ENTRY

Source

Reprinted with permission by The Oryx Press, 2214 N. Central Ave., Phoenix, AZ 85004.

As the example indicates, six notations are used for descriptors: SN (scope note), USE or UF (used for), BT (broader term), NT (narrower term), and RT (related term). A scope note is a brief statement of the descriptor's intended usage. It may be used to recommend use of a more specific term of publication/document type or to mention an earlier thesaurus instruction or to clarify the meaning between the term and another descriptor or an identifier. It may be noted that an identifier is not structured or cross-referenced and is therefore not found in the *Thesaurus*.[14] It is used "to add a depth to subject indexing that is not always possible with Descriptors alone."[15] Identifiers may include acronyms, programs, coined terminology, community organizations, equipment names and numbers, geographic names, manufacturers, projects, tests, trade names, and concepts not yet represented by approved descriptors.[16]

The notation USE refers to non-used terms for indexing to the preferred descriptor. UF indicates that the term following the UF notation is not used for indexing. USE and UF are reciprocal notations and are used to solve problems of synonyms. The BT and NT notations, also used reciprocally, indicate a hierarchical structure of terms. BT lists terms that include the main descriptor as a sub-class, whereas NT lists terms considered to belong to sub-classes of the main descriptor. RT is used to specify a close conceptual, but not hierarchical, relationship between the main descriptor and terms following the notation RT.

A thesaurus lists controlled vocabularies of concepts,[17] the same as subject headings. Both thesauri and subject headings establish generic and hierarchical relationships among terms. There is seemingly not much difference between the two. All Information Access Company's online databases, such as NEWSEARCH, use the *Library of Congress Subject Headings*. However, thesauri are characterized by the following features:[18] (1) Thesauri are an outgrowth of natural language indexing. (2) The conventional subject headings are designed as aids to indexing only, whereas thesauri are designed from the searcher's point of view, providing access to specific topics with many facets. (3) Display of generic and hierarchical relationships among terms is clearly structured with BT and NT notations. (4) A thesaurus lists controlled vocabularies in a particular subject field; it does not cover the whole range of human knowledge. (5) Thesauri are for coordinate indexing, and, as such, numerous subdivisions and inverted headings exemplified in both the *Library of Congress Subject Headings* and *Sears List of Subject Headings* do not appear in the thesaurus.

A thesaurus is a return to the mainstream of subject headings. It encounters the same problems of conventional subject headings and has its own weaknesses as well. In general, advantages of the natural language system are disadvantages of controlled vocabularies. First, a searcher's view on the subject does not always correspond to the terms assigned by the indexer to the subject.[19] The familiarity of subject terms requires, therefore, training, and it may take months to be thoroughly familiar with a large controlled vocabulary.[20] Second, a decision process is required for inclusion, exclusion, revision, or addition of a term as controlled vocabulary.[21] A document with a term or concept that has not yet been accepted as controlled vocabulary will be missed. Markey and others identify six categories for which ERIC searchers may choose not to use controlled vocabularies:[22] (1) geographic areas; (2) recent topics; (3) specific names and objects; (4) value judgments, for example, exemplary, effective; (5) action statements, for example, eliminating, predicting, and (6) individual or psychological characteristics, for example, withdraw.

Last but not least, in contrast to conventional subject headings, which cover all fields of knowledge, a thesaurus is designed for use in a database or particular databases. Controlled vocabularies vary with databases. The search strategies used on one database might not be compatible with the other. On the other hand, free-text searching is compatible from database to database.[23] Readers will notice the difference in using the saving search mentioned in part two.

NOTES

1. Motiner Tauber and Associates, *Studies in Coordinate Indexing Documentation* (Washington, D.C.: Documentation Inc., 1953) pp. 37-46.

2. Ibid., 46.

3. Lorraine M. Mathies and Peter G. Watson, *Computer-Based Reference Service* (Chicago, Ill.: American Library Association, 1973) p. 125.

4. A. C. Foskett, *The Subject Approach to Information*, 4th ed. Hamden, Conn.: Linnet Books, 1982) pp. 18ff.

5. Ibid.

6. Karen Markey et al., "An Analysis of Controlled Vocabulary and

Free Text Search Statements in Online Searches," 4 *Online Review* (1980) 233-34.

7. Andrew E. Wessell, *Computer-Aided Information Retrieval* (Los Angeles, Calif.: Melville, 1975) p. 9.

8. Quoted in Douglas J. Foskett, "Thesaurus," 38 *Encyclopedia of Library and Information Science* (1980) 416.

9. Calvin N. Mooers, "The Indexing Language of an Information Retrieval System." in Wesley Simonton, *Information Retrieval Today*, papers presented at the Institute conducted by the Library School and the Center for Continuation Study, University of Minnesota, September 19-22, 1962 (University of Minnesota, 1963) p. 26.

10. *Management Contents Data Base Thesaurus* (Northbrook, Ill.: Management Contents, 1980, loose-leaf).

11. *Predicasts Terminal System User Manual* (Cleveland, Ohio: Predicasts, 1980, loose-leaf).

12. *Thesaurus of ERIC Descriptors*, rev. ed. (Phoenix, Ariz.: Oryx Press, 1980). 429p.

13. Barbara Booth, "A 'New' ERIC Thesaurus, Fine-Tuned for Searching," 3 *Online* (1979) 20-29.

14. Mathies and Watson, *Computer-Based Reference Service*, p. 23.

15. *Thesaurus of ERIC Descriptors*, p,. xv.

16. Mathies and Watson, *Computer-Based Reference Service*, p. 73; *Thesaurus of ERIC Descriptors*, p. xv.

17. Calvin Mooers, "The Indexing Language," p. 34.

18. Cf. F. W. Lancaster, "Vocabulary Control in Information Retrieval Systems" in Melvin J. Voigt and Michael H. Harris, eds., 7 *Advances in Librarianship* (1977) 12.

19. Lois Seulowitz, "All the News That's Fit to Printout," 1 *Online* (1977) 60.

20. F. W. Lancaster, "Vocabulary Control," p. 23.

21. Lois Seulowitz, "All the News," p. 58.

22. Karen Markey, "An Analysis of Controlled Vocabulary," pp. 231-32.

23. F. W. Lancaster, "Vocabulary Control," pp. 34-35,.

4

Databases
and
Producers

Currently, machine-readable databases are available in most fields in science and technology as well as in the social sciences. The field of humanities has not been well covered. The following chart indicating the number of databases by subject is based on a listing in *Online Review*.[1]

Science/Technology	Social Sciences	Humanities	General	Total
150	67	6	53	276
54.3%	24.3%	2.2%	19.2%	100%

Databases in science and technology dominate, constituting 54 percent of the total. In recent years, however, more social science databases have been made available to the public. The distribution of databases by subject will be noted in the next chapter. Commerical firms produce the most databases, followed by institutions and societies, and government agencies.

Databases available to the public are either directly produced and marketed by producers, or channeled through vendors, or both: (1) Examples of databases produced and directly marketed by producers are LEXIS and NEXIS of Mead Data Central. Other databases in this category include WESTLAW by the West Publishing Company and ELECTRONIC LEGISLATIVE SEARCH SYSTEM by Commerce Clearing House. (2) Databases marketed through vendors include those created by Information Access Company. IAC produces five databases, noted later, all marketed to users through DIALOG. (3) Databases produced and marketed directly by the producer and through vendors at the same time include Predicasts's databases and Disclosure, just to name a few.

All databases may be broadly classified into two categories:[2] (1) Access to other sources of information. Representative forms of this category are indexes and abstracts. (2) Sources of Information. This category provides users direct information, such as numeric, statistical, and census data, without referring to other sources. A large number of databases have print or microform counterparts; some are in full text. Others are available online only.

DATABASES WITH COUNTERPARTS

The online version often has more extensive coverage, and faster updating and searching features are unavailable in its print counterparts. It must be noted that some databases do not provide retrospective searching, such as GPO MONTHLY (a counterpart of the *Monthly Catalog*) since 1976, and MEDLINE since 1971. Their print counterparts should be consulted for earlier coverage. A listing of databases and their counterparts may be found in the directories mentioned in chapter two. Some representative databases with counterparts are described here.

The PAIS International Bulletin database contains citations to all fields of social sciences and is particularly strong in economics, public policy, public administration, and international relations. Though limited in retrospective coverage, it is comprehensive, being a combination of the records from the Print *PAIS* from 1976 onward and the *PAIS Foreign Language Index* since 1972.

The Educational Resources Information Center (ERIC) compiles the *Current Index to Journals in Education* (*CIJE*), an index to more than 700 journals, and its companion volume, *Resources in Education* (RIE), a listing of more than 10,000 items a year of published and unpublished materials relating to education. The ERIC database is the combination of both CIJE and RIE.

The Information Access Company produces five online databases: the Magazine Index (MI), the National Newspaper Index (NNI), the Legal Resource Index (LRI), Trade and Industry Index (TI), and Newsearch. Both MI and LRI have print counterparts. The Magazine Index is a cover-to-cover index of about 380 popular journals. It covers all articles, news reports, editorials, product evaluations, short stories, poetry, recipes, reviews, obituaries, letters to the editor, and columns. MI is also available in microform. The Legal Resource Index database indexes cover-to-cover over 700 law journals, six newspapers, and books and government publications from the Library of Congress MARC (MAchine Readable Catalogue Project) tapes as well as relevant law articles from Magazine Index, National Newspaper Index, and Trade and Industry Index. LRI's print counterpart, *Current Law Index*, contains all citations to "core" legal journal articles, a much more selective listing than the online version.

The National Newspaper Index is available both online and in microform. NNI indexes the *Wall Street Journal* (Western and Eastern editions), *Christian Science Monitor* (Western edition), and the *New York Times* (late an national editions). Disclosure II is more selective than its microfiche counterparts. The Disclosure database contains approximately 8,500 corporations that are required to submit to the Securities and Exchange Commission a series of reports that disclose the continuing status of their operation. The database does not, however, include management investment companies, investment trusts, exploration funds and partnerships, and real estate trusts and partnerships. Also excluded are companies that have not filed a 10-K (or 20-K or 20-F)[3] within the past twenty-four months. Full-text copies of reports of companies not included in the Disclosure database are available in microfiche or paper copy from the Disclosure's Demand Information Centers. The

Management Contents database has, however, a more extensive coverage than its counterpart in that abstracts are provided only online.

DATABASES ONLINE ONLY

Quite a few databases do not have counterparts. PATSEARCH, produced by Pergamon International Information Corporation, covers 700,000 U.S. patents issued since 1971 on all chemical, electrical, mechanical, and general patents. In the family of the Information Access Company, just mentioned, Trade and Industry Index (TI) and NEWSEARCH are available only online. TI indexes and selectively abstracts about 300 journals and has partial coverage of information from over 1,100 publications. It covers the following fields: manufacturing, finance, insurance, real estate, services, public administration, retail trade, oil and gas, mining, public utilities, transportation, wholesale trade, agriculture, forestry, fishing, and construction.

NEWSEARCH is the front runner of IAC's four online databases: (MI, NNI, LRI, and TI) and Management Contents. Items included in NEWSEARCH will last for about a month and will then be purged. At the time of purging, each contributing database, such as MI, is updated with the past month's records.

ABI/INFORM, called by its producer The Database for Decision Makers, is another database without a print or microform counterpart. The database, a Data Courier's product, indexes and abstracts over 400 journals in English on management and administration. Major areas of its coverage include accounting and auditing, banking, finance, economics, EDP systems and information science, insurance, taxation, marketing, personnel, real estate, and telecommunications. It also provides full-text retrieval service. Full text of about 90 percent of the journals can be retrieved online at a fee in addition to the regular connect charges.

The *New York Times* Information Bank began its operation in 1972. It gives detailed abstracts, not available elsewhere, of virtually all materials published in the *New York Times* and of selected materials from some sixty other newspapers and magazines, including popular periodicals, such as *Atlantic,*

Consumer Reports, The New Yorker, and *Sports Illustrated.* The database has been marketed by Mead Data Central since early 1983.

FULL-TEXT DATABASES

LEXIS is the first database commercially available with full-text information. Legal documents are divided into "libraries." For instance, its federal law libraries contain the full text of all U.S. district court decisions from 1960 to the present, U.S. Supreme Court decisions from 1925 to the present, and the United States Code.

The *New York Times*—On Line, introduced in 1981, captures, in full text, all types of stories from each weekday's final Late City Edition and the Sunday *New York Times* from June 1, 1980, onward. The database has four features, known as enhancements, not available in its counterparts: (1) terse summaries for each full-text story; (2) index terms for each story; (3) a complete bibliographic citation, including date, pagination, and type of materials; and (4) short descriptions of all illustrations, such as graphs, charts, pictures, and maps. The database omits some items, such as advertisements and classified sections, stock and bond tables, and illustrations. For these items, its print or microform counterparts must be consulted.

Other full-text databases include the *Harvard Business Review* database containing complete text of every article published from 1976 and citations and abstracts to articles from 1925, the *Kirk-Othmer Encyclopedia of Chemical Technology* database consisting of the entire twenty-four volumes and twenty-fifth supplement, and *Academic American Encyclopedia* database. As mentioned earlier, most journal articles in ABI/INFORM can be retrieved online. More full-text databases will be available.[4]

BRS (Bibliographic Retrieval Services) announced two full-text databases: IRCS Medical Science database covering thirty-two English-language journals in the field of medical and biomedical sciences and American Chemical Society Primary Journal database composed of eighteen major ACS journals. The growth of full-text databases is continuing, but slowly, primarily because of the high cost for retrieval as compared with the use of their print counterparts. Roberts estimates that a typical 4,000-word magazine article takes roughly 13 minutes to retrieve at a 300-baud terminal at a cost of about $18.[5]

INDEX TO DATABASE CONTENTS

One of the early problems in using the databases was the lack of an index to subject contents. Donati prepared in 1977 a twenty-five topic index to selected social science and related databases indicating the topic coverage of the data in three categories: small, moderate, and high.[6] Lockheed released in 1978 the first subject guide containing 600 index terms for 79 DIALOG data files.[7] It was later revised to include 94 data files.[8] The DIALOG subject guide was made available online in DIALINDEX (File 411) in 1980. The System Development Corporation developed in 1979 the File DBI (Data Base Index), an online master index to all its system databases. BRS introduced its online master index, called BRS/CROS. All these indexes help identify databases available in the system that contain a given term. They cannot, however, compare and identify databases other than their own.[9] Also lacking is a master index to all descriptors used in a system.

DATABASE SELECTION

In selecting databases, there are two factors to be considered: (1) the characteristics of the database, and (2) the nature of the library and the needs of users. The database subject, coverage, update frequency, size, growth rate, searching features, accuracy, and currency are the primary criteria for selecting a database. Williams lists the following criteria for consideration:[10] (1) contents, including subject and materials coverage and range; (2) time lapse, between the item as it appears in the primary source, in the secondary source (index), and finally in the database; (3) indexing and coding practices, such as free-language keywords, controlled thesaurus, or hierarchical vocabularies; and (4) size and growth rate.

Database quality is another factor for selection. Unfortunately, some databases do not have good quality control. Norton has experienced the lack of quality control of some databases, such as wrong accession number, incorrect information, updating delays, inconsistency of assigning subject terms, and incorrect date and page of the source.[11] In using the *Library and Information Science Abstracts* database, it is not difficult to find inconsistencies of spellings of authors' names and duplication of information. A study of recall of journal titles in ABI/INFORM database by using four methods in the DIALOG system found errors in variant spelling of titles and missing information in journal code, ISSN, and CODEN. The search for the title of one core journal resulted in only 21 out of 256 items recovered by using the Journal Title (JN) search.[12] It may be noted that because information contained in a database is invisible until it is retrieved on a screen or in hard copy, the evaluation of database quality is more difficult than is the case with its print or microform counterparts.

What databases are used depends on the nature of the library and the needs of users. A survey on the use of the *New York Times* Information Bank by ten academic, public, and state libraries indicates that for academic libraries the bank is not as useful as it is for public libraries.[13] There are two reasons why: (1) Other services such as Lockheed and System Development Corporation are more meaningful for the academic research libraries, (2) The major asset of the bank is its access to newsworthy facts, but academic research has not created a sufficient demand for such a service.[14] Atherton and Christian report a similar finding that special libraries are the most frequent and the academic libraries are the least frequent subscribers to the *New York Times* Information Bank.[15] In historical research, however, databases are infrequently used not only because of historians' attitudes toward machines but also because of their different needs.[16]

There is an identifiable core of databases. The selection of these databases can answer most of the inquiries in a given subject. According to a survey by *Advanced Technology Libraries*, ERIC is the most frequently used file among academic and public libraries, followed by ABI/INFORM, MEDLINE,

PsycINFO, Chemical Abstracts, Management Contents, Compendex, NTIS, Magazine Index, Predicasts, and the Information Bank.[17] At the University of South Dakota serving a liberal arts community, 94.7 percent of the total number of requests were covered by 129 databases of which a majority, or 75.5 percent, were satisfied by 11 databases. Four databases—ERIC, PsycINFO, Comprehensive Dissertation Index, and Social Scisearch—accounted for 49.5 percent of the searching.[18] On the average, 61 percent of information was retrieved by a single database; a second database added 27.3 percent more, and the third database provided an additional 9.7 percent of the information.[19]

An analysis of ten databases on the subjects of "welfare," "corrective services," and "community development" revealed that 85 percent of the information on the subjects could be found in 5 databases, that is, ERIC, NTIS, PsycINFO, SSCI (Social Sciences Citation Index), and NCJRS (National Criminal Justice Reference Service), and that these databases were cost-effective in retrieving relevant documents.[20] A different finding, however, was reported on the use of 40 databases to retrieve citations on emergency management, a multidisciplinary field. No one database yielded over 19.3 percent of the total citations, but 5 databases supplied 60.7 percent recall and, for 80.6 percent to 89.3 percent recall, a search of 13 to 19 databases was necessary.[21]

For online searching courses at the library schools, 4 frequently used databases have been identified. They are, in rank of use, ERIC, 63 percent; PsycINFO, 27 percent; Social Scisearch, 25 percent; and NTIS, 19 percent.[22] In a study of the Computer-Assisted Literature Searching (CALS) project in historical research at Berkeley in 1978, of the 18 databases, the most frequently used were PsycINFO, ERIC, MEDLINE, BIOSIS, Magazine Index, NTIS, and Social Scisearch.[23]

NOTES

1. 6 *Online Review*, (1982) 353-90.
2. Cf. *Directory of Online Databases* (Santa Monica, Calif.: Cuadra

Associates, 1979-). The *Directory* classifies databases into reference databases and source databases. Reference databases may be of bibliographic or referral nature; source databases contain the original source or information.

3. These are forms filed with the Securities and Exchange Commission by public companies that trade their securities on the New York Stock Exchange, American Stock Exchange or Over-the-Counter. See *A Guide to SEC Corporate Filings* (Bethesda, Md.: Disclosure, 1982) 24p.

4. Carol Tenopir, "Full-text, Downloading and Other Issues," 108 *Library Journal* (1983) 1111-13.

5. Steven K. Roberts, "Online: A Smorgasbord of Services," *Today: The Videotex/Computer Magazine* (November 1983) 24.

6. Robert Donati, "Selective Survey of Online Access to Social Science Data Bases," 68 *Special Libraries* (1977) 400-1.

7. Lockheed Missiles and Space Company, *Subject Guide to DIALOG Databases* (DIALOG, October 1978).

8. Lockheed Missiles and Space Company, *Subject Guide to DIALOG Databases* (DIALOG, April 1979).

9. Carol Tenopir, "Distribution of Citations in Databases in a Multidisciplinary Field," 6 *Online Review* (1982) 405.

10. Martha E. Williams, "Criteria for Evaluation and Selection of Data Bases and Data Base Services," 66 *Special Libraries* (1975) 563.

11. Nancy Prothro Norton, "Dirty Data: A Call for Quality Control," 5 *Online* (1981) 40.

12. Bruce L. Keck, "An Investigation of Recall in the ABI/INFORM Database with Searching by Journal," 5 *Online Review* (1981) 396.

13. Rhoda Garoogian, "Library Use of the New York Times Information Bank: A Preliminary Survey," 16 *RQ* (1976) 61-63.

14. Ibid.

15. Pauline Atherton and Roger W. Christian, *Librarians and Online Services* (White Plains, N.Y.: Knowledge Industry, 1977) pp. 12-13.

16. Joyce Duncan Falk, "Computer-Assisted Reference Service in History," 21 *RQ* (1982) 344.

17. 12 *Advanced Technology Libraries* (1983) 1-2.

18. John Edward Evans, "Database Selection in an Academic Library: Are Those Big Multi-File Searches Really Necessary," 4 *Online* (1980) 36.

19. Ibid.

20. V. X. Sharma, "A Comparative Evaluation of Online Databases in Relation to Welfare and Corrective Services, and Community Development," 6 *Online Review* (1982) 311-12.

21. Carol Tenopir, "Distribution of Citations," pp. 412-13.

22. Carol Hansen Fenichel and Stephen Paul Harter, *Survey of Online Searching Instruction in Schools of Library and Information Science* (Dublin, Ohio: OCLC, 1981) pp. 38-39.

23. Evelyn-Margaret Kiresen and Simone Klugman, "The Use of Online Databases for Historical Research," 21 *RQ* (1981) 345.

5

Database Vendors

Vendors market database search services to the public. Some databases are for in-house use only and are not available to the public. According to *Online Review*, 274 databases are publicly available worldwide from 11 vendors in 5 countries.[1] The vendors are

England
> BLAISE
> Data-star
> Pergamon Infoline

France
> Questel

Germany
> Dimdi
> INKA

Italy
> ESA Information Retrieval Services (ESA-IRS)

USA
> Bibliographic Retrieval Services (BRS)
> DIALOG Information Services
> National Library of Medicine (NLM)
> System Development Corporation (SDC) Search Service (now SDC Information Services)—ORBIT (On-Line Retrieval of Bibliographic Information Timeshared)

Four vendors in the United States supply 217 databases of the 274 databases available, constituting 79.2 percent. Nearly three-fourths of the total, or 204 databases, are channeled to the public through DIALOG, SDC's ORBIT, and BRS. The United States dominates the database world.

The three vendors, DIALOG, BRS, and SDC, overlap in their supply of databases by roughly 20 percent. In others, they are exclusively from one or another. DIALOG has the most databases. By subject, SDC has a noticeable stress on science and technology, particularly chemistry and patents; whereas BRS has maintained a balanced development in science and technology as well as in the social sciences. The following chart indicates the distribution of subject fields.[2]

SUBJECT FIELDS DISTRIBUTION

	DIALOG	SDC	BRS
Science/Technology	75	41	28
Social Sciences	67	11	41
Humanities	6	0	2
General	41	11	13
Total	189	63	84

THREE SUPERMARKETS

DIALOG, SDC, and BRS are also called the database super-markets because of the large number and variety of databases available through them. DIALOG is the most popular, followed by BRS and SDC. About 60 percent of the libraries surveyed held subscriptions to three or more vendors.[3] Addresses and phone numbers for the three supermarkets of databases are listed here:

DIALOG Information Services
3460 Hillview Avenue
Palo Alto, CA 94304
415/858-3785
800/227-1960
800/982-5838 in California

SDC Information Services
System Development Corporation
2500 Colorado Avenue
Santa Monica, CA 90406
213/820-4111
800/421-7229
800/352-6689 in California

Bibliographic Retrieval Services (BRS)
1200 Route 7
Latham, NY 12100
518/783-7251
800/833-4707
800/553-5566 in New York

DIALOG, developed by the Lockheed Palo Alto Research Laboratory, had its initial application in 1967 when a DIALOG terminal was installed at the NASA Ames Research Center, Moffett, California. It began operation to the public in 1972 with a single database. As of January 1979, 95 databases were maintained. By May 1981, the number of databases increased to 142, an increase of 49 percent in a span of one and half years. In 1981, Lockheed's DIALOG became a subsidiary of Lockheed under a new name, DIALOG Information Services. By the end of 1983, DIALOG had over 180 databases with 80 million searchable records.[4] It is now the largest vendor in the field.

The System Development Corporation, an outgrowth of RAND's System Development Division, was established in 1968 as a not-for-profit organization.[5] SDC was contracted to work on an interactive database for the Advanced Research Projects Agency (ARPA) of the U.S. Department of Defense. The ARPA project later developed into the ORBIT system. SDC's ORBIT search service became commercially available in 1973. It grew steadily, but for some reason nine databases were withdrawn from the system in 1981.[6] In 1983, SDC Search Service was renamed as SDC Information Services. Over sixty databases are available from SDC.

BRS, a division of Indian Head, Inc., began its operation in 1976 with the purpose of filling the wide gap between the cost of database search services supplied by the public sector and those offered through the private sector.[7] It provides services to a national user community at a competitively low cost. In 1983, there were over eighty databases available from BRS. BRS is also expanding its databases in business. A dozen or so databases available from BRS are business or business related.

SERVICE FEATURES OF THREE SYSTEMS

Searching features of the three systems will be discussed in part two. Their service features are briefly described here:

Fees

There is no initial fee or minimum charge in DIALOG. Fees are charged for actual use. There are three types of fees: (1) Online computer connect time ranges from $15 to $300 per hour, depending on databases. (2) Offline print rates for each full record range from 10 cents to $5 in the Disclosure database to $50 in the CLAIMS/CITATION database. (3) Online display rates per full record in some databases range from 10 cents to $55. Discounts are provided for active use of the system in four categories of contract: (1) Standard contract provides a $5 to $25 discount per connect hour depending on the number of hours used, with a minimum of five connect hours per month. (2) Discount contract provides a larger discount to single password users for a minimum of at least $200 per month over a six-month time period. (3) Group contract provides an additional discount to a group of users for at least $500 per month with five passwords. (4) Subscription contract gives significant hourly discounts to users for a minimum of $2,500 a year.

SDC does not charge an initial or subscription fee either. There are three kinds of fees: (1) Online computer connect time rates range from $40 to $125 per hour. (2) Offline print rates range from 5 cents to 90 cents per record, depending on databases and the format. (3) Online display rates range from 5 cents to 20 cents per record. Discounts are given in three plans: (1) Monthly minimum plan in eleven steps ranges from a $2 to $20 discount per connect hour for monthly connect amounts starting from $200. (2) Annual subscription plan in eight steps varies from a $2 to $15 discount per connect hour for annual connect amounts starting from $3,500. (3) Automatic volume discount plan in ten steps, ranges from a $5 to $20 discount per connect hour starting from five hours a month.

BRS requires an initial subscription fee, but recently it has offered open access as an option. The basic connect hour rate for open access is $35. There is an initial password fee of $50, which is applicable to any searching done within the first three months. The subscription fee is proportionately reduced in four levels depending on usage as shown:

Level 1: $750 for 25 connect hours annually or $30 per hour

Level 2: $1,500 for 60 connect hours annually or $25 per hour

Level 3: $2,400 for 120 connect hours annually or $20 per hour

Level 4: $3,800 for 240 connect hours annually or $16 per hour

There is also available a group or mini-group membership access at a discounted rate for groups that can guarantee the use of a minimum number of connect hours per month among their membership.

In addition, BRS charges other fees: (1) royalties in most databases from $4 to $75 per connect hour, (2) royalties for on-line display in some databases ranging from 5 cents to 40 cents per citation, (3) royalties for offline prints in some databases, ranging from 2.5 cents to 75 cents per citation, (4) offline printing rate, which varies depending on the number of pages and citations, and citations charges which vary according to the format, and (5) offline searching, which is a flat charge in some databases. There are also flat-rate fees for such databases as California Union List Periodicals.

All three systems give special rates for classroom use. Both DIALOG and SDC charge a flat $15 per connect hour including telecommunication fees. BRS charges $8 per connect hour plus telecommunication and any applicable database royalty fees. These special rates limit use to certain databases.

Access

DIALOG, SDC, and BRS can be accessed by direct dial over telephone lines or via telecommunication networks: TELENET, TYMNET, and IN-WATS. DIALOG and BRS can also be accessed through the UNINET telecommunication network. In the BRS system, for instance, the communication cost is calculated as follows: direct dial, $3 per connect hour; UNINET, $8 per connect hour; TELENET, $8 per connect hour; TYMNET, $11 per connect hour; and IN-WATS, $26 per connect hour.

Operating Hours

DIALOG is available 120 hours per week with 22 hours per day from Monday through Thursday 10 P.M.—8 P.M. Pacific time), 20 hours on Friday (10 P.M.—6 P.M.), and 12 hours on Saturday (6 A.M.—6 P.M.). SDC operates 130 hours per week with 23.5 hours per day Monday through Thursday (7:15 A.M.—6:45 A.M. Pacific time), 17 hours on Friday (12 Noon—5 P.M.), 11 hours on Saturday (5 A.M.—4 P.M.), and 8 hours on Sunday (4 P.M.—12 Midnight). BRS has the longest hours of operation. It can be accessed 149 hours per week, with 22 hours per day Monday through Saturday (6 A.M.—4 A.M. Eastern time), and 17 hours on Sunday (6 A.M.—2 P.M., 7 P.M.—4 A.M.).

User Education and Training

Each system provides user education and training programs. DIALOG offers two programs: (1) system seminar, a one-and-a-half-day session to train beginners; (2) subject seminar, a half-day session for advanced training and updating. There are three kinds of training programs in SDC: (1) a one-and-a-half-day session; (2) a one-day session; and (3) review, advanced, and special-subject seminars, conducted in either half-day or one-day sessions. BRS training programs, one-day or half-day sessions, consist of (1) introductory system training, (2) system update sessions, (3) database-specific workshops, and (4) special BRS seminars. All three systems provide customized training service, that is, these programs can be conducted at users' sites. It may be noted that producers of databases also offer their own training programs.[8]

Vendor Databases

Vendors produce their own databases for different purposes. DIALOG Chemical Information System consists of CA SEARCH

(Files 308, 309, 310, 311, 320), CHEMNAME (File 301), CHEM-SEARCH (File 30), and CHEMSIS (Files 328, 329, 330, 331). CHEMNAME, CHEMSEARCH, and CHEMSIS are produced jointly by DIALOG and the Chemical Abstracts Service, providing users with various approaches to search chemical substances. Also to facilitate searching, DIALOG produced DIALINDEX (File 411), a master index to DIALOG databases mentioned earlier. A dozen or so ONTAP (ONline Training and Practice) databases, such as ONTAP ABI/INFORM (File 215), ONTAP CHEMNAME (File 231), ONTAP ERIC (File 201), and ONTAP PTS PROMT (File 216), are used for training and practicing. For information about DIALOG's services, there is CHRONOLOG NEWSLETTER (File 410), the online version of DIALOG's *Chronlog*. DIALOG PUBLICATIONS (File 200) is available for online ordering of DIALOG publications.

The SDC system has produced the following databases: DBI, a master index to all SDC databases; LIBCON on monographic literature and some non-profit materials cataloged in the Library of Congress; NUC/CODES (National Union Catalog codes), a union list of serials for holdings cited in the File CASSI, the *Chemical Abstracts Service Source Index*; ORBIT for other maintenance and housekeeping functions; and ORBCHEM and ORBPAT, both for search qualifiers in a number of databases.

Quite a few databases are produced by BRS. They are, for instance, BRS/CROS (CROS), a master index to all BRS databases; BRS/BULLETIN (BULL), an online version of the *BRS Bulletin* for latest news; PRE-MED (PREM) for current clinical medicine from 108 core medical journals; School Practices Information File (SPIF), a resource file of programs, practices, and instructional materials.

Other Service Features

Selective Dissemination of Information (SDI) is another service of the three systems. In some databases, searching will be automatically performed for the user every time the selected database is updated. The private file is another. All three systems make available the private file program. The system will create a private database for in-house use, and all records created in the file are searchable by using the system's retrieval software. Currently, online ordering of full-text documents from a number of databases is only available in DIALOG and SDC.[9] After November 1982, the LEXIS/NEXIS users were able to use the terminal provided by Mead Data Central to access DIALOG databases. There is, however, a telecommunication fee of $5 per hour, in addition to standard DIALOG charges. The electronic message is another service feature of the three systems.

SDC has developed the ORBIT SearchMaster software for micros. The software features automatic logon and logoff, saving the search strategy for later use, and instructional prompts for easy use. It also enables the user to store the search results and subsequently have them edited, formatted, and printed with a commericial word processing package. At the time of this writing, SDC is testing and has not yet marketed the software.

In 1983, BRS marketed a software product, BRS/SEARCH for private files. It is available for purchase or lease. BRS/SEARCH has two versions: (1) The mainframe version is used to run on BRS online database service and operates on IBM and IBM-compatible equipment. (2) The micro/mini version, written in C programming language, can run on any computer on the UNIX system of Bell Laboratories. BRS/SEARCH can handle up to 16 million documents per database, 65,000 paragraphs per document, 255 sentences per paragraph, and 255 words per sentence. It enables direct loading of databases and online updating. As compared with BRS, it has other capabilities too, such as left-hand truncation, NEAR positional operator, online scanning and sorting, and the use of numeric value in finding documents of particular years.

Services to Microcomputer Users

For the purpose of marketing its service to microcomputer users, DIALOG introduced Knowledge Index, which allows personal computer users access to a limited number of its databases in the evenings and on weekends at reduced rates.[10] Likewise, BRS launched the BRS/After Dark program available only in the evenings and on weekends.[11] Both Knowledge Index and BRS/After Dark and their search features will be noted in chapters nine and eleven, respectively. For medical professionals and students, BRS also offers BRS/COLLEAGUE providing access to bibliographic references in medical science and complete text of 24 medical textbooks. BRS/COLLEAGUE and BRS/After Dark have similar search features.

OTHER VENDORS

Besides DIALOG, SDC, and BRS, other vendors that provide various database services to the public include

CompuServe Information Service
CompuServe, Inc.
5000 Arlington Centre Boulevard
Columbus, OH 43220
614/457-8650
800/848-8990

Dow Jones News/Retrieval
P. O. Box 300
Princeton, NJ 08540
609/452-1511
800/257-5114

I. P. Sharp
Box 418, Exchange Tower
2 First Canadian Place
Toronto, Ontario M5X 1E3, Canada
416/364-5361

Infoline
Pergamon International Information Corporation
1340 Old Chain Bridge Road
McLean, VA 22101
703/442-0900
800/336-7575

Mead Data Central
P. O. Box 933
Dayton, OH 45401
513/859-1611
800/227-4908

The Source
1616 Anderson Road
McLean, VA 22102
703/821-6660
800/336-3366

VU/TEXT Information Services
P. O. Box 8558
Philadelphia, PA 19101
215/854-8297

CompuServe and The Source are two of the best-known information utilities, providing various services not limited primarily to bibliographic searching.[12] They can be used for correspondence, games, electronic shopping, private files, programming, and other purposes. CompuServe's service may be summarized as follows: (1) news, weather, and sports from major newspapers and news services; (2) business and financial information; (3) games and entertainment, including electronic games and reviews of theaters, books, and movies; (4) home information, such as nutrition, gardening, home decorating, automobile maintenance, family health, and education; and (5) personal computing for software exchange, programming languages, word processing, line printer, art gallery, and so forth. It is menu-structured. The main menu consists of six categories, namely Home Services, Business and Financial, Personal Computing, Services for Professionals, User Information, and Index.

Rates vary depending on the standard or prime services. The rate for standard service is $5 per connect hour up to 300 baud with no monthly minimum charge. The prime service rate is $22.50 per connect hour up to 300 baud with a minimum monthly charge of two hours. There is an additional surcharge for using the telecommunication network ranging from $2 to $20 per hour depending on services and locations. CompuServe also charges for online disk storage, premium program, and line printer. Standard service hours are from 6 P.M. to 5 A.M., all day Saturday, Sunday, and announced holidays. The prime service is available from 8 A.M. to 6 P.M. weekdays.

The Source is produced by the Source Telecomputing Corporation, a subsidiary of The Reader's Digest Association. It entered the market in 1979 primarily as a source of information.[13] The Source is also structured in menus. Its main menu has eight categories: News and Reference Resources, Business/Financial Markets, Catalogue Shopping, Home and Leisure, Education and Career, Mail and Communications,

Creating and Computing, and Source*Plus. The system provides such services as electronic mail; information on air schedules, stock markets, shopping, wine, and cinema; education, from learning a foreign language to mathematics, statistics and computer programming; United Press International wire service, *New York Times* news summary, *New York Times* consumer databases; and software on pre-programmed financial routines. In addition, business and financial databases are available under Source*Plus at a higher rate.

The rate for The Source varies. It ranges from $7.75 for evenings, weekends, and holidays to $35 for daytime up to 300 baud depending on locations. For instance, in the continental United States, it charges $7.75 per connect hour up to 300 baud from 6 P.M. to 7 A.M., Monday to Friday, weekends, and holidays. A higher rate is charged for using Source* Plus.

Dow Jones News/Retrieval provides nearly twenty databases in four broad areas, namely, business and economics news, financial and investment, quotes, and general news and information services. They are mostly Dow Jones databases, such as Dow Jones News, *Wall Street Journal* Highlights Online, Current Quotes, and *Wall Street Week* Online. Other databases channeled through Dow Jones include Disclosure II and *Academic American Encyclopedia*. All databases are menu-structured. But free-text searching is also available in Dow Jones News database. Dow Jones News was first offered as a private file accessed from BRS in early 1981. After March 1, 1983, the free-text version of Dow Jones News was accessed only from Dow Jones, but its search features remain basically those of BRS. The user who is familiar with BRS search should have no difficulty in using the free-text version of Dow Jones News.

Dow Jones can be accessed 22 hours per day, 7 days a week from 6 A.M. to 4 A.M. Eastern time as prime time. For non-prime time users, the operating hours are from 6:01 P.M. through 4 A.M. Eastern time, Monday through Friday, weekends, and holidays. Fees vary depending on the prime time or non-prime time and usage plans. Three plans are available: standard, blue chip, and executive. Rates for 300-baud users range from 40 cents to $1.20 per connect minute in prime time and from 10 cents to 90 cents per connect minute in non-prime time. In addition, there are subscription fees and other fees such as communication charges. Also available are rates for academic customers. For 300-baud users, rates are from 10 cents to 80 cents depending on time and database. Rates for academic customers include communication charges, and there is no monthly fee.

I. P. Sharp supplies primarily business numeric data. Some 100 databases of more than 30 million time series are available to the public. A time series is composed of "data or observations that are evenly spaced over time."[14] The series may be daily, weekly, monthly, or annual. It must have a beginning date, an ending date, and a frequency. I. P. Sharp's databases fall into four broad subject categories, namely, finance, economics, aviation, and energy.[15] Most of the databases are structured in I. P. Sharp's MAGIC system. It is conversational with a prompted series of menus. Free-text searching in those databases is not available. I. P. Sharp is operating 24 hours a day, Monday through Saturday, and 6 hours on Sunday. The fee for 300-baud users is $60 per connect hour. There is no minimum charge. Rates for class use are also available.

Mead Data Central markets the first full-text public database, LEXIS. The LEXIS system developed as a result of a cooperative venture between OBAR, a non-profit organization of Ohio lawyers, and Mead Data Central. It contains legal information divided into libraries, and each library is organized into files. LEXIS also provides Auto-Cite, Shepard's Citations, and Matthew Bender's publications. MDC's other system is NEXIS. NEXIS is a full-text, general news and business service containing information from newspapers, magazines, news wires, and reference works. The reference works include the *Encyclopaedia Britannica* and the *Federal Register.*

The LEXIS/NEXIS system also includes others databases, such as LEXPAT, a full-text patent search service, and NAARS (National Automated Accounting Research System), a financial and accounting database including over 8,000 annual reports for listed and over-the-counter companies, selected proxy statement information, and financial reporting practices. In 1983 MDC acquired the exclusive right to market databases of the *New York Times* Information Service. Five databases are currently available from MDC: (1) the *New York Times*, a full-text database; (2) Advertising and Marketing Intelligence (AMI), information from trade and professional publications on advertising, marketing, and related fields; (3) Deadline Data on World Affairs, geographical data on the countries of the world, the United States, and world organizations; (4) Information Bank on current affairs, business, economics, and social and political information published in the *New York Times* and selected materials from other newspapers and magazines; and (5) Today, a daily service of news summary and update.

Mead Data Central is operating from 3:00 A.M. to 2:00 A.M. (Eastern time), Monday through Friday, and 7:30 A.M. to 10 P.M. on Saturday and Sunday. Its pricing policy consists of many components, such as monthly library access, monthly equipment, peak and off-peak connect time, number of connect hours, search surcharge, offline printing, and one-time charge. It has been the practice of MDC to require its own terminals to access the system. The use of dedicated terminals is generally considered not economical because the terminals cannot be used to connect with other systems. It is a particular burden to those libraries having other terminals for *New York Times* Information Service because they must purchase or lease MDC terminals if they wish to continue using those databases.[16] As a first step to allow access to its databases through any terminals, MDC announced recently that limited availability of its services can be accessed through IBM Personal Computers and Displaywriters and 3101 terminals.[17] MDC terminals can be used to connect with DIALOG. There is a telecommunication fee in addition to DIALOG's charges.

VU/TEXT Information Services, a Knight-Ridder Company, began its operation in 1983. It offers full text online of newspapers and other publications. As of June 1983, the following databases are available from VU/TEXT: *Philadelphia Inquirer* (January 1980–   ), *Washington Post* (April 1983–   ), *Lexington* (Ky.) *Herald-Leader, Academic American Encyclopedia,* and Mediawire, a public relations news wire service throughout the mid-Atlantic. VU/TEXT can be accessed by telephone or via telecommunication systems. Its pricing structure ranges from $30 to $100 per connect hour depending on the databases and user's options.

VENDOR SELECTION

In selecting vendors, Atherton and Christian list the following technical features for consideration: availability of natural language commands; ease of logging in and logging off; type of search available—author, title, key words, and so forth; speed and cost of communication options (300 and 1,200 baud); ease of access to free-text search in record; degree of logic offered; times of available service; and printing and display options.[18] Blue even prepared a detailed list of questions for selection in thirteen categories, which include database creation, availability of service, hardware, software, storage, input/output, user training, user procedures and aids, and maintenance.[19] Of the factors that may influence the user's attitude toward a particular vendor, the following four are worth noting: (1) the availability of subject fields and the range of coverage, (2) ease of use, (3) the retrieval result, and (4) costs.

Subject Fields and Coverage

Haines suggests four factors in choosing a vendor: complete coverage, largest data file, number of multidisciplinary or subject databases, and proximity searching.[20] If a particular discipline is stressed, the vendor with the largest number of databases in the discipline and with the databases most in need will likely be the first choice. For retrospective or current information, database coverage, its growth, size, and update will be the primary factors for assessment. It may be noted that the difference in proximity searching which will be noted in part two, as pointed out by Haines, has been minimized in major vendors since SDC introduced the feature.

Ease of Use

There is no consensus on the criteria by which to judge ease of use. Krichmar suggests the following:[21] (1) the difficulty (or ease) of memory recall of a given command and/or its mnemonic versions, (2) the physical awkwardness (or lack of it) of actually entering a given command at the terminal. . . the need to re-member (or not to remember) any fixed order or sequence of argument values following a command... not completely understanding the meaning or purpose of a command. . .

In addition, the user may consider as a factor for ease of use the length of training required, brief and unambiguous commands, the number of errors, and easily understood messages.[22] A survey of online searchers' perceptions and attitudes toward the command (or user) languages of DIALOG and SDC indicates that a majority of users preferred DIALOG for two major reasons: (1) SDC's ORBIT system has fewer files than DIALOG, and (2) "the perceived awkwardness of ORBIT's STRINGSEARCHing and term expansion."[23] But of the three commercial vendors—DIALOG, SDC, and BRS-SDC was considered easiest to use, being the "most human."[24]

Retrieval Result

The user may also consider the retrieval result as a factor in choosing a vendor. Williams mentions as criteria for evaluation and selection of database services the standard internal format, data elements in the printout or display, arrangement of data elements on the output, and options available for sorting the output.[25] The print commands and the availability of customized format may affect the user's attitude toward a system. As one study points out, the printing format flexibility and printed documentation are better developed in SDC.[26] It appears, however, that differences in the use of print commands in the three systems are insignificant, and most users do not consider the inflexibility of the printing format a major concern because of the availability of a number of pre-formatted options. In some databases, items retrieved can be sorted in logical arrangement, such as alphabetical order by author or title or in descending order by sales volume. In all major systems, offline sorting is available. At present, only DIALOG has the feature of online sorting.

Costs

In the study of the three commerical online vendors, SDC's prices and costs were higher than those of DIALOG and BRS because of, in some cases, the higher rates of telecommunication that SDC charged.[27] SDC's discounts for 100 hours of monthly use were less than those of DIALOG and BRS.[28] Overall, BRS had the lowest rates, but its lowest rates were offset by the inability to perform online retrospective searching in some large databases.[29] The study also points out that SDC used more paper in a printing terminal.[30] A similar finding is reported from a comparative study of DIALOG and SDC in six databases in which the "time availability," savings in connect time cost, and savings in keystrokes by an experienced searcher were rated in favor of DIALOG.[31]

Over years of improvement and refinement, most searching features, such as display of terms, truncation, and proximity searching, have been made available in major vendors, and all the vendors provide easy access to their systems. Command languages and protocols are considered friendly. As differences in using the systems become less distinct, most of the criteria suggested by Atherton, Blue, and others have now become either standard or minor concerns. The choice of a particular vendor appears to depend more on factors of subject fields available, range of coverage, and costs than on technical searching aspects of the systems.

NOTES

1. 6 *Online Review* (1982) 353-90.

2. Based on *DIALOG Database Catalog* (DIALOG, July 1983), *ORBIT Database* (SDC), May 1983), and *Directory and Database Catalog* (BRS, 1983), including forthcoming databases.

3. 12 *Advanced Technology Libraries* (1983) 1.

4. Roger K. Summit, "DIALOG—A Forward Look," 11 (12) *Chronolog* (1983) 231.

5. For a brief history of SDC's ORBIT, see *ORBIT User Manual*, p. 1.

6. 9 *Searchlight* (November/December 1981).

7. Richard V. Janke, "Business on BRS—Focus on Predicasts," 6 *Database* (1983) 33-50.

8. Kristyn Kuroki, "Online Regional and On-Site Training Opportunities in the Lockheed, SDC and BRS Systems and Their Databases," 3 *Online* (1979) 36-49.

9. For a guide to document ordering through DIALOG and SDC, see Mary Margaret Gibbs and George A. Laszio, "Document Ordering

Through Lockheed's DIALOG and SDC's ORBIT—A User's Guide," 4 *Online* (1980) 31-38.

10. 10 (12) *Chronolog* (1982) 240-41.

11. 6 (11) *BRS Bulletin* (1982) 1.

12. For a synopsis of selected information utilities, see Elizabeth Ferrarini, "The Information Utilities," 1 *Linkup* (1983) 14.

13. *MAGIC User's Manual* (Toronto, Ontario, Canada: I. P. Sharp, 1980), p. 3.

14. See *Financial and Economic Data Bases Reference Guide* (Toronto, Ontario, Canada: I. P. Sharp, 1983) p. 143; David Keith, "The Database of I. P. Sharp," 6 *Database* (1983) 51-61.

15. Hollis Vail, "The Source Today," 8 *ASIS Bulletin* (1982) 21.

16. Maureen Corcoran, "Mead Data Central and "All the News That's Fit to Print' " 7 *Online* (1983) 32-35; Carol Tenopir, "Full-Text, Downloading, and Other Issues," 108 *Library Journal* (1983) 1111.

17. 11 (8) *Advanced Technology Libraries* (1983) 1.

18. Pauline Atherton and Roger W. Christian. *Libraries and Online Services* (White Plains, N.Y.: Knowledge Industry, 1977) p. 36.

19. Richard I. Blue, "Questions for Selection of Information Retrieval Systems," 3 *Online Review* (1979) 78-83.

20. Judith S. Haines, "Experiences in Training End-user Searches," 6 *Online* (1982) 15.

21. Albert Krichmar, "Command Language Ease of Use: A Comparison of DIALOG and ORBIT," 5 *Online Review* (1981) 227-28.

22. Ibid., 229-30.

23. Ibid., 233.

24. Ryan E. Hoover, "A Comparison of Three Commercial Online Vendors," 3 *Online* (1979) 21.

25. Martha E. Williams, "Criteria for Evaluation and Selection of Data Bases and Database Services," 66 *Special Libraries* (1975) 563.

26. Irwin Weiss, "Evaluation of ORBIT and DIALOG Using Six Databases," 67 *Special Libraries* (1976) 579.

27. Ryan E. Hoover, "A Comparison," p. 10.

28. Ibid.

29. Ibid.

30. Ibid.

31. Irwin Weiss, "Evaluation of ORBIT and DIALOG," 67 *Special Libraries* (1976) 579.

6

Managing the Online Searching Service

The inauguration of online searching service requires planning and investment in equipment, resources, and personnel. Decisions have to be made as to the needs of online service, how to provide the service, who is to do it, when to do it, and where to do it. The needs of users and potential users of online service and the user's ability to pay, if charged, must be assessed.[1] Also involved in establishing the service are problems of selecting equipment, calculating the cost for the library, determining whether the cost will be recovered, planning office routines, and evaluating the implications for library operation.

EQUIPMENT

For online searching, a telephone, a terminal, and a modem, if the terminal does not have a built-in modem, are three essentials. The telephone is used to connect the terminal with a computer either directly or via telecommunication networks. The user may find the following book useful for information on modems and terminals: *Online Terminal/Microcomputer Guide and Directory 1982-83*, 3rd ed., Weston, Conn.: Online, 1982, 286p; updated by supplements in 1982 and 1983. The *Guide and Directory* contains feature articles, specifications for print and video terminals, microcomputers, modems, and six directories

(U.S. sales, U.S. service, U.S. brokers sales, U.S. brokers service, international sales, and international service).

The Modem

The modem, an acronym for modulator-demodulator translates signals into tones that can be transmitted over ordinary phone lines. Computers generate digital information, but phone lines can only transmit voice or analog information. A modem converts digital information into analog information or vice versa, so that data can be transmitted through phone lines to and from the computer.[2] A modem is connected with the terminal by an interface RS-232C cable. Computers handle data by bits. Most computers transmit parallel data, that is, a group of bits transmitted simultaneously over separate lines. Regular phone lines do not provide multiple lines to transmit parallel data. The use of the RS-232C is to serialize parallel data into logical sequence and to enable transmission of each bit one at a time.[3]

There are three basic kinds of modems: (1) acoustic coupler, (2) direct-connect, and (3) intelligent.[4] The most widely used modem is an acoustic coupler, which holds the telephone handset. It is either a separate unit with a cable to connect with the terminal or a built-in unit of the terminal. The advantage of a separate unit is that the modem can be used for other terminals. The direct-connect modem can be plugged into a modular phone jack without the acoustic coupler. The intelligent modem can be programmed to do auto-logon, auto logoff, and auto-search. Modems must be compatible with industry standards. At 300-baud, they must have a Bell 103 modem and at 1200 baud with either a Bell 212A or a VADIC 3400 modem.

The Terminal

The terminal, a typewriterlike device, is used to enter and receive information from a computer. In selecting a terminal, factors to be considered include (1) cost, (2) kinds, (3) buying or leasing, (4) maintenance, (5) portability, (6) speed, (7) compatibility with communication networks, (8) ease of operation, (9) printout quality, and (10) noise level.[5]

Kinds of Terminals

There are in general two kinds of terminals: a CRT (Cathode-ray tube), also called VDT (Visual display terminal), and a printer. For a CRT terminal, the following features should be considered:[6] (1) a large number of display lines (twenty-four or more), (2) a line width of seventy-three to eighty characters, (3) availability of interface for use with an attached hard-copy printer, and (4) ability to display lower-case alphabets. A CRT is cheaper than a printer, and its display on the screen can be seen by many people. Its major drawback is that it cannot retain the search results for later viewing.

Use of the CRT has raised questions about its impact on the health of its users. Abnormal pregnancies and birth defects were reported among women working with CRT's.[7] Although there is no conclusive evidence of the relationship between the use of a CRT and health hazards, Miller has compiled an annotated bibliography on the subject and provided some guidelines for using CRT's from the ergonomic point of view.[8]

Terminal Functions

Functionally, terminals fall into three categories: communication, intelligent, and programmable. The communication terminal simply transmits and receives information. The intelligent terminal has a limited ability for programming, editing, formatting, and data entry. The programmable terminals have software support, such as personal computers, with capability of connecting to the databases.

Terminal Speed

The terminal's speed is measured by BPS (bits per second), CPS (characters per second), or baud (signals), that is, the number of bits, characters, or signals transmitted or received per second. A high-speed terminal is more expensive than a low-speed one. The high cost is, however, offset by using less connect time. It is estimated that if more than thirty searches are performed each month, the use of high-speed terminals is more cost-effective.[9]

Printout Quality

A thermal non-impact printer creates dot matrix characters on special heat-sensitive paper.[10] It operates with less noise compared with the impact printer. The non-impact printer does not, however, produce good quality hard copy. Another limitation is that it can only make single copies. For a clearer impression, an impact printer should be used. The impact printers are of two types: dot matrix and character. A dot matrix impact printer makes characters as clusters of dots on any paper through a ribbon. A character impact printer produces sharp typewriterlike characters. The impact printers are more expensive than the non-impact printers. An impact printer equipped with changeable print wheels is one of the top grades currently available in the market.

BASIC COSTS

One should be aware of four basic costs for providing the online service:

(1) Terminal cost—the cost to purchase or lease a terminal with its related expenses, such as the maintenance contract. The price for a terminal has been stable and competitive in some models. Radio Shack's PT-210 portable terminal with built-in acoustic coupler capable of connecting to communication networks costs about $500. There is a sizable price range between the low-speed and fast terminals. For instance, the list price of a Texas Instrument's 745 portable (30 CPS) is $1,515; whereas, a Texas Instrument's 785 portable featuring 120 CPS has a list price of $2,200, a difference of $685. The price for leasing a terminal ranges from $85 to $150 per month.

(2) Communication usage—the telephone charge to connect the terminal with the computer either directly or via telecommunication networks.

(3) Computer time—the time connected with the system. Once the computer is connected, the user is charged with connect time, whether he or she is actually using the computer or merely pondering search strategies. Fees vary depending on the databases as noted in the previous chapter.

(4) Online display and/or offline prints. In some databases, there is a charge for online display. The offline print rate per full record in the DIALOG system ranges from 10 cents to $50.

Besides direct costs, other costs include support costs, such as furniture, site preparation, promotional materials, print reference sources; and overhead costs, such as those for administering the service and the facilities.[11] The unit cost of online searching varies. At Lockheed, the cost per search was found to average $47.[12] An average search was $25 at Kodak Research Laboratories.[13] A much lower cost per search was reported at Purdue, which averaged $8.41 per search in 1979-1980.[14] The University of Pennsylvania calculated an average cost per search at $25, in addition to the costs for equipment, training, or general overhead.[15] The discrepancy of cost is primarily because different methods are used to figure the cost. The cost will be lower if indirect costs, such as administrative overhead and salary, are excluded.

Fee Recovery

One of the issues facing libraries, particularly public libraries, is whether it is justifiable to charge end users a fee for the online service. The opposing camps are strongly divided, and the proponents for free service cite the long history of public libraries during which there is scanty evidence for the pricing of services directly to the library user.

Despite the argument for free service, an overwhelming majority of libraries charge users some, most, or all costs of online searching. Drake criticized those persons who urged access to information at no cost as confusing the issue of free access to information with that of free provision of information.[16] According to Drake, in many instances the cost charged to users is more than justified because of the time saved and the retrieval of citations that could not be found in a manual search.[17] In a recent survey of publicly supported libraries, 709 libraries do charge fees to users, constituting 72 percent of the total libraries surveyed.[18] The *Advanced Technology Libraries* reported in its survey that 85 percent of the academic libraries surveyed passed along charges to their patrons, and a majority of public libraries, except where prohibited by law as it is in New York, charged the patrons for the connect fees.[19]

Methods for fee recovery vary. Some completely pass the cost over to the users; some charge fees according to a fixed schedule; others charge only the vendor usage fee; and still others charge a certain amount of fees above cost. In a DIALIB project to examine the public library as a "linking agent" between the public and the databases, a fixed fee schedule of $5 was set up for a "standard search" in the DIALOG system, that is, a search restricted to a single database with no more than ten search sets and twenty offline prints.[20] The program of the Metropolitan Reference and Research Agency (METRO) in New York City provided DIALOG service to public library patrons and charged a prorated share of the fixed expenses for searches done on behalf of its members, but no administrative costs were charged.[21]

At Purdue University libraries, fees are established to recover the vendors' usage charges and indirect costs, such as computer terminal supplies, terminal maintenance, search analysts' initial and follow-up training, and user manuals.[22] A 20 percent fee is added to the user's bill (50 percent for non-university users) to recover actual indirect costs so that the service can be provided without a large subsidy or loss.[23] At M.I.T. libraries, all direct costs and administrative overhead are passed to users, and some are charged for the time of a specialist during the appointment.[24] The user and the specialist work together during a typical appointment, which lasted 57 minutes, of which 37 minutes were spent online. The actual average cost to the user was $45.84 for computer connect costs and administrative costs, and, if they applied, $7.84 for the time of the specialist and $20.75 for offline printouts.[25] A survey of 200 users revealed that 77 percent of the 92 responses found the service to be worth the charges.[26]

Personnel Selection and Training

Atherton and Christian state that one of the key elements for start-up consideration of online searching is personnel selection and training.[27] Because online searching is an extended reference service, the reference department of a library will be the primary unit of the service. Any librarian with a logical mind and with no preconceived notion against machines will be a suitable choice to be trained for the new service.

Training of personnel to do searching is costly. The training programs fall into three categories: (1) Vendors' or producers' training workshops or seminars. All major systems and many producers sponsor training workshops and seminars. For instance, DIALOG charges $135 per person for a one-and-a-half-day session. (2) Professional development or continuing education training programs offered by users' groups, institutions, and associations. In general, this consists of a one-day workshop with or without hands-on practice. (3) Formal training offered by library science schools. Fenichel and Harter have identified three patterns of this kind of training:[28] (a) a single course devoted entirely to online searching, (b) online searching as a major component, 40 to 60 percent, of another course, and (c) full integration of online searching into all the general reference and subject bibliography courses. The first approach is considered the prevalent one.

Physical Facilities

Space and physical facilities are another major component of the online service. Since the operation of terminals is noisy and since interviews with end users are in most cases necessary, a separate room or a space away from the reading area deserves consideration. Physical facilities include wiring, installment of telephone, furniture, forms for the online service, and shelves for print reference sources.

IMPACT ON THE LIBRARY OPERATION

The online searching service extends the resources of the library beyond its walls. Though physically not in the library, the databases constitute, in essence, a part of the library resources because they can be accessed as if they were in the library holding. As such, their existence should be reflected in the library catalog. The traditional concept of cataloging only for in-house materials and for "object in hand" has to be changed.

Discussion of cataloging machine-readable data files (MRDF) began in the 1960s.[29] In 1970, a Subcommittee on Rules for Machine-Readable Data Files was formed to study the bibliographical control of MRDF in the library catalog. A final report of the subcommittee was released in 1976, and as a result, the second edition of the *Anglo-American Cataloguing Rules* (AACR2) included in its ninth chapter rules on machine-readable data files.[30] According to AACR2, MRDF refers to "a body of information coded by methods that require the use of a machine (typically, but not always, a computer) for processing." The definition is broad enough to include bibliographical databases, but it appears that the framers of chapter nine did not have in mind the application of the rules to bibliographic databases accessible through vendors.

The application of AACR2 is inadequate for the following situations: (1) same database with different titles used by vendors; (2) same database with different sizes marketed by vendors; (3) varied parallels, either broader or narrower, or lack of some features in the counterpart of a database or vice versa; and (4) same database with different abbreviations or file numbers for access. Other problems include the amount of detail needed to describe the database and the number of added entries to be used.

At the Airlie House Conference in Cataloging and Information Services, three levels of description for each data source were suggested: standard cataloging information, file content, and physical characteristics.[31] Taking file content, for example, how much detail should be provided? Should all searching features and fields or paragraphs of a unit record in the database be described? The added entries pose another problem. Are added entries required for vendors and for a series of databases, such as DIALOG's Chemical Information System, which consists of four databases? Serious consideration should be given to the following aspects for cataloging the databases:

1. Title with medium designator in the bracket, parallel title, and other titles

2. The parallel with notes describing differences and range of coverage

3. Search title (abbreviations for access) or file number for access

4. Period of coverage—most databases, updated and cumulated periodically, can be treated as serials with open entries

5. Added entries for vendors

6. Added entries for a series of databases

Another impact on the library operation is the database's relationship with its print or microform counterpart. Online service complements the traditional library service, and at the same time, it duplicates with its print or microform counterparts,. Many databases are current, but some of them have selective coverage only. For retrospective and full coverage, their print or microform counterparts are indispensable. If both databases and their counterparts have the same coverage, the availability of databases appears to have an impact on their counterparts.

In a report prepared for the Commission of the European Communities on "the impact on user charges of the extended use of online information services," Barwise presented three empirical findings:[32] (1) Subscription to printed abstracts, journals, and indexes showed no increase and in many cases declined largely because of economic factors. (2) The impact of online retrieval on print subscriptions had been small. The growth of online mainly reflected an increase in the volume of searches, rather than a switch from the use of printed materials. (3) There was much uncertainty about how much online usage would grow. Lancaster and Goldhor revealed a similar result.[33] They reported that reasons for cancellation of subscriptions were not due to the availability of online searching. Nine out of 102 subscriptions, or 8.8 percent, cancelled were solely due to the availability of online access; 60 cancellations, or 58.8 percent, were not influenced by the availability online. The authors contended that availability of online access had so far a rather minor effect in causing libraries to cancel subscriptions to print on paper. It must be noted, however, that the 8.8 percent cancellations may very well increase, if more databases with the same coverage as their counterparts become available.

Online databases have an impact on their print counterparts in two obvious ways: (1) In searching capabilities, databases are superior to their counterparts. To single out a particular language, to identify a certain type of document, to limit publications to a particular year, and to confine searching in different modes cannot be done easily by manual searching. Some databases even provide statistical computation in addition to information. In Predicasts's databases, the user can tabulate, index, graph, correlate, and regress the economic statistical data.[34] (2) For less-used print indexes and abstracts, their counterparts, online databases, serve as a good standby. Since most databases use "charge as you go basis," substituting online use for subscription to less frequently used print products may be more cost-effective. The Center for the Study of Youth Development, Boys Town, rarely uses popular materials and so relies on the Magazine Index database and the Information Bank rather than their print counterparts; and the use of the *American Statistics Index* database in one year totalled 2.17 hours, a definite saving over subscriptions to its counterpart.[35] On the other hand, there is perhaps a need to use the print counterpart, which is less expensive than the database. In 1983, Gale Research began monthly publication of *Business Publications Index and Abstracts* as a print counterpart of the Management Contents database in view of the limited use of the database because of high cost, searching skill, and equipment.

The traditional reference service has experienced perhaps most strongly the impact of online service. Its performance must be changed to ensure effective online searching. We shall now turn to that topic.

NOTES

1. David M. Max, *On-line Bibliographic Search Services* (Washington, D.C.: Association of Research Libraries, Office of University Library Management Studies Occasional Paper, no. 4, 1976). Max is perhaps the first handbook for starting an online searching service. See also Ryan E. Hoover, "Computer Aided Reference Service in the Academic Library," 3 *Online* (1979) 28-41.

2. Steve Franzmeier, " 'Ma' Bell's System," 1 *Linkup* (1983) 18; Rick Hosking, "Serial Data Transmission," 1 *Linkup* (1983) 42.

3. Eric Balkan, "The RS-232 Interface," 1 *Linkup* (1983) 38-39.

4. Brian McDermott, "Looking at Modems," 1 *Linkup* (1938) 15-17.

5. Mark S. Radwin, "The Intelligent Person's Guide to Choosing a Terminal for Online Interactive Use," 1 *Online* (1977) 12-18. Radwin lists five decisions and five checkpoints for choosing a terminal. Also see David Grossman, "How to Choose a Terminal," paper presented at Online 1979, Atlanta, Ga., on November 9, 1979.

6. Radwin, "The Intelligent Person's Guide."

7. Willie Schatz, "Do CRTs Kill," 83 *Datamation* (1983) 56.

8. Bruce R. Miller, "Radiation, Ion Depletion, and VDTs: Healthful Use of Visual Display Terminals," 2 *Information Technology and Libraries* (1983): 151-58.

9. David Grossman, "How to Choose a Terminal"; A. L. Moore and S. R. Pyrce, eds., *Chicago Online Users Introductory Guide* (Chicago, Ill.: COLUG, 1978) p. 17. It is also considered to be economical to use a 1,200-baud terminal, if over 42 searches are done per month at an input and output ratio of 1:9. *See* John Wish et al., "Terminal Costs for On-line Searching," 33 *College and Research Libraries* (1977) 391-97.

10. For a discussion of the printers, refer to Janet Bruman, "Physical Requirements: Terminals, Printers, and Furnitures" in James J. Manoleny, ed., *Online Searching Technique and Management* (Chicago: American Library Association, 1983) pp. 38-40.

11. Jean E. Koch, "A Review of the Costs and Cost-Effectiveness of Online Bibliographic Searching," 10 *Reference Service Review* (1982) 59-60.

12. Stanley A. Elman, "Cost Comparison of Manual and Online Computerized Literature Searching," 66 *Special Libraries* (1975) 12-18.

13. Judith S. Haines, "Experiences in Training Searchers," 6 *Online* (1982) 17.

14. Katherine M. Markee, "Economies of Online Retrieval," 5 *Online Review* (1981) 439-44.

15. James A. Cogwell, "On-line Search Services: Implications for Libraries and Library Users," 39 *College and Research Libraries* (1978) 277.

16. Miriam A. Drake, "Impact of On-line Systems on Library Functions" in Allen Kent and Thomas J. Garvin, eds., *The On-Line Revolution in Libraries* (New York: Marcel Dekker, 1978) p. 112.

17. Ibid., 102-3.

18. Mary Jo Lynch, *Financing Online Search Services in Publicly Supported Libraries* (Chicago, Ill.: American Library Association, 198) p. 24.

19. 12 *Advanced Technology Libraries* (1983) 1.

20. Roger K. Summit and Oscar Firschein, "Fee for Online Retrieval Service in a Public Library Setting" in 12 *Proceedings of the ASIS Annual Meeting* 1975) p. 155.

21. Alice E. Ahlgren, "Providing On-Line Search Services" in 12

Proceedings of the ASIS Annual Meeting (1975) p. 156.

22. Markee, "Economics of Online Retrieval," p. 438.

23. Ibid., 441-44.

24. Alan R. Benefeld et al., "User Receptivity to Fee-for-Service Computer-Based Reference in a University Community" in 12 *Proceedings of the ASIS Annual Meeting* (1975) p. 151.

25. Ibid.

26. Ibid.

27. Pauline Atherton and Roger W. Christian, *Librarians and Online Services* (White Plains, N.Y.: Knowledge Industry, 1977) p. 32.

28. Carol Fenichel and Stephen Paul Harter. *Survey of Online Searching Instruction in Schools of Library and Information Science* (Dublin, Ohio: OCLC Development Division, 1981) pp. 38-39; for a summary of the findings, see Stephen P. Harter and Carol H. Fenichel, "Online Searching in Library Education," 23 *Journal of Education for Librarianship* (1982) 3-22.

29. Marilyn Nasatir, "The Cataloging and Classification of Machine-Readable Data Files," 1 *Cataloging and Classification Quarterly* (1980) 26-27.

30. *Anglo-American Cataloguing Rules* (Chicago: American Library Association, 1978) pp. 201-16.

31. Nasatir, "Cataloging and Classification," pp. 32-33.

32. P. Barwise, "The Impact on User Charges of the Extended Use of Online Information Services," 10 *Information Reports and Bibliographies* (1981) 3-29.

33. F. W. Lancaster and Herbert Goldhor, "The Impact of Online Services on Subscriptions to Printed Publications," 5 *Online Review* (1981) 307-10.

34. Joanne Tysenhouse, "The Pleasures and Pitfalls of the Predicasts Computational System," 4 *Online* (1980) 26-29.

35. James Sweetland, "Using Online Systems in Reference Work," 3 *Online* (1979) 19.

7

Reference Service and Online Searching

Online searching is an extended reference service. The use of computers necessitates new approaches to the traditional reference service. Reference interview becomes more important than ever. The presence of the patron, not required in the traditional reference service, is regarded to be helpful in searching; and the pre-search preparation involves additional work before using the computer. Most mistakes and some false moves in searching can be eliminated by a carefully planned search strategy. There are two obvious reasons for these approaches.[1] First is cost. Once the computer is connected, the fee for using the computer and the communication network is charged. Second, in natural-language searching, any word can be searched as a subject. The word, related word, synonym, near synonym, acronym, and abbreviation of a subject must be searched. The patron, particularly one who knows the subject, will be the most important source for the accurate word, related words, synonyms, and so forth.

REFERENCE INTERVIEW

In online searching, it is recommended that every request go through the process of reference interview. Reference interview helps establish specific need, ameliorate mistakes, and minimize the chance of failure, thus ensuring high relevancy and reducing cost. And a series of terms or words for searching can be more effectively built with the help of the patron in the interview.

The stress on the teaching role of librarians was a catalyst in the development of reference service, and the instructional aspect has long functioned as a part of it. This role requires that librarians provide guidance and direction in the use of information rather than in the end product. Today, librarians give less weight to the instructional function. They spend more time dealing with access to materials and provision of information. In online searching, the instructional function appears to be entirely eliminated from the reference service. Although it has been suggested that searchers familiarize patrons with features of online searching, including the use of Boolean logical operators and the basic properties of set theory,[2] it is doubtful that a searcher should spend time instructing the patron on some of the basics of searching. However, presence of the patron during searching is generally favored, because the patron can often provide useful information for searching and refining search strategies and for post-search review.[3]

Online searching requires not only knowledge of the subject field and the databases but also the searching skills acquired over a considerable amount of time. The cost is prohibitive for a patron who is unfamiliar with the system, the database, the search strategy, and the search language to work at a keyboard. It is also financially unfeasible for the librarian to instruct the patron how to use the terminal to do searching. The role of an intermediary is a new dimension of the traditional reference service in that the patron is not allowed to use the reference source, the database. The patron must rely on the reference librarian to retrieve information. That librarians are seen as valuable resources is regarded by Atherton to be the most important impact on library patrons.[4]

PRE-SEARCH PREPARATION

For cost-effectiveness, online searching requires preparation before connecting with the system. Markee considers that the end product of searching will be better and the computer connect time will be less, if an appropriate amount of time is spent in preparing the search strategy.[5] The preparation consists of two essential components: (1) The needed information, including the subject and search range and scope. The searcher must be sure about the subject matter to be searched; range of search, such as language, period, type of materials, titles of journals, number of citations, output format; and approximate cost the user is willing to pay. (2) Search strategy, the logical sequence of the process, including the selection of database(s), the system(s), free-text searching, controlled vocabulary searching, listing of terms to be searched, and so forth. Somerville mentions fourteen common components of the interview to determine the needed information.[6]

1. Use interpersonal communication and negotiation skills.
2. Discuss subject with user.
3. Determine if a computer search is the appropriate way to answer the question.
4. Make sure that you understand the question.
5. Determine comprehensiveness of the search question.
6. Identify limits to be placed on the search.
7. Select database(s) or system.
8. Identify additional sources.
9. Identify main concepts and develop search strategy.
10. Anticipate potential problems.
11. Determine alternative strategies.
12. Determine citation output.
13. Discuss confidentiality.
14. Conduct post-search review.

The fourteen points actually deal with three stages of online searching: pre-search interview, pre-search strategy, and post-search review.[7] Most libraries require the user to fill out a request form to specify needs and the range of the search. The form may include search topic, description of search subject and terminology, broad or narrow search, number of citations requested, range of period of the subject coverage, language limitations, type of materials, number of periodicals searched, cost range acceptable to the patron, agreement to pay, and status of the user, if cost schedule varies according to user's status, for example, faculty, student, or non-resident. A sample search request form is reproduced for reference.

DePaul University Library

Computer Index Search Service-Request Form

Name_____   Date_____

Address____ _____   Phone: Home_____

                                                        Office_____

Faculty_____ Graduate Student_____Undergrad. Student_____Staff _____

Department or major_____   Social Security # _____

Search Topics:

Give a detailed statement of your research problem. Describe the subject using the most specific terminology possible. Define terms which have a special mean-ing in your request. Be sure to mention any aspects which would not be acceptable.

_____

_____

_____

_____

If known, list any relevant citations or the names of authors who have written on this topic:

_____

_____

_____

Which printed indexes have you searched on this topic? List any relevant keywords or thesaurus terms that you used.

_____

_____

_____

_____

Have you had a computer search done before?   Yes____ No_____

If yes, was the search on this topic?   Yes____   No _____

Results needed no later than_____

(over)

```
Database preference, if known_____

Would you like to be present when the search is performed?  Yes_____ No _____
(Search can be scheduled Monday through Friday between 9:00 and 4:30)

Please check the statement below which most nearly defines your expectations for
this search:

        _____ A broad search, producing a relatively long list of citations,
               including most relevant ones but also some irrelevant items.

        _____ A narrow search, producing a short list of primarily relevant citations,
               probably missing some relevant onces.

Maximum number of citations acceptable _____

If available, do you wish to receive printed abstracts for the citations in the
bibliography you receive?   Yes_____ No _____

Limitations and restrictions (check where applicable):

     Language:  English only _____Others (specify)_____
     Date:  Most recent year only _____ All available _____Other_____
     Categories: Human only_____ Animal only_____ Other_____
                 Female only _____Male only _____Race/Nationality_____
                 Age_____Grade level_____
                 Geographic region_____

     Type of documents excluded:  Journal articles _____Dissertations_____
        Conference reports_____ Books_____ ERIC Documents_____ Other_____

     Concepts, terms, or categories to be excluded:

                 AUTHORIZATION TO CHARGE FOR COMPUTER LITERATURE SEARCH

I hereby authorize the DePaul University Library to perform the online search(es)
specified and agree to pay for one half the amount of terminal connect time,
offline prints, and mailing fees.  If the fee of faculty or staff is to be paid
by departmental funds a signed authorization form must be completed and returned
at the time of the search.  I realize that the DePaul University Library cannot
guarantee that references of interest will be retrieved or that those which are
retrieved will be highly relevant.  I also understand that the charges must be
paid at the time of the search even if no relevant items are found.

Signed_____
```

Reprinted with the permission of the DePaul University Library.

PREPARATION OF SEARCH STRATEGY

Online searching requires concept analysis and logical thought processes. Dolan and Kremin reject the attitude that anyone can run a computer search.[8] In their view, a searcher should be able to analyze concepts and funnel every search request, no matter how complex, into only two concepts.[9] A searcher should have a combination of traits, namely, concept analysis, flexibility of thinking, ability to think in synonyms, anticipation of variant word forms and spellings, and self-confidence.[10]

Search strategies vary. Frequently mentioned ones are building blocks, successive fractions, and citation pearl growing, as shown in the chart.[11]

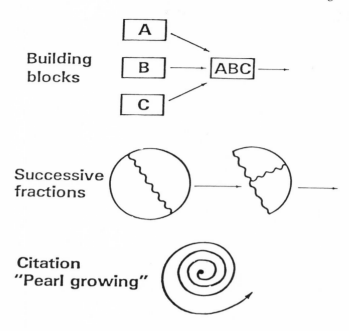

Building blocks refers to the method of building concepts and searching terms under each concept to find results. If the concept and terms are not precise, use the method of citation pearl growing to find a few clues by which to develop other search strategies. The strategy of successive fractions reduces the size of search results. But the most popular method is building blocks. Its operation can be illustrated in a simple form as follows.

Concept A	Concept B	Concept C
Terms		
(including synonyms	AND	AND
and	OR	OR
related terms)	NOT	NOT

For instance, in searching on "automobile safety for adults," the user will build concepts, such as automobile, safety, and adults, and then terms under the three concepts. An example is:

Concept A		Concept B		Concept C
Auto	A	Safe	A	Adult
Autos	N	Safety	N	Adults
Automobile	D	—	D	Man
Automobiles				Men
Truck				Woman
—				—

The user combines the terms under each concept for either narrow or broad results by using operators AND, OR, and NOT. For convenience of searching, a search worksheet should be used. The worksheet may include the name of the patron, date of appointment, free-text terms(s), thesaurus descriptor(s), databases expected to be used, and search strategies.

Online searching is not to search a concept but relevant terms. In free-text searching, terms related to the concept, synonyms or not, should be searched to achieve a large recall. The searcher must develop a strategy to build terms and to execute the strategy. The building blocks search may be from broad to narrow or vice versa.[12] For a broad result, a large number of terms under possibly relevant concepts are selected and combined in various ways. If too few references are retrieved, select less specific terms or delete some concepts. In the search example cited here, assuming not many references are retrieved by searching terms under three concepts, delete concept C for a large result, although the result will not be precisely relevant. In a narrow search, only terms most likely to be of relevance to the topic are selected. If too many references are retrieved, combine concepts by using AND or NOT logical operators, or restrict the search by other factors, such as language, date, and document type.

SEARCH LOG AND OTHER FORMS

For accounting and statistical purposes, and for maintaining the operation within the budget, a search log and other forms should be kept for online searching. The search log lists date, name of the patron, department, title or subject, databases, time online, offline prints, citations retrieved, total costs, charge number, notes, and so forth.[13] A sample form is included here.

DePaul University Library
Campus _____

COMPUTER SEARCH LOGBOOK

Month ____ Year ____ Page ____

Date	Name	Status	Search-er	Database	Vendor	Session No.	Elapsed Terminal Time	Citations Received	Offline Services Requested	Charges		
										Total	Paid	Method

Reprinted with the permission of the DePaul University Library.

Other forms essential to online searching include an evaluation form and a payment notice or invoice. The evaluation form is used by the patron to assess the effectiveness of online searching. Feedback from the patron serves as a valuable guide to refining and improving online searching services. The payment notice or invoice is used to notify the patron of the charges for online searching. The use of various forms in online searching is an added work load for the traditional reference service. For sample forms, reference may be made to Daniels.[14] Based on forms collected from a number of libraries, Daniels presents four sample forms: search request, invoice, database evaluation and search request log, with detailed explanations on the search request form. Sample forms are also found in Atherton and Christian, and Hoover.[15]

NOTES

1. Arleen N. Somerville, "The Pre-Search Reference Interview—A Step by Step Guide," 5 *Database* (1982) 32.

2. Ibid., 34; Douglas R. Knox and Marjorie M. K. Hlava, "Effective Search Strategies," 3 *Online Review* (1979) 148-52.

3. Oscar Firschein, "Use of Online Bibliographic Search in Public Libraries: A Retrospective Evaluation," 2 *Online Review* (1978) 41-55.

4. Pauline Atherton and Roger W. Christian, *Librarians and Online Services* (White Plains, N.Y,.: Knowledge Industry, 1977) p. 9; Alan E. Bayer and Gerald Jahoda, "Effect of Online Bibliographic Searching on Scientists' Information Style," 5 *Online Review* (1981) 323-33.

5. Katherine M. Markee, "Economics of Online Retrieval," 5 *Online Review* (1981) 444; Knox and Hlava, "Effective Search Strategies," p. 148.

6. Arleen Somerville, "The Pre-Search Reference Interview," pp. 34-36.

7. Jacquelin A. Gavryck, "Teaching Concept Identification Through the Use of the Thesaurus of ERIC Descriptors," 4 *Online* (1980) 31-34.

8. Donna R. Dolan and Michael C. Kremin, "The Quality Control of Search Analysis," 3 *Online* (1979) 11.

9. Ibid., 9.

10. Ibid.

11. Robert E. Buntrock, "The Effect of the Searching Environment on Search Performance," 3 *Online* (1979) 12. Others add lowest postings and most specific facet approaches. See Carol H. Fenichel and Thomas

H. Hogan, *Online Searching: A Primer* (Marlton, N.J.: Learned Information, 1981) pp. 72-74; Charles T. Meadow and Pauline (Atherton) Cochrane. *Basics of Online Searching* (New York: John Wiley, 1981) pp. 136-41.

12. Betty K. Oldroyd and Charles L. Citroen, "Study of Strategies Used in On-Line Searching," 1 *Online Review* (1977) 301.

13. Donald T. Hawkins and Carolyn P. Brown, "What Is an Online Search?" 4 *Online* (1979) 16.

14. Linda Daniels, "A Matter of Form," 2 *Online* (1978) 31-39.

15. Atherton and Christian, *Librarians and Online Services*; Ryan E. Hoover, *The Library and Information Manager's Guide to Online Services* (White Plains, N.Y.: Knowledge Industry, 1980).

Part Two

8

Basic Procedures of Online Searching

The search in an online system consists of four basic procedures: logon, search, result, and logoff.

LOGON PROCEDURE

The logon procedure involves two major steps: (1) the user connects the terminal with the system and (2) then identifies himself or herself as a legitimate user. The most commonly used method to connect the system is by dial access. The searcher dials a telephone number to connect the terminal with the system either directly or through a telecommunication network, such as TELENET or TYMNET.

In general, three pieces of equipment are used: a telephone, a modem (if not a built-in unit), and a terminal. Switches on both the modem and the terminal should be adjusted depending on their models to ensure proper connection. Using the DIABLO Systems Comdata modem and Hytype II printer terminal for 300-baud and full duplex users as an example, their switches should be adjusted as follows:

Modem

Switch	Adjusted
ECHO	OFF
COPY	OFF

Terminal

Switch	Adjusted
SCROLL	ON
SPACING	10
LINES/INCH	6
FEED	1
FUNCTIONS	NORMAL
MODE	PRINT
DUPLEX	FULL
RATE	30
LINE	LINE
PARITY	NO

Basic steps to connect the system are as follows:

1. Turn on power to the terminal and to the modem, if it is not a built-in unit of the terminal.

2. Dial the telephone number of the system for direct connection or the telephone number for a telecommunication network node closest to your location.

3. Place the telephone headset on the modem, an acoustic coupler, after a high-pitched tone is received. The tone indicates that the telecommunication network can be connected.

4. Give a terminal model identifier. The identifier varies depending on the terminal model and the telecommunication network.

5. Enter the system number or code, equivalent to an institution's address.

6. Identify yourself as a legitimate user by giving your assigned password, after the system is connected.

As an illustration, to use TELENET to connect the system requires the following steps:

1. Dial a local TELENET telephone number.

2. Hear the high-pitched tone, then place the telephone handset in the acoustic coupler and press the carriage return twice.

3. A TELENET herald, the terminal port address, and a prompt, TERMINAL = , will be displayed. The prompt is used to identify the terminal node. On most terminals, simply press the carriage return once; there is no need to identify the terminal model.

4. TELENET will respond with the @ sign to indicate that TELENET is ready to connect with the system. Type C for connect, skip a space, and type the system address.

Using a terminal is similar to using a typewriter. Thus, anyone who can type should be at ease in using the terminal. There are, however, some key functions that a user must understand in order to have the terminal perform properly. Here is a reproduction of the keyboard of a Texas Instrument's printer terminal.

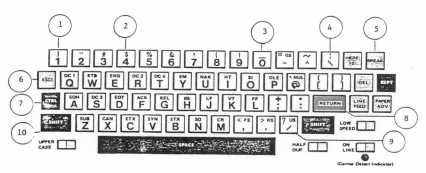

Courtesy of Texas Instruments.

Some key functions of the terminal should be noted:
The numerical key (1) and the lower case letter "1" key are not interchangeable.
The numerical 0 key (3) and letter "O" key are not interchange able either.
The control key (7) and the H key are used to correct an error in input. Hold down the control key and press the H key, called the control H method, and the system will respond in backspace and thus erase the error. The user may type the correct letter(s) over the incorrect one(s). You may use this method to bring you back to the error as many times as necessary.
The break key (5) is used to instruct the system to stop proceeding. Press the break key, followed by a carriage return (8) (optional depending on the system); the system will stop proceeding and responds with a new prompt. In BRS, the break function can only serve to stop online printing.

The carriage return ⑧ is used to request the system to respond. Be sure to press the carriage return after you have given your command and wish the system to respond. The system will not respond until the carriage return is pressed.

The backspace key, if there is one, is used to correct errors. Errors can be corrected by backspacing to the error and simply typing the correct letter(s) over the incorrect one(s).

The escape key ⑥ is used to erase the entire line. In DIALOG, you may press the escape key followed by a carriage return to erase the entire line, or simply press the carriage return twice.

The backward slash key "\" ④ is used to correct individual characters. In SDC's ORBIT, you may use the back\slash, one slash for each error of character, and type the correct one(s) following the backward slash(es).

In ORBIT, the dollar sign key ② followed by a carriage return, is used to erase an entire line.

The question mark key ⑨ followed by a carriage return is used in BRS to erase an entire line.

A beginner often forgets to press the carriage return after completing a command. The system will not respond to commands until the carriage return is pressed. Also, a beginner is often overly eager to give a command without waiting for a prompt sign or a user cue. If the prompt does not appear, the system is not ready to receive any command.

The system's output provides, in general, six categories of messages:

The display of a prompt sign tells the user that the system is ready to receive instructions. The format of prompt varies. The question mark "?" is used in DIALOG. In ORBIT, the prompt "USER:" appears. BRS uses "__:" as a user cue on most terminals.

Current awareness messages announce such things as new features, unavailability of databases, and price changes. These messages are given immediately after the system is connected.

Some messages tell the user what to do next. For instance, after the system is connected, BRS responds: "ENTER DATA BASE NAME__:." In ORBIT, the message, "SPECIFY NUMBERS, ALL, OR NONE," appears after display of each term truncated. The user is told to make a selection.

Error messages indicate that the user has made an error in input. Two examples serve as an illustration. DIALOG will respond with "Bad password . . .," if the user enters an incorrect password. In BRS, input of a wrong paragraph qualifier will be given the statement "INVALID PARAGRAPH NAME, PROCESSING WILL CONTINUE."

Some messages tell the user that the system has completed its function according to the user's instructions. For instance, if the user enters a cancellation command of "AUDIT," the ORBIT system having completed the execution will respond with "SEARCH AUDITING IS NO LONGER IN EFFECT."

Some messages display the result of searching.

SEARCH PROCEDURE

The searcher employs various strategies seeking desired information. A search procedure involves basically two steps: (1) selection of a database and (2) searching of desired terms. To a great extent, searching features in the three systems are comparable. All systems require file selection before searching for desired information. The user must select files, one at a time, to do searching. In all systems, each search operation will result in a set or search statement giving number of records or postings. The set numbers are given in a consecutive order. They enable the user to do further searching by combining the set numbers with each other or the set numbers with other search terms. The set numbers are also essential for printing results.

Each system has its own master index to all databases available from the system. If the searcher is not certain which database(s) should be used, he or she may seek help from the master index. The master index serves as a clue to the number of postings on a desired term in different databases, thus enabling the searcher to select the databases with a substantial number of postings on a desired term. All systems feature free-text searching, that is, all words, with exceptions, in the text are searchable. The searcher may also search descriptors or controlled vocabularies in most files.

The use of Boolean and positional operators is available in each system. Boolean operators are used to coordinate and combine words and terms; whereas positional operators are used to retrieve records that contain words or terms in a specified order or sequence. In some databases, the use of positional operators is preferred to simple Boolean logical operators because the former achieve higher relevancy and precision. It must be noted that an ideal method in one database does not necessarily work the same way in other databases.

The record, known as the unit record, is divided into a number of fields or paragraphs, such as title, author, and language fields. Most fields or paragraphs are searchable. Illustrated here are sample records of the ERIC database from three vendors. Fields or paragraphs are indicated.

DIALOG

Accession number and Cheringhouse accession no.	EJ253769 EA514723
Title	Solar in the Snow Belt.
Source	American School and University, v54 n2 p54-55 Oct 1981
Availability	Available from: Reprint: UMI
Language	Language: English
Document type	Document Type: JOURNAL ARTICLE (080); PROJECT DESCRIPTION (141)
Abstract	Two schools in New York's snow belt region are using solar energy to heat their swimming pools. (Author)
Descriptors	Descriptors: Cost Effectiveness; *Educational Facilities Improvement; Elementary Secondary Education; *Heating; *Solar Radiation; *Swimming Pools

SDC's ORBIT

```
-1-
AN   - EJ253769
CHAN- EA514723
TI   - Solar in the Snow Belt
SO   - American School and University; v54 n2 p54-55 Oct
       1981 (Oct1981)
IS   - CIJMAR82
DT   - 080; 141
LA   - English
IT   - Cost Effectiveness; *Educational Facilities
       Improvement; Elementary Secondary Education;
       *Heating; *Solar Radiation; *Swimming Pools
AB   - Two schools in New York's snow belt region are using
       solar energy to heat their swimming pools. (Author)
```

```
AN EJ253769.
TI Solar in the Snow Belt.
SO American School and University; v54 n2 p54-55 Oct 1981. Oct81.
LG EN..
IS CIJMAR82.
CH EA514723.
PT 080; 141.
AV Reprint: UMI.
YR 81.
MJ Educational-Facilities-Improvement. Heating. Solar-Radiation.
   Swimming-Pools.
MN Cost-Effectiveness. Elementary-Secondary-Education.
AB Two schools in New York's snow belt region are using solar energy to
   heat their swimming pools. (Author).
```

A search can be confined to a particular field or paragraph, the component of a unit record, by using a qualifier. For instance, in DIALOG and ORBIT, the use of /TI, a title qualifier, after a term will limit the searching of the term to titles only. The same result will be achieved by using .TI. after the term in BRS. Searching for a string of words or characters, known as stringsearch, is also available. The use of ADJ in BRS instructs the system to search terms right next to each other and in that order. In addition, searching can be limited by date of publication, language, type of documents, and so forth. Each system also features truncation, that is, the use of a term stem to retrieve all terms beginning with that stem and capability of combining free-text subject searching with non-subject searching.

To search controlled vocabularies, also called index terms in ORBIT and descriptors in DIALOG and BRS, a thesaurus if available should be consulted before the search is begun. To search a single word as a controlled vocabulary, a qualifier to limit the search in the field of controlled vocabularies must be used to distinguish it from the word in a free-text search. The use of a qualifer is not required in searching of multiwords as controlled vocabularies. If a search for multiwords results in zero postings, in DIALOG and ORBIT, it can be assumed that they are not used as controlled vocabularies. In BRS, to search multiwords as controlled vocabularies, a hyphen should be used in between words as discussed in chapter eleven.

RESULT PROCEDURE

The user requests the system to present the search result in a chosen format. There are two: (1) pre-formatted and (2) tailored user's option. In the pre-formatted option, fields or paragraphs of a unit record to be presented are predetermined. For instance, the use of the format number 6 in most fields in DIALOG will present the title and DIALOG accession number of a unit record. Since the format is predetermined, no change can be made. In a user's option format, on the other hand, the user may designate any field or paragraph of a unit record to be presented. In BRS, for instance, the user may use AU for author display only, and AU,TI for author and title display.

Results of the searching can be presented either online or offline. There is online sorting available in some databases in DIALOG. This is a convenient feature, for the user may arrange the result, such as alphabetical by author or by sales growth in descending order. In practically all fields, record retrieval is in first-in last-out order. The first item to be retrieved is the latest one stored in the system. In a file where online sorting is available, the searcher may rearrange online the record in first-in and first-out order.

LOGOFF PROCEDURE

The searcher instructs the system to discontinue. The system will respond with such information as the date, time for beginning and ending of search, total time of search, and cost, depending on the system. The user may reconnect the system after discontinuance, without re-dialing, by simply re-entering its address. This method can also be used to change from one system to another. After logoff, when a ready for connection sign such as @ in TELENET displays, the user may connect with the other system by entering the system's address.

The next three chapters are essentially manuals for basic searching in DIALOG, SDC, and BRS, respectively. They serve as an introduction to the commands fundamental to searching in each system and to the variations of searching techniques.

9

Basic DIALOG Searching

This chapter is prepared for 300-baud and full duplex users in basic DIALOG searching. For details, reference should be made to *Guide to DIALOG Searching*, Palo Alto, Calif.; DIALOG Information Retrieval Services, 1979, loose-leaf. Updated by supplementary pages.

The *Guide* provides "a comprehensive presentation of the essential elements of the DIALOG online retrieval system, the many databases accessible through it, and the special features of the DIALOG Information Retrieval Service" (preface). It explains in detail the procedures of logon, selection, search, result, and logoff. The *Guide* also includes (1) a glossary, brief definitions of some sixty terms; (2) technical notes and DIAL-INDEX; (3) search aids for use with DIALOG databases, a listing of guides and search aids for each database with full bibliographic citations, and some with annotations; and (4) an index. Also included are Yellow Sheets and Blue Sheets. The Yellow Sheets provide information on DIALOG's Dialorder service. The Blue Sheets are separate pages in blue color on database description and features, a very convenient and easy to use search aid. A sample page of the Blue Sheet of File 1 is reproduced here.

FILE 1

ERIC
DIALOG FILE 1

SAMPLE RECORD

```
  DIALOG Accession Number ───────────────────────────────────────────  AN=
      ED178312  SE029137
  CH=    Guidelines for Teaching Mathematics K-12. ◄──────────────  /TI
  AU=──►Flax, Rosabel; And Others
  CS=──►Kansas State Dept. of Education, Topeka. Div. of Education Services.
  PY=   Jun 1979    91p.; Best copy available
         EDRS Price - MF01/PC04 Plus Postage.
  LA=──►Language: English
  DT=──►Document Type: Teaching Guide (052)
  CP=──►Geographic Source: U.S./ Kansas
  JA=──►Journal Announcement: RIEMAR80
  GL=──►Government: State
         This guide is intended to provide a basic outline for developing local ⎫
         mathematics programs.  It was developed to give Kansas mathematics teachers from │
         grades K-12 minimal sequential experiences in implementing the skills, values, │
         and concepts of the mathematics program.  The guide contains objectives, a ├◄── /AB
         checklist of topics appropriate for each grade level, and a human resources │
         guide which provides the names of individuals willing to serve as technical │
         assistants to local school districts. (MK)                                    ⎭
         Descriptors:   *Directories/   *Elementary  School  Mathematics/   Elementary ⎫
         Secondary Education/  Guidelines/ *Mathematics Curriculum/  *Resource Teachers/ ├◄── /DE
         *Secondary  School Mathematics/  *State Curriculum Guides/  State Departments of │
         Education                                                                       ⎭
         Identifiers: *Kansas ◄──────────────────────────────────────────  /ID
```

SEARCH OPTIONS

BASIC INDEX

SUFFIX	FIELD NAME	EXAMPLES	
None	Basic Index (Includes Abstract, Descriptor Identifier, and Title)	E SKILLS	S RESOURCE?
/AB	Abstract	S MATHEMATICS(W)PROGRAM?/AB	
/DE	Descriptor[1]	S MATHEMATICS CURRICULUM/DE	
/ID	Identifier[2]	S KANSAS/ID	
/TI	Title	S TEACHING(F)GUIDELINES/TI	

[1]Also /DE*, /DF, /DF*.
[2]Also /ID*, /IF, /IF*.

ADDITIONAL INDEXES

PREFIX	FIELD NAME	EXAMPLES	
AN=	Clearinghouse Number	E AN=VT203158	S AN=SE029137
AU=	Author	E AU=BOOKER, E	S AU=FLAX, R?
CH=	Clearinghouse Code	E CH=VT	S CH=SE
CN=	Contract/Grant Number[3]	E CN=NIDA	S CN=NIDA-5-H81-DA-01496-03
CP=	Country of Publication[3,4]	E CP=JAPAN	S CP=U.S.
CS=	Corporate Source[3]	E CS=BBB10844	S CS=KANSAS(F)CS=STATE(F)CS=EDUCATION
DT=	Document Type[3]	E DT=TEACHING GUIDE	S DT=052
GL=	Government Level[3,4]	E GL=FOREIGN	S GL=STATE
JA=	Journal Announcement	E JA=CIJMAY80	S JA=RIEMAR80
JN=	Journal Name	E JN=LIBRARY	S JN=READING HORIZONS
LA=	Language[4]	E LA=FRENCH	S LA=GERMAN
PN=	Bureau/Project Number[3]	E PN=BR	S PN=BR-7-0883
PY=	Publication Year	E PY=1964	S PY=1979
RN=	Report Number[3]	E RN=ADM	S RN=ADM-79-678
SP=	Sponsoring Agency[3]	E SP=INST	S SP=BABCOCK(W)SP=FOUNDATION
UD=	Update	E UD=8003	S UD=9999
ZZ=	Rotated Descriptors	E ZZ=ABILITY	(Select from EXPAND display)

[3]RIE records only.
[4]For records from 1979 to the present.

LIMITING

SUFFIX	FIELD NAME	EXAMPLES	
/ED	Accession Numbers and/or RIE Subfile	LIMIT 1/080788-999999/ED	LIMIT 4/ED
/EJ	Accession Numbers and/or CIJE Subfile	LIMIT 5/082165-999999/EJ	LIMIT 8/EJ
/AVAIL	Document Available from EDRS	LIMIT 6/AVAIL	
/UNAVAIL	Document Not Available from EDRS	LIMIT 14/UNAVAIL	
/MAJ	Major Descriptor or Identifier	LIMIT 7/MAJ	
/MIN	Minor Descriptor or Identifier	LIMIT 9/MIN	

SORTING

SORTABLE FIELDS	EXAMPLES
Online (.SORT) and offline (PRINT). AU,CS,JN,PY,TI	.SORT 8/1-56/JN/PY PRINT 15/5/1-129/AU

FORMAT OPTIONS

NUMBER	RECORD CONTENT	NUMBER	RECORD CONTENT
Format 1	DIALOG Accession Number	Format 5	Full Record
Format 2	Full Record except Abstract	Format 6	Title and DIALOG Accession Number
Format 3	Bibliographic Citation	Format 7	Bibliographic Citation and Abstract
Format 4	Abstract and Title	Format 8	Title and Indexing

DIRECT RECORD ACCESS

PREFIX	FIELD NAME	EXAMPLES	
None	DIALOG Accession Number	TYPE ED178312/6	PRINT EJ207531/5

1-2   (Revised December 1980)

For features of a particular database, DIALOG Information Retrieval Services publishes *Guide to DIALOG Databases*, a separate publication for each database. For instance, the "Guide to ERIC File" (June 1980, 36p.) consists of the Blue Sheet, search examples, format options, search aids, and document retrieval. DIALOG's *Chronolog*, a serial published since 1973, is a must for current information on any changes and new features of the DIALOG service.

In addition, users may find useful two other DIALOG publications: (1) *Pocket Guide to DIALOG Information Retrieval Service* (1983, 16p.), a manual in a nutshell, listing command summary, basic search features, search-save feature, command entry and output features, troubleshooting, logon and logoff, and DIALOG databases; and (2) *Database Catalog* (January 1983, 46p.), a listing of databases accessible through DIALOG with a brief note about each.

For convenience of use, this chapter is preceded by contents with numbers in parentheses which refer to pages in the *Guide to DIALOG Searching*. The chapter also includes a section of DIALOG's new service, Knowledge Index.

Contents

2. Article Type (AT =) and Journal (JN =)
3. Publication Date (PY =, PD =)
4. Company (HN =, BN =, CO =) and Product
    (PC =)
5. Update (UD =)
6. Statistical Data (QC =)

IV. Knowledge Index
    A. Logon Procedure
    B. Search Procedure
    C. Result Procedure
    D. Logoff Procedure

*Numbers in parentheses refer to pages in the *Guide to DIALOG Searching*.

I. BASIC PROCEDURE
A. Logan Procedure

The DIALOG system can be accessed through several communication options. Direct dialing over standard telephone lines and communication networks, such as TELENET, TYMNET, and UNINET, are the most commonly used methods.

TELENET, TYMNET, and UNINET Procedures

The user dials a TELENET, TYMNET, or UNINET number and obtains a high-pitched tone indicating that the system can be connected. The user then inserts the telephone handset in the acoustic coupler of the terminal.

TELENET procedure

The User Enters	The System Responds
(CR) (CR)	TELENET XXX XXX
	Terminal =
(CR)	@
C 415 20 (CR)	415 20 CONNECTED ENTER YOUR DIALOG PASSWORD XXXXXXXX
Password (CR)	

Terminal = is for a terminal identifier. See DIALOG's *Guide* T-5 for various identifiers. On most terminals, just a carriage return without the terminal identifier can be used. 415 20 is one of DIALOG's addresses via TELENET. Other DIALOG addresses for access via TELENET include 415 48, and 213 170. An overflow routing of calls is instituted, that is, all calls made to either the 415 20 or 415 48 address will automatically route to the 213 170 address if the address chosen has full ports. After the password is entered followed by a carriage return, the system defaults on File 1 (ERIC) and displays logon date, time, and port.

TELENET logon example

```
TELENET
312 3J

TERMINAL=

@c 415 20

415 20 CONNECTED

ENTER YOUR DIALOG PASSWORD
████████  LOGON File1 Wed 30may84 10:05:20 Port868
```

TYMNET procedure

The User Enters	The System Responds
	please type your terminal identifier
E	-XXXX-XXX-
	please log in:
DIALOG (CR)	DIALOG; call connected
	ENTER YOUR DIALOG PASSWORD
	XXXXXXX
Password (CR)	

The terminal identifier E will not be shown. The identifier varies. See DIALOG *Guide*, T-N.

TYMNET logon example

```
please type your terminal identifier
-3151-052-
please log in: dialog


DIALOG: call connected


ENTER YOUR DIALOG PASSWORD
████████  RECONNECT File1 Wed 30may84 10:16:51 Port094
```

UNINET procedure

The User Enters	The System Responds
	L?
(CR).(CR)	UNINET pad XXX port XX
	Service.
DLG (CR)	•
	XXXX XXX connected to XXXXXXX
	ENTER YOUR DIALOG PASSWORD
	XXXXXXXX
Password (CR)	

UNINET Logon example

```
L?
uninet pad 1415 port 05
service : dlg


*u001 000 connected to 41500026


ENTER YOUR DIALOG PASSWORD
████████  RECONNECT File1 Wed 30may84 10:19:44 PortOBD
```

B. Search Procedure

Commands or instructions can be given in three different forms: word(s), letter(s), and symbolic abbreviation(s). The basic commands, such as BEGIN, EXPAND, SELECT, COMBINE, and TYPE may be substituted by B, E, S, C, and T, respectively, or by symbols such as ! for BEGIN, '' for EXPAND, # for SELECT, $ for COMBINE, and ' for TYPE.

There are two types of indexes for searching: (1) Basic Index for searching by subject and (2) Additional Index for searching in all other fields. The Basic Index consists of, in most files, words from titles, words assigned as subject terms, and words from abstracts. Except stop words (see DIALOG *Guide*, T-17), all words contained in the fields of title, abstract, descriptors, and identifiers can be searched. It must be noted that words in descriptors are controlled vocabularies. If a descriptor is known, SELECTing the descriptor is preferred to achieve search relevancy and precision. The Additional Index includes all other non-subject fields, which are designated by a two-letter prefix code. This will be discussed in section III.

1. BEGIN and .FILE

The BEGIN command is used to specify the database for searching. It begins a new set of numbers of searching, initiates the clock time of the specified database, and erases the previous search history. If the user working on File 1 wishes to erase previous search history in the same database, the user simply enters the command BEGIN 1, that is, to begin File 1. The system will erase all search history and begin a new set of numbers of searching in the same database. Each DIALOG database is designated by a number. For database numbers, see Blue Sheet, *Pocket Guide*, and *Database Catalog*, mentioned earlier.

The BEGIN command differs from the .FILE command (note a period before FILE) which is used to switch the file. The .FILE command resets the time clock, but continues the search history. It allows to return to the previous file for continuing search and for a printout of the search result.

BEGIN command example

```
? begin 10
          30may84 10:20:42 User27019
   $0.27  0.018 Hrs File1*


File10:AGRICOLA - 1979-84/Apr & 1979 Supplemental
See File 110(thru 1978)
          Set Items Description
   ---  -----  -----------
```

The system initiates the date and clock time of the specified file, displays the user number, cost, and time used in the previous file, previous file, and the number of searching items performed in the previous file, if any, and specifies the file initiated and its period of coverage. In addition, three columns and logical operators in parentheses are given. The three columns are *set* number, number of *items* of the term or terms contained in the file, and *description*, that is, term also known as index-term.

.FILE command example

```
? .file 10
          30may84 10:27:24 User27019
   $1.53  0.102 Hrs File1*


File10:AGRICOLA - 1979-84/Apr & 1979 Supplemental
See File 110(thru 1978)
```

2. EXPAND and PAGE

The use of the EXPAND command is to instruct the sytem to display the alphabetically related search terms of twelve lines of listing, with a temporary EXPANDed serial number, up to fifty terms. For each EXPAND listing are given the listing number (called an EXPAND number) in sequence, the number of items or postings, and postings of subject-related terms, if any. A word "more" at the end of a listing indicates that the listing is not complete. For additional listings, use the PAGE command. The serial number E3 usually designates the term EXPANDed. The terms or how many postings are contained in the file or if searching of a particular term or terms results in no postings. Examples follow:

```
? expand swim
Ref Items   Index-term                      R T
E1      2   SWII
E2      1   SWILL
E3     48  *SWIM
E4      1   SWIM FOR YOUR LIFE
E5      1   SWIMBLADDER
E6      6   SWIMMER
E7     33   SWIMMERS
E8    423   SWIMMING                         4
E9     81   SWIMMING POOLS                   4
E10     1   SWIMNASTICS
E11     3   SWIMS
E12     1   SWIMSUITS
                                       -more-
? expand safe
Ref Items   Index-term
E1      1   SAFARIS
E2      1   SAFAVI
E3    842  *SAFE
E4      2   SAFE DRINKING WATER ACT
E5     12   SAFE SCHOOL STUDY
E6      1   SAFE SCHOOL STUDY
               REPORT TO CONGRESS
E7      2   SAFE STREETS ACT
E8      1   SAFEBEING
E9      1   SAFEGARDS
E10    97   SAFEGUARD
E11    12   SAFEGUARDED
                                       -more-
? page
Ref Items   Index-term                      R T
E12    61   SAFEGUARDING
E13   243   SAFEGUARDS
E14     1   SAFEKEEPING
E15     1   SAFELIGHT
E16   118   SAFELY
```

```
E17     57   SAFER
E18      1   SAF RIS
E19     25   SAFEST
E20   5278   SAFETY                        28
E21      1   SAFETY CODES
E22      2   SAFETY DIRECTORS
E23    961   SAFETY EDUCATION              14
                                  -more-
```

The display of related terms (RT) can be made by using the EXPAND En command. The sytem will present a list of terms in the thesaurus as follows. The online display of the thesaurus is a unique feature of DIALOG.

```
? e safety
Ref Items   Index-term                RT
E1      1   SAFERIS
E2     25   SAFEST
E3   5278  *SAFETY                     28
E4      1   SAFETY CODES
E5      2   SAFETY DIRECTORS
E6    961   SAFETY EDUCATION           14
E7    221   SAFETY EQUIPMENT            5
E8          SAFETY GLASSES             1
E9      1   SAFETY IN OUTDOOR
            ADVENTURE PROGRAMS
E10         SAFETY PROVISIONS          1
E11     1   SAFETYING
                                -more-
? e e3
Ref Items   Index-term              Type RT
R1   5278   SAFETY                       28
R2          SAFETY PROVISIONS      U   1
R3     44   AGRICULTURAL SAFETY    N   3
R4    322   FIRE PROTECTION        N  11
R5    417   LABORATORY SAFETY      N   8
R6    150   OCCUPATIONAL SAFETY AND
            HEALTH                 N  13
R7    396   SCHOOL SAFETY          N  11
R8    418   TRAFFIC SAFETY         N   5
R9    607   ACCIDENT PREVENTION    R   6
R10   593   ACCIDENTS              R   9
R11    78   ALARM SYSTEMS          R  22
                                -more-
```

Compare the result with the term "safety" listed in the *ERIC Thesauraus*:

SAFETY   *Jul. 1966*
        CIJE: 493   RIE: 705
UF   Safety Provisions
NT   Agricultural Safety
        Fire Protection
        Laboratory Safety
        School Safety
        Traffic Safety
RT   Accident Prevention
        Accidents
        Alarm Systems
        Consumer Protection
        Design Requirements
        Fallout Shelters
        Health
        Injuries
        Poisoning
        Radiation
        Refugees
        Safety Education
        Safety Equipment
        Security Personnel
        Traffic Accidents

Reprinted with permission by The Oryx Press, 2214 N. Central Ave., Phoenix AZ 85004.

3. SELECT

There are two methods of using the SELECT command. By using the indirect method, the user uses the EXPAND command first and then SELECTs the desired term. The direct method is to search the term or terms without using the EXPAND command. For each SELECT command, the system responds with a search set number and postings contained in the file. The set number is in consecutive order to the end of the search session, or the BEGIN command is entered. As mentioned earlier, the BEGIN command will begin a new set of searches. SELECT examples are given:

Indirect method

```
? expand swimming
Ref Items  Index-term                    RT
E1     6   SWIMMER
E2    33   SWIMMERS
E3   423  *SWIMMING                        4
E4    81   SWIMMING POOLS                  4
E5     1   SWIMNASTICS
E6     3   SWIMS
E7     1   SWIMSUITS
E8     1   SWIMWEAR
E9     3   SWINBURNE
E10    1   SWINBURNE INSTITUTE OF
               TECHNOLOGY (AUSTRAL
E11    4   SWINDLE
                                       -more-
? select e3
           1    423 SWIMMING
? expand safety
Ref Items  Index-term                    RT
E1     1   SAFERIS
E2    25   SAFEST
E3  5278  *SAFETY                         28
E4     1   SAFETY CODES
E5     2   SAFETY DIRECTORS
E6   961   SAFETY EDUCATION               14
E7   221   SAFETY EQUIPMENT                5
E8         SAFETY GLASSES                  1
E9     1   SAFETY IN OUTDOOR
               ADVENTURE PROGRAMS
E10        SAFETY PROVISIONS               1
E11    1   SAFETYING
                                       -more-
? select e3
           2   5278 SAFETY
```

Direct method

```
? select swimming
           1    423 SWIMMING
? select safety
           2   5278 SAFETY
```

The search result is given a set number in sequence. The last search result indicates that in search set number 2, there are 5,278 items that contain the term "safety."

4. COMBINE

The COMBINE or C command is used to compare sets of entries and then create a new set. Three Boolean operators are used: OR, AND, and NOT. Boolean operators are executed in the following sequence: NOT's are executed first, followed by AND's; OR's are executed last. If more than one Boolean operator is used and if there is a priority in execution, parentheses must be used to specify which Boolean operator is executed first. Boolean operators in parentheses are executed first. An example is

```
File1*:ERIC - 66-84/May
        Set Items Description
        --- ----- -----------
? s boys
          1  4414 BOYS
? s girls
          2  4063 GIRLS
? s schooling
          3  3156 SCHOOLING
? c 1 or 2
          4  5747 1 OR 2
? c 1-2/or
          5  5747 1-2/OR
? c (1 or 2) and 3
          6    47 (1 OR 2) AND 3
```

The COMBINE command for set number 4 can be simplified by using "c 1-2/or" shown in set number 5. The statement for set number 6 specifies that set number 1 (boys) and set number 2 (girls) will be executed first and then COMBINEd with set number 3 (schooling), resulting in postings that contain boys schooling or girls schooling. It must be noted that the COMBINE command is used to combine set numbers only.

5. SuperSELECT and SELECT STEPS

The SELECT and COMBINE commands used in the search procedure just mentioned can be entered in a single command by either one of the three methods: (1) the use of semicolons, (2) SuperSELECT, and (3) SELECT STEPS. The use of semicolon will be discussed in section II-B-4 later. The SuperSELECT is used to perform SELECT and COMBINE operations in a single SELECT statement as shown in the following example:

```
File10:AGRICOLA - 1979-84/Apr & 1979 Supplemental
See File 110(thru 1978)
          Set Items Description
          --- ----- ------------
? s (rice or wheat) and (butter or margarine)
                9863 RICE
               15175 WHEAT
                 529 BUTTER
                 128 MARGARINE
          1      27  (RICE OR WHEAT) AND (BUTTER OR MARGARINE)
```

The single SELECT statement can also be used to retrieve EXPANDed numbers and to combine them with other search terms, for example.

```
File1*:ERIC - 66-84/May
          Set Items Description
          --- ----- ------------
? e swimming
Ref Items  Index-term                RT
E1     6   SWIMMER
E2    33   SWIMMERS
E3   423  *SWIMMING                  4
E4    81   SWIMMING POOLS            4
E5     1   SWIMNASTICS
E6     3   SWIMS
E7     1   SWIMSUITS
E8     1   SWIMWEAR
E9     3   SWINBURNE
E10    1   SWINBURNE INSTITUTE OF
              TECHNOLOGY (AUSTRAL
E11    4   SWINDLE
                             -more-
```

```
? s e3, e6 and safety
            425 E3, E6
                E3: SWIMMING
            5278 SAFETY
      1     72 E3, E6 AND SAFETY
```

The use of E3, E6 with a comma to separate the two assumes the Or relationship, that is, E3 or E6. The set number can be executed with any search term in a single SELECT statement. If a set number is used in the SELECT statement, the character "S" must proceed the set number. An example is given:

```
? s s1 and schools
   71577 SCHOOLS   (EDUCATIONAL INSTITUTIONS AT ALL LEVELS (
2     14  S1 AND SCHOOLS
```

The SELECT STEPS or S STEPS or SS command is a modified version of SuperSELECT. It performs the same functions as instructed in a SuperSELECT command except that the SELECT STEPS command gives a set number to each of the operations. Each term in the set can be used later in the same file without rekeying it. Compare the example that follows with the one in SuperSELECT mentioned earlier.

SELECT STEPS command example

```
File10:AGRICOLA - 1979-84/Apr & 1979 Supplemental
See File 110(thru 1978)
        Set Items Description
        --- ----- -----------
? ss (rice or wheat) and (butter or margarine)
         1  9863 RICE
         2 15175 WHEAT
         3   529 BUTTER
         4   128 MARGARINE
         5    27 (1 OR 2) AND (3 OR 4)
```

6. .COST

The .COST command is used to obtain a record of intermediate cost estimate during the course of the search. The cost message will also be displayed after each BEGIN, END, END/SAVE, END/SAVETEMP,. FILE, and LOGOFF command.

.COST command example

```
? .cost
          30may84 10:39:24 User27019
   $0.36  0.024 Hrs File10 4 Descriptors
```

The system responds with date, time, user number, cost, time used, file number, and the number of search sets executed in the file.

C. Result Procedure

1. TYPE (or DISPLAY)

The TYPE or T command is used to display records online from the search result. It is entered in a sequence of set number, format number, and item number(s) separated by two slashes. For example, by entering "TYPE 9/6/1-2, 8" the system will display the first two and the eighth records in format 6 of set number 9.

TYPE command example

```
? t 5/6/1-2, 8
5/6/1
84139491  84004290  Holding Library: AGB
   Fish protein concentrate as a
      protein supplement in four baked products

5/6/2
84115286  84005346  Holding Library: AGL
   Comparative vitamin B-6 bioavailability
      from tuna, whole wheat bread and
      peanut butter in humans (Pyridoxine)

5/6/8
83054403  82001112  Holding Library: AGB
   Food use and perceived food meanings of the elderly
```

Record numbers may be either consecutive or non-consecutive, or both. In addition, numbers need not be sequential. For formats available in each file, refer to the Blue Sheets. In the ERIC file, formats available are

Format 1	DIALOG accession number
Format 2	Full record except abstracts
Format 3	Bibliographic citation
Format 4	Abstract and title
Format 5	Full record
Format 6	Title and DIALOG accession number
Format 7	Bibliographic citation and abstract
Format 8	Title and indexing

The most frequently used formats are format 3 and format 5. The TYPE command is used only with a set in the same file in which it was created.

2. PRINT

The PRINT or PR command is used to order search results to be printed at the system site and sent to the user. In entering PRINT 5/5/1-45, the user orders printing of the first forty-five records in format 5 of set number 5.

D. Logoff Procedure

The logoff procedure is used to instruct the system to disconnect. Simply enter LOGOFF (no space between log and off) and press the carriage return once; the system will be disconnected.

Logoff example via TELENET

```
? logoff
            30may84 11:35:26 User27019
    $0.38   0.025 Hrs File82 1 Descriptor

LOGOFF 11:35:29

415 20 DISCONNECTED 00 00

@
```

The system responds to the LOGOFF command with date, hour, user number, cost, time used, file number, and the number of searching items performed in the file. For temporary interruption in searching, the user may use the LOGOFF HOLD command to instruct the system to save the search operations for a period of ten minutes. The search operations will not be erased after the system is reconnected within the time limit.

E. Tutorial Commands

Tutorial commands are used to obtain immediate tutorial information. All tutorial commands are specified, a listing of which can be obtained by using the ?EXPLAIN command shown here.

EXPLAIN command

```
? ?explain
Valid EXPLAIN commands are:
Basic Commands:
  ?BEGIN      ?ENDSDI     ?MAPRN      ?SCREEN
  ?COMBINE    ?EXPAND     ?ORDER      ?SELECT
  ?COST       ?KEEP       ?PAGE       ?SFILES
  ?DISPLAY    ?LIMIT      ?PRINT      ?SORT
  ?DS         ?LIST       ?REVIEW     ?TYPE
  ?ENDSAVE    ?LOGOFF
                     :*:*:
News/Status:
  ?DIALINDX  ?FILESUM    ?ONTAP      ?SUBSCRIP
  ?DISCOUNT  ?HELP       ?RATES      ?SUPPLRS
  ?EXPLAIN   ?INSTRUCT   ?SCHEDULE   ?TOLLFREE
  ?FILES     ?MESSAGE    ?SDI        ?TRUNCATE
  ?FILESAZ   ?NEWS       ?SEMINARS   ?UPDATE
                     *:*:
Telecommunication Access:
  ?ACCESS    ?DIALNET    ?SABD       ?TRANSPAC
  ?DARDO     ?FINNPAK    ?TELENET    ?TWX
  ?DATAPAC   ?IDAS       ?TELEPAKD   ?TYMNET
  ?DATEX     ?NORPAC     ?TELEPAKS   ?UNINET
             ?PSS        ?TELEX      ?WATS
                  :*:*:
```

```
File Information:
 ?FIELDn*  ?FILEn*   ?LIMITn*  ?RATESn*
 *Enter desired file# in place of the n
              :*:*:*
Training (DIALOG Service):
 ?TRAIN (For information on DIALOG
         training sessions, including
         descriptions of particular
         training sessions.)
              *:*:*
Training (Database Suppliers):
 ?ANZNEWS  (Australia/New Zealand)
 ?CANNEWS  (Canada)
 ?EURNEWS  (Europe)
 ?KINONEWS (Kinokuniya Japan)
 ?MMCNEWS  (Masis Japan)
 ?USNEWS   (United States)
              *:*:*
Online User Group News:
 ?CANOUG   ?OUGNEWS  ?MMCOUG   ?USOUG
 ?EUROUG
```

?COST command

```
? ?cost
The .COST command may be entered at any
time during a search session.  The re-
sponse will give elapsed time and cost
estimates since last BEGIN command.
              ***
```

II. SEARCH VARIATIONS

A. Modified SELECT Commands

1. The Use of Truncation

In SELECTing, the word can be truncated at the end or in the middle, and the number of characters truncated can be specified. The use of truncation enables a user to select a term stem with a specified or unspecified number of characters to appear at the end of the term stem or embedded within it. A truncated stem can be used to search up to a thousand different terms with the specific root in a single command.

The symbol ? is used for truncation. Examples are

SWIM?   for any number of characters after the word SWIM
SWIM??   limited to one character after the word SWIM
SWIM????? limited to four characters after the word SWIM
M?N   for any one character embedded in the word

Similar to ORBIT's "MM " display, noted in chapter ten, the use of SS and E commands in DIALOG will display all words truncated, such as

```
? ss swim?
              1    458 SWIM?
? e
Ref Items   Index-term              RT
E1     48   SWIM
E2      1   SWIM FOR YOUR LIFE
E3          *SWIM?
E4      1   SWIMBLADDER
E5      6   SWIMMER
E6     33   SWIMMERS
E7    423   SWIMMING               4
E8     81   SWIMMING POOLS         4
E9      1   SWIMNASTICS
E10     .   SWIMS
E11     1   SWIMSUITS
E12     1   SWIMWEAR
                              -more-
```

2. The Use of Suffix Codes

Suffix codes are two-letter codes used for restricted searching. The following are four suffix codes used in most files:

/TI   for searching the term in titles only
/AB   for searching the term in abstracts only
/DE   for searching the term in descriptors only
/ID   for searching the term in identifiers only

In using the suffix code, a slash / must be entered between the term and the suffix code. Both the EXPAND and the SELECT commands can use suffix codes, and more than one suffix code can be used in the same EXPAND or SELECT command.

EXPAND command with suffix codes

```
? e safety/ti, de
Ref Items  Index-term               RT
E1    57  SAFER
E2    25  SAFEST
E3  5278 *SAFETY                    28
E4   961  SAFETY EDUCATION          14
E5   221  SAFETY EQUIPMENT           5
E6        SAFETY GLASSES             1
E7        SAFETY PROVISIONS          1
E8     1  SAFIADDIN
E9     2  SAFIRE
E10    5  SAFRAN
E11    3  SAG
E12   38  SAGA
                            -more-
```

EXPAND command with one suffix code

```
? e safety/de
Ref Items  Index-term               RT
E1  5278 *SAFETY                    28
E2   961  SAFETY EDUCATION          14
E3   221  SAFETY EQUIPMENT           5
E4        SAFETY GLASSES             1
E5        SAFETY PROVISIONS          1
E6  4184  SALARIES   (EARNINGS PAID
             AT FIXED INTERVAL      17
E7  2882  SALARY
E8        SALARY DIFFERENTIALS
             (1968 1980)            1
E9        SALARY RAISES             1
                            -more-
```

SELECT command with suffix codes

? s swimming/ti, ab
        2   334 SWIMMING/TI, AB

? s swimming/id
        3   2 SWIMMING/ID

? t 3/5/1
3/5/1
EJ121745 SP503765
AAHPER Standards for Instructors of Competitive Swimming--A Curriculum
Guide
Cramer, John L.; And Others
Journal of Physical Education and Recreation, 46, 5, 47-50   May 1975
Language: ENGLISH
  Descriptors: *Physical Education; *Swimming; *Athletic Coaches;
*Evaluation Criteria; Higher Education; Athletics; Teaching Skills;
Curriculum Guides
  Identifiers: *AAHPER Standards for Instructors of Competitive Swimming

The code /DE is used to search the term contained in the field of descriptors, disregarding its order of occurrence. The search of the term SAFETY/DE, for example, will retrieve documents in which such descriptors as SAFETY, SAFETY EDUCATION, SCHOOL SAFETY, and SAFETY EQUIPMENT are indexed. If the search is limited to SAFETY as a major descriptor, /DF (descriptor full), instead of /DE, should be used.

3. The Use of Full-Text Operators

It is intended to restrict text searching of multiwords other than the bound words, that is, multiwords not recorded in the descriptor or identifier fields. The full-text operator is inserted in parentheses between the search words, with or without spaces, to search specified word adjacency throughout the text. Some operators are noted:

(W) for searching terms on either side of the operator to be adjacent and in the specified order
(nW) for searching terms with a specified distance, such as one or two intervening words between terms
(C) analogous to using the SELECT and AND commands
(L) available in those files that have hierarchically related descriptor terms. Its use will automatically restrict the search to the descriptor field
(F) for terms to be within the same field, but in any order

Examples of using Boolean and full-text operators in ERIC

```
? s library and science
                18773 LIBRARY
                56633 SCIENCE
            1   2684   LIBRARY AND SCIENCE
? s library science
            2    961 LIBRARY SCIENCE
                        (STUDY AND PROFESSION OF THE ADMI
? s library(w)science
            3   1216 LIBRARY(W)SCIENCE
? s library(2w)science
            4   1319 LIBRARY(2W)SCIENCE
? s library(c)science
```

```
     5   2684 LIBRARY(C)SCIENCE
? s library(l)science
     6    961 LIBRARY(L)SCIENCE
? s library(f)science
     7   2366 LIBRARY(F)SCIENCE
```

Set number 6 using full-text operator (L) is the same as the searching descriptor in set number 2; whereas set number 5 using operator (C) is the same as using AND in set number 1.

B. Other Search Strategies

1. LIMIT and LIMITALL

The LIMIT command is used to reduce by specified criteria the number of items in a set after the search. Its availability and criteria vary. In File 11, PsycINFO, for instance, limiting criteria include four fields: /ENG for English language, /FRN for non-English language, /ANIMAL for animal subject, and /HUMAN for human subject. In some files, the use of prefix codes can achieve the same result as LIMITing. Again in File 11, the prefix LA = ENGLISH for English language is equivalent to the file's suffix /ENG. The LIMIT command is entered as LIMIT set number/criterion. In contrast to the LIMIT command, the LIMITALL (or LALL) command is used before the search. It restricts all subsequent sets of items according to the criterion given by the LIMITALL command. The LIMITALL command must be cancelled by using the LIMITALL/ALL or LALL/ALL command, if it is no longer needed. The LIMITALL command will be automatically cancelled by the BEGIN or LOGOFF command. The example illustrates the use of LIMIT to confine previous search set number 2 (library science) to the field of major descriptors.

```
? l 2/maj
          8    551   2/MAJ
? t 8/2/1
8/2/1
EJ293579   IR512164
   The Golden Age of American Librarianship.
   Bobinski, George
```

```
Wilson Library Bulletin, v58 n5 p338-44 Jan      1984
Available from: UMI
Language: English
Document Type: REVIEW LITERATURE (070)
Descriptors:   *Federal Aid;  Federal Legislation;  History;
*Libraries;  Library Associations;  *Library Education;
Library Facilities;   Library Schools;  *Library Science;
*Philanthropic Foundations;  Private Financial Support
Identifiers: American Library Association; *Library Developm
```

It retrieves records with major descriptors as indicated by an asterisk.

2. The Saving Search

The saving search features repeating operations from one file to another with compatible vocabularies. Two procedures may be mentioned: standard and temporary.

END/SAVE, .EXECUTE, .RECALL, and .RELEASE commands are used for the standard saving search. A serial number will be given by using the END/SAVE command, after a search strategy has been completed. The system is instructed to repeat the search strategy by using the .EXECUTE command with the serial number. The standard saving search is available for use permanently. It can be .RECALLed and .EXECUTEd at any time, until it is .RELEASEd.

For a temporary saving search, use END/SAVETEMP and .EXECUTE commands. The temporary saving search will last for re-use all week long until it is deleted every Friday night.

END/SAVETEMP command example

```
? b10
          30may84 10:57:29 User27019
    $2.03  0.135 Hrs File1* 13 Descriptors


File10:AGRICOLA - 1979-84/Apr & 1979 Supplemental
See File 110(thru 1978)
        Set Items Description
        --- ----- -----------
? ss (rice or wheat) and (butter or margarine)
```

```
       1  9863 RICE
       2 15175 WHEAT
       3   529 BUTTER
       4   128 MARGARINE
       5    27  (1 OR 2) AND (3 OR 4)
? end/savetemp
Serial#T35U
            30may84 10:59:17 User27019
    $0.47  0.031 Hrs File10 4 Descriptors
```

A serial number of T35U is acquired.

File switch: .EXECUTE and .EXECUTE STEPS command example

```
? b18
            30may84 10:59:46 User27019
    $0.14  0.009 Hrs File10


File18:F & S INDEXES - 79-84/JUL (UD=8407W5)
(Copr. PREDICASTS Inc. 1984)
          Set Items Description
          --- ----- -----------
? .execute t35u
              5615 RICE
              7997 WHEAT
              1064 BUTTER
               219 MARGARINE
                 3  (1 OR 2) AND (3 OR 4)
         1       3 SERIAL# T35U
? .execute steps t35u
         2  5615 RICE
         3  7997 WHEAT
         4  1064 BUTTER
         5   219 MARGARINE
         6     3  (2 OR 3) AND (4 OR 5)
```

A beginner should be aware of two situations: (1) The use of saving search will save all previous searches in the file whether they are needed or not. (2) The .EXECUTE STEPS command will not give a set number to each of the operations, unless previous searches saved were performed in the SELECT STEPS operation.

3. .SORT

Several databases have the sorting feature. The .SORT command is used to instruct the system to sort records in a specified order before they are displayed. In entering ".SORT 1/1-30/au,a" the system is instructed to arrange in alphabetical order by author in ascending order the first thirty records of set number 1. An example of using .SORT in the ERIC file is

```
? s library science
          1    961 LIBRARY SCIENCE
                        (STUDY AND PROFESSION OF THE ADMI
? .sort 1/1-30/au, a
          2     30  1/1-30/AU, A
? t 2/3/1-3
2/3/1
EJ285621
   Education in Library Conservation.
   Banks, Paul N.
   Library Trends, v30 n2 p189-201 Fall
   1981

2/3/2
EJ293579
   The Golden Age of American Librarianship.
   Bobinski, George
   Wilson Library Bulletin, v58 n5 p338-44 Jan
   1984
   Available from: UMI

2/3/3
EJ293574
   Educating Special Librarians.
   Clough, M. Evalyn; Galvin, Thomas J.
   Special Libraries, v75 n1 p1-8 Jan
   1984
   Available from: UMI
```

4. Stacking Commands

Several commands can be combined in a single statement by use of semicolons to separate each command. Following is an example of stacking commands using three commands—BEGIN, SELECT, and TYPE—separated by semicolons in one statement.

```
? b6; s swimming and safety; t 1/3/1
           30may84 11:05:25 User27019
    $0.71  0.047 Hrs File1* 1 Descriptor

File6:NTIS - 64-84/Iss12
(Copr. NTIS)
           Set Items Description
           --- ----- -----------
                807 SWIMMING
                62647 SAFETY
           1    92  SWIMMING AND SAFETY
1/3/1
1036168  AD-D010 694/8
  Ground Fault Detector and Shutdown System
  (Patent)
  Tucker, L. W. ; Nelson, F. E.
  Department of the Navy, Washington, DC.
  Corp. Source Codes: 001840000; 110050
  Report No.: PAT-APPL-6-360 524; PATENT-4 410 925
  Filed 22 Mar 82 patented 18 Oct 83    6p
  Supersedes PAT-APPL-6-360 524, AD-D009 373.
  This Government-owned invention available for U.S.
licensing and, possibly, for foreign licensing. Copy of
patent available Commissioner of Patents, Washington, DC
20231 $1.00.
  Languages: English   Document Type: Patent
  NTIS Prices: Not available NTIS
  Journal Announcement: GRAI8407
```

5. DISPLAY SETS

The DISPLAY SETS or DS command is used to view a summary of the search history. The search statements in section I-B-4 can be summarized by using the DISPLAY SETS command, such as

```
? display sets
Set Items Description
  1  4414 BOYS
  2  4063 GIRLS
  3  3156 SCHOOLING
  4  5747 1 OR 2
  5  5747 1-2/OR
  6    47 (1 OR 2) AND 3
```

C. Multiple Database Subject Search

Online subject search across databases became available in File 411 DIALINDEX in 1980. All DIALOG data files are grouped into more than thirty subject categories, such as AGRICULT (AGRICULTURE/FOOD), BIOSCI (BIOSCIENCES), and BUSCO (BUSINESS COMPANIES). The use of File 411 involves three steps: (1) selecting File 411, (2) selecting files category, and (3) selecting search terms in a single statement.

Step 1

```
? b 411
          30may84 14:19:02 User30172
   $0.30  0.012 Hrs File1*
   $0.10  Telenet
   $0.40  Estimated Total Cost


File411:DIALINDEX(tm)
(Copr. DIALOG Inf.Ser)Nc.)
```

Step 2

```
? s files agricult

File10:AGRICOLA - 1979-84/Apr & 1979 Supplemental
File50:CAB Abstracts - 72-83/Dec
File60:CRIS USDA - 75-84 Apr
File110:AGRICOLA - 70-78/Dec

          File Items Description
          ---- ----- -----------
```

Step 3

```
? s butter or margarine
        (10)
                529 BUTTER
                128 MARGARINE
                618  BUTTER OR MARGARINE
        (50)
               7126 BUTTER
```

```
        934 MARGARINE
       7497  BUTTER OR MARGARINE
  (60)
         51 BUTTER
         10 MARGARINE
         58 BUTTER OR MARGARINE
 (110)
       1168 BUTTER
        224 MARGARINE
       1342 BUTTER OR MARGARINE
```

III. ADDITIONAL INDEX SEARCH

A. The Use of Additional Index

The Additional Index provides another approach to database search. In some files, such as File 22 (EIS Industrial Plants) and File 92 (EIS Non-manufacturing Establishments), the use of Additional Index is preferred, since the availability of free-text search in these files is limited. The Additional Index is used to limit the search to a specific field or fields designated by a two-letter prefix code directly followed by the sign of =. The Additional Index varies with files. Refer to DIALOG's Blue Sheets for database descriptions. There are over 400 fields in Additional Index in DIALOG databases.

The user may use either the indirect or the direct method. In the indirect method, the user uses the EXPAND command first to display a listing of terms preceded by suffix codes and then SELECTs the desired number(s). Or, the user may prefer the direct method, if the search term is known. It is advisable to use the Additional Index in conjunction with the Basic Index for a broader result of search.

B. Prefix Codes Search

The Additional Index search is designated by a prefix code plus the = sign. Below are selected prefix codes for Additional Index searching.

1. Author (AU =)

The prefix code AU = is used to search authors.

Indirect method: EXPAND AU= command

```
? b1
                30may84 11:10:10 User27019
      $0.96  0.064 Hrs File1* 3 Descriptors


File1*:ERIC - 66-84/May
            Set Items Description
            --- ----- -----------
? e au=li, tze-c
Ref Items  Index-term
E1      1  AU=LI, PETER S.
E2      1  AU=LI, TING-KAI, ED.
E3        *AU=LI, TZE-C
E4      2  AU=LI, TZE-CHUNG
E5     ·2  AU=LI, VIRGINIA C., ED.
E6      1  AU=LI, WAI-KEE
E7      1  AU=LI, WANG
E8      2  AU=LI, WEN L.
E9      2  AU=LI, WEN LANG
E10     1  AU=LI, XIAOJU
E11     1  AU=LI, Y. C.
E12     2  AU=LI, YING-CHE
                                  -more-
? s e4
             1      2 AU=LI, TZE-CHUNG
```

Direct method: SELECT command

```
? s au=li, tze-chung
             2      2 AU=LI, TZE-CHUNG
```

2. Article Type (AT =) and Journal (JN =)

In the following example, the EXPAND command is used to view article types in File 111. In the second part, using SuperSELECT to search Kissinger as a subject and to select EXPANDed 2, biography as article type, and the journal name, the *New York Times*, results in thirty-one postings of biographies of Kissinger published there.

```
? e at=
Ref Items  Index-term
E1          *AT=
E2  53464  AT=BIOGRAPHY
E3   1852  AT=CALENDAR
E4  38703  AT=COLUMN
E5  17778  AT=EDITORIAL
E6    653  AT=EVALUATION
E7   4656  AT=ILLUSTRATION
E8  21962  AT=LETTER
E9  20709  AT=OBITUARY
E10     5  AT=PHOTOGRAPH
E11 49732  AT=REVIEW
E12  1186  AT=TRANSCRIPT
                              -more-

? s kissinger and e2 and jn=new york times
                645 KISSINGER
              53464 AT=BIOGRAPHY
             417254 JN=NEW YORK TIMES
          1    31   KISSINGER AND E2 AND JN=NEW YORK TIMES
```

3. Publication Date (PY=, PD=)

The prefix code for the field of publication varies. For instance, in File 1 (ERIC), prefix PY= is used. The example searches materials on library science published in 1982.

SuperSELECT with PY=

```
? s library science and py=1982
                961 LIBRARY SCIENCE
                    (STUDY AND PROFESSION OF THE ADMI
              28719 PY=1982
          1    54   LIBRARY SCIENCE AND PY=1982
```

File 51 (Food Science and Technology Abstracts) uses the prefix code PD= for publication date. In the next example, the system is instructed to search materials on either butter or wheat published in 1982.

SELECT STEPS with PD =

```
? ss butter and pd=1982
        1   6114 BUTTER
        2  15692 PD=1982
        3    313  1 AND 2
```

4. Company (HN =, BN =, CO =) and Product (PC =)

The user may search headquarters name, branch name or company name, and product code in some files. Product codes are a classified scheme to designate each product by code. For instance, PC = 314 is a code for footwear. It is further divided by categories, such as PC = 314 2 for house slippers and PC = 314 3 for men's nonrubber footwear. The search for a broad code includes all categories under the code. For product codes in Predicasts databases, refer to *Predicasts Users Manual.*

In the first example, the system is instructed to EXPAND headquarters name Interco in File 22 (EIS Industrial Plants) and SELECT the EXPANDed number 4. The second example is used to search and combine the branch name of Interco truncated with set number 1, which is the headquarters name of Interco Inc. In SELECTing set number, the character "S" must precede the number to distinguish it from literal number 1. The third example searches information on Avis Rent-A-Car in File 18 (PTS) F&S Indexes), by EXPANDing the company name and then SELECTing the EXPANDed numbers 7 and 8.

EXPAND HN = and SELECT commands

```
? e hn=interco
Ref Items  Index-term
E1      1  HN=INTERAND CORP
              (HX=19095)
E2     13  HN=INTERCHECKS INC
              (HX=21808)
E3         *HN=INTERCO
E4    101  HN=INTERCO INC
              (HX=03252)
```

```
E5       1   HN=INTERCOASTAL STEEL
             CORP  (HX=31124)
E6       7   HN=INTERCOLE INC
             (HX=03253)
                                    -more-
? s e4
         1   101 HN=INTERCO INC  (HX=03252)
```

SELECT STEPS BN = command

```
? ss bn=interco? or s1
         2    28 BN=INTERCO?
         3   128  2 OR 1
```

EXPAND CO = and SELECT commands

```
? e co=avis
Ref Items  Index-term              RT
E1       3   CO=AVIONS TRANSPORT
             REGION                  2
E2       3   CO=AVIQUIPO
E3      30  *CO=AVIS                 3
E4       7   CO=AVIS (AUSTRALIA)
E5       2   CO=AVIS FLOWERS
             WORLDWIDE
E6       1   CO=AVIS INTNL
E7      10   CO=AVIS RENT-A-CAR      1
E8       3   CO=AVIS RENT-A-CAR (UK)
E9       1   CO=AVIS UK
E10      1   CO=AVISTON LUMBER
                                    -more-
? s e7, e8
         1    13 E7, E8
             E3: CO=AVIS
```

For product code search, the following example uses the Additional Index together with free-text searching to find information on shoe companies in File 22 and to sort the records retrieved by sales revenue in descending order.

SELECT with PC = , .SORT, and TYPE commands

```
? ss pc=314 or footwear?
          1    586 PC=314
          2    581 FOOTWEAR?
          3    623 1 OR 2
? .sort 3/1-100/sd, d
          4    100 3/1-100/SD, D
? t 4/4/1-2
4/4/1
158358
  HERMAN JOSEPH M SHOE CO

    3143    MENS FOOTWEAR, EXCEPT ATHLETIC

    SALES MIL $ :    063.0       INDUSTRY Z :    02.76
    EMPLOYMENT :    6 (500-999)

4/4/2
150593
  TONY LAMA CO INC

    3143    MENS FOOTWEAR, EXCEPT ATHLETIC

    SALES MIL $ :    057.5       INDUSTRY Z :    02.52
    EMPLOYMENT :    6 (500-999)
```

5. Update (UD =)

The prefix code UD = is used for recent additions. Four characters after an equal sign are used. The first two represent the year, and the last two are sequential; for instance, in a file updated monthly, these would be from 01 to 12. UD = 9999 can be used; it always corresponds to the most recent addition to a file. Examples of using UD = in File 1 are

```
? ss library science and ud=8301
          1    961 LIBRARY SCIENCE
                        (STUDY AND PROFESSION OF THE ADMI
          2   2294 UD=8301
          3     10 1 AND 2
```

```
? ss library science and ud=9999
        4    961 LIBRARY SCIENCE
                    (STUDY AND PROFESSION OF THE ADMI
        5   3043 UD=9999
        6      3  4 AND 5
```

6. Statistical Data (QC =)

In some databases, the Additional Index QC= is available for statistical data. QC stands for quick code. Statistical data are arranged by broad subject, each being designated by a code, such as QC = POPM for male population. For a listing of QC codes, refer to *Predicasts Users Manual*. Here is an example of using stacking commands, BEGIN, SELECT QC=, and TYPE, for male population in File 82.

```
? b82; s qc=popm; t 1/5/1
         30may84 11:34:01 User27019
  $0.81   0.054 Hrs File1* 4 Descriptors


File82:PTS US Time Series - 83/QTR3
(Copr. PREDICASTS Inc. 1983)
          Set Items Description
          --- ----- -----------
            1     1 QC=POPM
1/5/1
799253  Predicasts 84/01/30  (POPM)  United States
   Male Population. population.  .

                YEAR    MIL  people

                1957    84.456
                1958    85.876
                1959    87.305
                1960    88.632
                1961    90.045
                1962    91.304
                1963    92.548
                1964    93.774
                1965    94.835
```

1966	95.640
1967	96.313
1968	97.125
1969	98.000
1970	99.271
1971	100.738
1972	101.984
1973	102.962
1974	103.890
1975	104.876
1976	105.859
1977	106.880
1978	107.963
1979	109.132
1980	110.373
1981	111.423
1982	112.5
1983	113.7
1984	115.0
1985	116.2
1986	117.4
1987	118.5
1995	125.6

```
GROWTH RATE= 0.9%
CC=1USA    PC=e122100    EC=510
```

IV. KNOWLEDGE INDEX

The following are two indispensable references for using Knowledge Index: *Knowledge Index User's Workbook*, Palo Alto, Calif.: DIALOG Information Services, 1982, loose-leaf. Updated by supplementary pages, *Knowledge Index News* v. 1, no,. 1—, 1983–, Palo Alto, Calif.: DIALOG Information Services.

The *Workbook* consists of five parts as an introduction to Knowledge Index, searching techniques, and procedures for ordering copies of documents. At the end of each part is a worksheet to review commands and practice. Answers to exercises are given in appendixes, which include a glossary, subject guide, information on interfacing computers with Knowledge Index, TELENET and TYMNET numbers (UNINET added recently), and suggested answers to worksheet exercises. The *News*, a quarterly publication, provides up–to–date information on Knowledge Index services. Knowledge Index is organized in eleven broad subjects called sections. Each section has at least one database. The database contains citations with or without abstracts. One database, Corporate News, contains complete articles. The eleven sections (designated by a four-character label) are Agriculture (AGRI), Business Information (BUSI), Computers and Electronics (COMP), Corporate News (CORP), Education (EDUC), Engineering (ENGI), Government Publications (GOVE), Magazines (MAGE), Medicine (MEDI), News (NEWS), and Psychology (PSYC).

A. Logon Procedure

Knowledge Index can be accessed either by direct dial over standard telephone lies or via TELENET, TYMNET, or UNINET telecommunication networks. Refer to the procedure mentioned in section I-A of this chapter. The procedure for connecting with Knowledge Index via TELENET is shown as an example.

The User Enters	The System Responds
(CR) (CR)	TELENET XXX XX Terminal =
(CR) *	@
C 41548K (CR)	415 48K CONNECTED
	DIALOG INFORMATION SERVICES PLEASE LOGON
Account number (CR)	ACCOUNT NUMBER: XXXXXXXX
Password (CR)	LOGON AT XXXXXXX WELCOME TO KNOWLEDGE INDEX

* Identifier varies. On most terminals, a simple carriage return without entering a terminal identifier can be used.

TELENET procedure example

```
TELENET
312 3J

TERMINAL=

@c 41548k


415 48K CONNECTED

DIALOG INFORMATION SERVICES
PLEASE LOGON:
?████████
ENTER PASSWORD:
?████████

WELCOME TO KNOWLEDGE INDEX
Accounting starting at 18:55:39 EST
```

B. Search Procedure

Although Knowledge Index has limited searching capabilities as compared with DIALOG, many DIALOG searching features, such as free-text searching, Boolean logical operators, truncations, combination of set numbers with term, and combination of EXPANDed numbers with term, are all available. There are only a dozen or so commands to be grasped. Five commands are basic to searching:

BEGIN or B   to select a specified section
EXPAND or E   to display a portion of the terms indexed in a database
FIND or F   to search a database and find results, has a similar function of SuperSELECT mentioned in section I-B of this chapter
PAGE or P   to bring more of a record on display
HELP or H   to request explanation online of commands

Below are examples of searching:

BEGIN command to select section EDUC

```
?begin educ
 5/30/84  18:56:10 EST
Now in EDUCATION (EDUC) Section
  ERIC (EDUC1) Database
```

EXPAND command

```
?expand swimming
Ref Items  Index-term
E1     6  SWIMMER
E2    33  SWIMMERS
E3   423 *SWIMMING
E4    81  SWIMMING POOLS
E5     1  SWIMNASTICS
E6     3  SWIMS
E7     1  SWIMSUITS
E8     1  SWIMWEAR
E9     3  SWINBURNE
E10    1  SWINBURNE INSTITUTE OF
             TECHNOLOGY (AUSTRAL
E11    4  SWINDLE
              For more, enter PAGE
```

FIND command to combine EXPANDed numbers and term resulting in seventy-three postings in set number 1.

```
?find e2, e3 and safety
            430 E2, E3
                E3: SWIMMING
           5278 SAFETY
      S1    73  E2, E3 AND SAFETY
```

The use of truncation

```
?find swim? and safety
            458 SWIM?
           5278 SAFETY
      S2    73  SWIM? AND SAFETY
```

To combine set number and term

```
?find s1 and children
   71094 CHILDREN  (AGED BIRTH THROUGH APPROXIMATELY 12 YEA
      S3    18 S1 AND CHILDREN
```

Knowledge Index has also the Additional Index search feature. Refer to section III for Additional Index and its use. Only author (AU = (and journal (JN =), two prefix codes, are available in Knowledge Index. Examples are

Author search

```
?find au=tanoue, karen y.
       S4     1 AU=TANOUE, KAREN Y.
```

Journal search

```
?find jn=sea grant today
       S5     3 JN=SEA GRANT TODAY
```

C. Result Procedure

The DISPLAY or D command followed by a set number is used to display search results. There are only three options of forms, namely Short or S for short version, Medium or M for medium version, and Long or L for long version. The short version consists of title and citation number only. The medium version contains the bibliographic details. The long version will retrieve the entire citation plus abstract if available. But, in Knowledge Index, results are displayed one at a time. The DISPLAY command is entered in a sequence of set number, form, and item number separated by two slashes.

Set number 2, short form, first item

```
?display s2/s/1
            Display 2/S/1
EJ282099
  Planning Facilities.
```

Set number 2, medium form, first item

```
?display s2/M/1
          Display 2/M/1
EJ282099
  Planning Facilities.
  Flynn, Richard B., Ed.; And Others
  Journal of Physical Education, Recreation & Dance, v54 n6
p19-38 Jun
  1983
  Available from: Reprint: UMI
```

Set number 2, long form, first item

```
display s2/l/1
          Display 2/L/1
J282099   SP513010
  Planning Facilities.
  Flynn, Richard B., Ed.; And Others
  Journal of Physical Education, Recreation & Dance, v54 n6
19-38 Jun        1983
  Available from: Reprint: UMI
  Language: English
  Document Type: JOURNAL ARTICLE (080);   PROJECT DESCRIPTION
141); SERIAL (022)
  Nine articles give information to help make professionals in
ealth, physical education, recreation, dance, and athletics
ore knowledgeable about planning facilities. Design of
atatoriums, physical fitness laboratories, fitness trails,
ymnasium lighting, homemade play equipment, indoor soccer
renas, and dance floors is considered. A safety/security
hecklist is included. (PP)
  Descriptors: Athletic Equipment; Dance; *Design Requirements;
Facility Planning; Flooring; Lighting Design; *Physical
ducation Facilities; Physical Fitness; Safety; Soccer; Swimming
ools; Trails
  Identifiers: *Natatoriums
```

D. Logoff Procedure

The LOGOFF command is used to disconnect with the system, as shown in the following example.

?logoff
 5/30/84   19:02:22 EST
Session Total: 0.114 Hours $ 2.74   User U44066

415 48K DISCONNECTED 00 00

10

Basic SDC's ORBIT Searching

This chapter is prepared for 300-baud and full duplex users in basic ORBIT searching. The user should consult frequently the vendor's two publications: *ORBIT User Manual*, rev. ed., Santa Monica, Calif.: System Development Corporation, 1982, loose-leaf. *Quick-Reference Guide*, Santa Monica, Calif.: System Development Corporation, loose-leaf. Updated by supplementary pages.

The *ORBIT User Manual* and the *Quick-Reference Guide* are companion volumes. The *Manual* provides procedures of search in detail for the ORBIT system. It consists of four parts: (1) an introduction to the ORBIT system, (2) commands used in the ORBIT system, (3) time and storage overflow conditions, and (4) searching techniques. Appendixes include ORBIT commands—a listing of commands, synonyms and abbreviations, and their functions—and ORBIT program messages. The *Quick-Reference Guide* consists of two parts. The first is a summary of the *ORBIT User Manual*. The second part describes databases accessible through ORBIT. For each database is given a general description, sample record, record description, and searching tips. Pages of sample records and record description of ERIC database are reproduced here.

```
AN  - ED127411
CHAN- UDØ16256
TI  - IMPACT OF TITLE I: A DECADE OF PROGRESS
AU  - MOORE, TERRY E.; TURNER, W.E.
OS  - WICHITA UNIFIED SCHOOL DISTRICT 259, KANS.
SO  - MAR 1976; 1Ø7PP
IS  - RIE76DEC
AV  - EDRS PRICE MF-$Ø.83 HC-$6.Ø1 PLUS POSTAGE.(2 MF).
DT  - R (RESEARCH & TECHNICAL REPORTS)
IT  - COMMUNITY INVOLVEMENT; *ECONOMICALLY DISADVANTAGED; EDUCATIONAL
      ASSESSMENT; *EDUCATIONAL NEEDS; EDUCATIONAL RESEARCH; *ELEMENTARY
      SECONDARY EDUCATION; INTERAGENCY COOPERATION; NONPUBLIC SCHOOL
      AID; PARENT PARTICIPATION; PARTICIPANT CHARACTERISTICS; *PROGRAM
      DEVELOPMENT; *PROGRAM EFFECTIVENESS; PROGRAM EVALUATION; SCHOOL
      DISTRICTS; SCHOOL INTEGRATION; SCHOOL SYSTEMS
ST  - *ELEMENTARY SECONDARY EDUCATION ACT TITLE I; ESEA TITLE I;
      *KANSAS (WICHITA)
AB  - THE WICHITA, KANSAS ELEMENTARY SECONDARY EDUCATION ACT TITLE I
      PROJECT WAS BEGUN DURING THE 1965-66 SCHOOL YEAR AS A DIVERSIFIED
      ATTACK ON THE PROBLEMS OF DISADVANTAGED PUPILS. OVER THE PAST 1Ø
      YEARS, THE PROJECT HAS EVOLVED TO ONE WHICH CONCENTRATES FUNDS ON
      A SMALL NUMBER OF PROGRAMS. SUPPORTIVE SERVICES HAVE BEEN
      ELIMINATED IN FAVOR OF INSTRUCTIONAL PROGRAMS. THE SIZE OF THE
      TITLE I TARGET POPULATION HAS BEEN REDUCED IN COMPARISON TO
      EARLIER YEARS. THE TITLE I PROJECT HAS CONTRIBUTED TO THE SUMMER
      SCHOOL PROGRAM THROUGH COURSES AND THE PROVISION OF TUITION
      SCHOLARSHIPS. TITLE I PROGRAMS HAVE HAD A MAJOR IMPACT UPON THE
      WICHITA SCHOOL SYSTEM AND THE COMMUNITY AT LARGE. ONE OBVIOUS
      EFFECT IS SAID TO HAVE BEEN THE PUBLICITY IT HAS BROUGHT TO THE
      WICHITA COMMUNITY. THROUGH A CLOSE, COOPERATIVE RELATIONSHIP, THE
      TITLE I PROGRAM HAS GREATLY INFLUENCED THE WICHITA SCHOOL SYSTEM.
      THE TITLE I PROJECT HAS CONSISTENTLY ENCOURAGED AND SUPPORTED
      PARENTAL AND COMMUNITY INVOLVEMENT IN THE PROGRAMS. CHILDREN
      ATTENDING PAROCHIAL SCHOOLS, INSTITUTIONS FOR THE DELINQUENT, AND
      HOMES FOR THE NEGLECTED HAVE BEEN INCLUDED IN THE PROGRAMS. MOST
      IMPORTANTLY, THE PROJECT HAS BROUGHT ABOUT AN INCREASED AWARENESS
      OF THE SPECIAL NEEDS OF DISADVANTAGED PUPILS. (AUTHOR/JM)
```

```
AN  - EJ142244                                           (CIJE)
CHAN- UD5Ø4614
TI  - STATE PRODUCTION OF SOCIAL KNOWLEDGE: PATTERNS IN GOVERNMENT
      FINANCING OF ACADEMIC SOCIAL RESEARCH
AU  - USEEM, MICHAEL
SO  - AMERICAN SOCIOLOGICAL REVIEW; 41; 4; 613-629 (AUG 1976)
IS  - CIJE76
IT  - *FINANCIAL SUPPORT; *GOVERNMENT ROLE; *POLICY FORMATION;
      *RESEARCH PROJECTS; *RESEARCH UTILIZATION; *SOCIAL SCIENCES;
      STATE ACTION; STATE FEDERAL SUPPORT; SOCIAL FACTORS; STATE
      AGENCIES
AB  - FIVE DISTINCT AIMS UNDERLYING FEDERAL SUPPORT OF ACADEMIC
      SOCIAL RESEARCH ARE HYPOTHESIZED, AND A DIFFERENT OBSERVABLE
      FUNDING PATTERN IS ASSOCIATED WITH EACH ONE. CONCLUDES WITH A
      POSSIBLE EXPLANATION FOR THE GOVERNMENT'S INTEREST IN PRODUCING
      SOCIAL KNOWLEDGE FOR THE ADVANCEMENT OF SOCIAL SCIENCE.
      (AUTHOR/AM)
```

ERIC RECORD DESCRIPTION

SEARCH QUALIFIER	ELEMENT NAME	PRINT/STRS QUALIFIER	STANDARD PRINT COMMANDS		
			PRINT	TRIAL	FULL
--	Basic Index *(Single words from TI, IT, ST, AB)*	--	-	-	-
/IT	Index Terms *(IT and ST)*	IT	-	X	X
/IW	Index Term Words *(single words from IT, ST)*	--	-	-	-
(IN IT)	Supplementary Terms	ST	-	X	X
/TI	Title	TI	X	X	X
(IN BI)	Abstract	AB	-	-	X
/AN	Accession Number	AN	X	X	X
/FS	File Segment	--	-	-	-
/CHAN	Clearinghouse Accession Number	CHAN	-	X	X
/CC	Category Codes	--	-	-	-
/AU	Authors	AU	X	-	X
/OS	Organizational Source	OS	X	-	X
/SPO	Sponsoring Organizational Source	SPO	-	-	X
/LO	Location	LO	-	-	X
/JC	Journal Citation Name	--	-	-	-
Ranging	Publication Year (PY)	--	-	-	-
/IS	Issue	IS	X	-	X
/NU	Numbers	NU	-	-	X
/DT	Document Type	DT	-	X	X
/LA	Language	LA	X	-	X
/UP	Update Code	--	-	-	-
/AV	Availability	AV	X	-	X
--	Source *(includes JC and PY)*	SO	X	-	X
--	Notes	NO	X	-	X
/LPA	Legislative Program Area	LPA	X	X	X

SDC also published the *Self-Instruction Workbook*, compiled by Kris Kuroki Thurman (1982). The workbook gives instructions on beginning-level commands and techniques with thirteen exercises. For a listing of databases accessible from SDC, refer to SDC's *ORBIT Databases*, a catalog, frequently updated. The catalog describes briefly each database and its producer, size, coverage, update frequency, and cost. *Handy Guide to the ORBIT Information Retrieval System* (Santa Monica, Calif.: SDC Information Services, 1983) is a new publication outlining the system's service and procedures for logon, search, result, and logoff. For current information on the system and databases, any changes and new features, refer to *Searchlight*, a periodical published by SDC since 1973.

For convenience of use, this chapter is preceded by contents with numbers in parentheses which refer to pages of the *ORBIT User Manual*.

Contents

*Numbers in parentheses refer to pages in SDC's *ORBIT User Manual.*

I. BASIC PROCEDURE

A. Logon Procedure

The ORBIT system can be accessed through either direct dial or communication networks, such as TELENET and TYMNET.

TELENET and TYMNET Procedure

The user dials a TELENET or TYMNET number and obtains a high-pitched tone indicating that the computer can be connected. The user then inserts the telephone handset in the acoustic coupler of the terminal.

TELENET procedure

The User Enters	The System Responds
(CR) (CR)	TELENET
	XXX XXX
	Terminal =
(CR)	@

TELENET procedure

The User Enters	The System Responds
C 213 33 (CR)	213 33 CONNECTED
/LOGIN user ID (CR)	YOU ARE ON LINE XXX
	HELLO FROM SDC/ORBIT . . . ENTER SECURITY CODE: XXXXXXXX
Security code (CR)	

The identifier for Terminal = varies. On most terminals, just a carriage return without the terminal identifier can be used.

TELENET Logon example

```
TELENET
312 3.50

TERMINAL=

@c 213 33


213 33 CONNECTED
/login librosem

YOU ARE ON LINE LEB

HELLO FROM SDC/ORBIT IV.  (05/30/84  12:27 P.M.
                          PACIFIC TIME)

ENTER SECURITY CODE:
●●●●●●●●●●
```

TYMNET procedure

please type your terminal identifier

	The System Responds
E	-XXXX—XXX-
	please log in:
(CR)	user name:
SDC (CR)	password:
ORBIT (CR)	remote: call connected
/LOGIN user ID (CR)	YOU ARE ON LINE XXX
	HELLO FROM SDC/ORBIT . . .
	ENTER SECURITY CODE:
	XXXXXXXX
Security code (CR)	

The identifier varies. The terminal identifier E and the password OBBIT will not be shown.

TYMNET logon example

```
please type your terminal identifier
-3151-073-
please log in:

user name: sdc

password:

remote: call connected
/login librosea

YOU ARE ON LINE LA1

PROG:
ENTER SECURITY CODE:
●●●●●●●●●
```

Note that in the ORBIT system, the user is asked to *login*; in DIALOG the user will *logon*; and in BRS the user will *sign-in*. These are generically referred to as logon procedures.

As the examples indicate, a security code, in addition to the user ID, is needed to connect the system as a double protection against unauthorized use. The ORBIT system asks for a security code each time the user logs on. At the first logon, the user must create a security code by entering what the user wants to use for a code of up to ten characters. For subsequent logon, when the system responds ENTER SECURITY CODE, enter the security code already created.

Creating a security code example

```
213 33 CONNECTED
/login librosep

YOU ARE ON LINE LEB

HELLO FROM SDC/ORBIT IV.  (05/30/84  12:30 P.M. PACIFIC TIME
YOU MUST CREATE A SECURITY CODE FOR THIS USERID.  ENTER A
SECURITY CODE OF UP TO  TEN(10) CHARACTERS AND CHECK THE
VERIFICATION MESSAGE CAREFULLY.
ENTER SECURITY CODE.

USER:
rosary

PROG:
****
USCLASS NEWLY UPDATED TO REFLECT PATENT CLASSIFICATION
CHANGES THRU 12/27/83
****
CANADIAN USERS:  FOR LATEST TRAINING SCHEDULE, ENTER EX
TRAINING CANADA.
****
CANADIAN USERS:  SEE NEWS.
****
STANDARD DRUG FILE (SDF) NOW RELOADED AND UPDATED! SEE NEWS
FOR DETAILS.
****
YOUR NEW SECURITY CODE IS ROSARY.
YOU ARE NOW CONNECTED TO THE ORBIT DATABASE.
FOR A TUTORIAL, ENTER A QUESTION MARK.  OTHERWISE, ENTER A
COMMAND.
```

To change a security code, the user enters the SECURITY command and the new security code of up to ten characters.

Change of security code example

USER:
security college

PROG:
YOUR NEW SECURITY CODE IS COLLEGE.

B. Search Procedure

Similar to DIALOG, the ORBIT system uses two approaches in searching: (1) the subject term or the Basic Index search, and (2) the subject-implicit and other types of search. The subject term search is used to search the subject term primarily in the Basic Index (BI). The Basic Index is constructed, in most files, from words from abstracts, words assigned as index terms, single words from the index terms, and words from titles. All words, except stopwords, contained in the Basic Index can be searched. Usually, stopwords in ORBIT are an, and, by, for, from, in, of, the, to, and with. The subject-implicit and other types of searches will be discussed in section III.

1. FILES, FILE, and TFILE

The FILES command is used to obtain a list of databases files available to the user's aid.

FILES command example

USER:
files

PROG:
YOU ARE NOW CONNECTED TO THE ORBIT DATABASE.
THE FOLLOWING DATABASES ARE AVAILABLE TO YOU:

ACCOUNTANTS	ASI	CAS-ED	CASSI	CDEX-ED
CIS	COMPENDEX	CRECORD	DBI	EINET
ENERGYLINE	ENVIROLINE	ERIC	GEOREF	GRANTS
INFORM	INSPEC	LABORDOC	LC/LINE	MDF/I
METADEX	NTIS	NUC/CODES	ORBCHEM	ORBIT
ORBPAT	PAPER	POWER	TROPAG	TSCA PLUS
TULSA	USPA	USP70	USP77	WATERLIT
WPI-ED				

The FILE command is used to select the database for searching. The effect of the FILE command is to enter a database, with a new set of search statements (SS), and to initiate the clock for the specified database. To enter a database, use the FILE command with the name of the database. For database names, see *Quick-Reference Guide* and *ORBIT Databases.*

FILE command example

USER:
file eric

PROG:
ELAPSED TIME ON ORBIT: 0.06 HRS.
YOU ARE NOW CONNECTED TO THE ERIC DATABASE.
COVERS RIE 1966 THRU APR (8404) AND CIJE 1969 THRU APR (8404)

*NOW PROXIMITY-SEARCHABLE! ENTER EX ERIC FOR SEARCHING
DETAILS!*

In the process of searching in a file, the user may switch to another file without erasing searches in the file by using the TFILE command. The TFILE command resets the clock, yet continues the search history with a temporary number assigned to each search statement. The effect of the TFILE command allows the user to return to the previous file and to retain all search statements previously acquired.

2. NEIGHBOR

The NEIGHBOR or NBR or EXPAND command is used if the user is not sure what terms and how many postings are in the file or if searching a particular term or terms results in no postings. The command has a similar function to that of DIALOG's EXPAND command; it displays five alphabetically related search terms with the entered term in the middle. If more than five terms are desired, enter the NEIGHBOR command, the term NEIGHBORed, and the number of terms desired. In each

NBR listing are given the listing number (called a SELECT number) in sequence and the postings. The sequence number continues in spite of change of files from logon to end of the search session. At the end of listings, the system asks "UP N OR DOWN N?"—how many additional terms up or down do you want to see. The user may request further terms by using UP or DOWN commands, with the number of terms specified, for example, DOWN 6 or UP 4. The DOWN command is optional; for DOWN listings, one can simply enter the number of terms desired, where 6 is the same as DOWN 6.

In the ORBIT system, the NEIGHBOR command has three main features: (1) Each NEIGHBORed term has its source indicated by a qualifier. For instance, "SWIM FOR YOUR LIFE/IT" indicates the term as an index term and "SWIMMER/TI" is a term from the title. The use of qualifiers will be further discussed in section II. (2) It can specify the number of terms displayed. It can also instruct the system to display terms in an up or down sequence. (3) More than one NEIGHBOR command can be given in a file before making selection of any term. There is no need to select immediately any term after each NEIGHBOR command, as in the case of the DIALOG system in which selection must be made after each term EXPANDed before other terms are EXPANDed, or the result of the term EXPANDed will be lost.

NEIGHBOR command in ERIC file (number of listings unspecified)

```
SS 1 /C?
USER:
nbr swimming

PROG:
SELECT# POSTINGS   TERM
     1        1     *SWIMMERS/IW
     2       33      SWIMMERS/BI
     3       92      SWIMMING/TI
     4      242      SWIMMING/IW
     5      175     *SWIMMING/IW
UP N OR DOWN N?
```

DOWN command example

```
USER:
down 3

PROG:
SELECT# POSTINGS   TERM
    6      423    SWIMMING/BI
    7        1    SWIMMING/OS
    8        1    SWIMMING/AV
UP N OR DOWN N?
```

DOWN command (only number of listings specified)

```
USER:
4

PROG:
SELECT# POSTINGS   TERM
    9      179    SWIMMING/IT
   10      130    *SWIMMING/IT
   11       81    SWIMMING POOLS/IT
   12       50    *SWIMMING POOLS/IT
UP N OR DOWN N?
```

NEIGHBOR command (number of listings specified)

```
USER:
nbr safety 8

PROG:
SELECT# POSTINGS   TERM
   13        1    SAFER, NANCY B./AU
   14        1    SAFERIS/BI
   15        1    SAFEST/TI
   16       25    SAFEST/BI
   17      969    SAFETY/TI
   18     3274    SAFETY/IW
   19     1781    *SAFETY/IW
   20     5248    SAFETY/BI
UP N OR DOWN N?
```

3. SELECT and SHOWSELECT

The SELECT or SEL command is used to select the number for the term from the SELECT list generated by the NEIGHBOR display. In SELECTing, the number may be consecutive or non-consecutive, or both, with or without commas, and numbers selected are executed in an OR relationship. For instance, SEL 3-7, 10 as shown in the example is to SELECT listing numbers 3 or 4 or 5 or 6 or 7 or 11. A search statement numbered in sequence will be displayed with postings of the terms. The user can do further searching by using Boolean operators to combine set numbers. The SHOWSELECT or SHOSEL command is used to display all terms in the SELECT list during the search session.

SELECT command from previous NEIGHBOR display example

```
USER:
sel 3-7, 10

PROG:
SS 1 PSTG (423)

SS 2 /C?
USER:
sel 20

PROG:
SS 2 PSTG (5248)
```

Boolean operators to combine numbered sets example

```
SS 3 /C?
USER:
1 and 2

PROG:
SS 3 PSTG (72)
```

4. FIND

There are two methods of searching. In the indirect method, the user uses the NEIGHBOR command first and then the SELECT command to select the desired terms. Or, the user may prefer the direct method by using the FIND or FD command. The use of the FIND command is, however, optional. The system automatically defaults to search mode.

Direct search in ERIC file example

```
SS 4 /C?
USER:
swimming and safety

PROG:
SS 4 PSTG (72)
```

The default to search mode differs from the procedure of the DIALOG system in which the commands SELECT and COMBINE, SuperSELECT or SELECT STEPS must be used.

Three Boolean operators, OR, AND, and AND NOT, are used in searching. They are executed automatically in the following sequence: AND's and AND NOT's are executed first, and OR's are executed last. If more than one Boolean operator is used and if there is a priority in execution, parentheses must be used to specify which terms should be grouped in an OR operator before they are executed in an AND operator with other terms or groups of terms. Boolean operators in parentheses are executed first. Examples are

Searching terms in ERIC file

```
PROG:

SS 1 /C?
USER:
boys
```

```
PROG:
SS 1 PSTG (4394)

SS 2 /C?
USER:
girls

PROG:
SS 2 PSTG (4039)

SS 3 /C?
USER:
schooling

PROG:
SS 3 PSTG (3129)
```

Boolean operators execution

```
SS 4 /C?
USER:
(1 or 2) and 3

PROG:
SS 4 PSTG (47)
```

Set number 4 of the search statement (SS) specifies that set number 1 (boys) and set number 2 (girls) are executed first then executed with set number 3 (schooling), resulting in postings that contain boys schooling or girls schooling. The user may directly enter the terms to be searched with parentheses specifying the priority of execution. The previous example can be entered as follows:

```
SS 5 /C?
USER:
(boys or girls) and schooling

PROG:
SS 5 PSTG (47)
```

The term searched can also be combined with search statement (SS) or set number. In this case, the characters "SS" must precede the set number with a space between the two.

Set numbers with a term example

```
SS 6 /C?
USER:
(ss 1 or ss 2) and schooling

PROG:
SS 6 PSTG (47)
```

If searches require extended processing time, called overflow conditions, the system will display for the user to choose a time prompt: "unprompted?/PROMPTED?CANCEL? (U/P/C)." If U or UNPROMPTED, is entered, the system will execute the search to completion without further interruption. Should P or PROMPTED be entered, the user will receive the same message at the next time if extended time for processing is again required. C or CANCEL is for the user to cancel processing.

5. The Cost Commands

There are six commands for online cost displays: AUTOCOST ON, AUTOCOST OFF, COST, COST FILE, COST PRINT, and COSTFILE DETAIL. The AUTOCOST ON command is used to display automatically each time the file is changed or the LOGOFF command is entered. The system responds to AUTOCOST ON with "AUTOMATIC DISPLAY OF SEARCH COSTS IS NOW IN EFFECT." The online cost display is shown in the example when the logoff command is entered:

```
PROG:
TERMINAL SESSION FINISHED 05/30/84  1:13 P.M.  (PACIFIC TIME)
ELAPSED TIME ON ERIC: 0.11 HRS.
$1.65 ESTIMATED COST CONNECT TIME.
$0.00 ESTIMATED COST OFFLINE PRINTS: 0
$0.00 ESTIMATED COST ONLINE PRINTS: 0
$1.65 ESTIMATED TOTAL COST THIS ERIC SESSION.
```

```
ELAPSED TIME THIS TERMINAL SESSION: 0.17 HOURS.
$2.55 ESTIMATED COST CONNECT TIME.
$0.00 ESTIMATED COST OFFLINE PRINTS: 0
$0.00 ESTIMATED COST ONLINE PRINTS: 0
$2.55 ESTIMATED TOTAL COST THIS TERMINAL SESSION.
PLEASE HANG UP YOUR TELEPHONE NOW.  GOOD-BYE!
213 33 DISCONNECTED 00 00
```

The AUTOCOST ON command may be cancelled by using the AUTOCOST OFF command. The COST command gives the user the session costs since logon, and the COST FILE command displays all charges since last file change with the file name indicated. Examples are

COST display

```
PROG:

SS 3 /C?
USER:

USER:
cost

PROG:
$2.25 ESTIMATED TOTAL COST THIS TERMINAL SESSION.
ELAPSED TIME THIS TERMINAL SESSION: 0.16 HOURS.
```

COST FILE display

```
SS 3 /C?
USER:
cost file

PROG:
$1.50 ESTIMATED TOTAL COST THIS ERIC SESSION.
ELAPSED TIME ON ERIC: 0.10 HRS.
```

The COST PRINT command is used for the number of an charges for offline and online prints since file change. The COSTFILE DETAIL command displays all charges since last file change as well as the total session costs.

C. Result Procedure

1. *PRINT FULL, PRINT, PRINT TRIAL, and PRINT SCAN*

There are three basic print commands: PRINT FULL or PRT FU, PRINT or PRT, and PRINT TRIAL or PRT TR. The PRINT FULL command gives one full record, unless the number to print is specified. The system responds to the PRINT command with five bibliographic citations. No index terms and abstracts are given. The PRINT TRIAL command gives two strategy-development prints to help the user revise the search strategy. Titles, index terms, category codes, and so forth are usually given in this command. In addition, the PRINT SCAN or PRT SCAN command is available in files that charge online display. It is used to display five documents with accession number and title only. There is no charge for display of the PRINT SCAN format. Below are examples of PRINT FULL, PRINT, and PRINT TRIAL used in the ERIC file.

PRINT FULL command

```
SS 1 /C?
USER:
swimming and safety

PROG:
SS 1 PSTG (72)

SS 2 /C?
USER:
print full

PROG:

-1-
AN  - ED235291
CHAN- UD023144
```

TI – Physical Education Curriculum Guide. Second and Third Grades. 1977-78

AU – Saul, Fran C.; Paris, Jalie

OS – Duval County Schools, Jacksonville, Fla.

SO – (1978); 485pp

NO – A publication of the Office of Curriculum Development.

LO – U.S.; Florida

IS – RIE84FEB

AV – EDRS Price – MF02/PC20 Plus Postage.(6 MF).

DT – 052

LA – English

IT – Behavioral Objectives; Curriculum Guides; Grade 2; Grade 3; *Gymnastics;
*Movement Education; *Perceptual Motor Learning; Physical Activities;
*Physical Education; Primary Education; Resource Materials; Skill
Development; *Swimming

AB – This physical education curriculum guide was developed for use in grade 2
and grade 3 in the Duval County Public Schools, Jacksonville, Florida. A
short discussion of administrative policies is followed by a suggested
yearly program and a listing of essential skills. The greater part of the
guide is devoted to sections on (1) movement education; (2)
perceptual-motor development; (3) gymnastics, stunts, and tumbling; (4)
relays; (5) swimming and water safety; (6) classroom and/or inclement
weather activities; (7) rhythms; and (8) additional activities. For each
of these sections, concepts, subconcepts, objectives, and activities are
given. In the section on perceptual- motor development, instructions for
screening for perceptual-motor problems are provided. The guide ends with
information on making equipment, lists of films for classroom use, and a
46-item list of reference books. (CMG)

PRINT command limited to one record

USER:
print '1

PROG:

-1-
AN - ED235291
CHAN- UD023144
TI - Physical Education Curriculum Guide. Second and Third Grades. 1977-78
AU - Saul, Fran C.; Paris, Jalie
OS - Duval County Schools, Jacksonville, Fla.
SO - (1978); 485pp
LQ - U.S.; Florida
IS - RIE84FEB
AV - EDRS Price - MF02/PC20 Plus Postage.(6 MF).

PRINT TRIAL command

USER:
print trial

PROG:

-1-
AN - ED235291
CHAN- UD023144
TI - Physical Education Curriculum Guide. Second and Third Grades. 1977-78
DT - 052
IT - Behavioral Objectives; Curriculum Guides; Grade 2; Grade 3; *Gymnastics;
      *Movement Education; *Perceptual Motor Learning; Physical Activities;
      *Physical Education; Primary Education; Resource Materials; Skill
      Development; *Swimming

-2-
AN - ED235281
CHAN- UD023131
TI - Physical Education Curriculum Guide. Pre-Kindergarten, Kindergarten,
      First Grade, 1977-78
DT - 052
IT - Athletic Equipment; Behavioral Objectives; Curriculum Guides; Early
      Childhood Education; Grade 1; *Gymnastics; Kindergarten; *Movement
      Education; *Perceptual Motor Learning; *Physical Activities; *Physical
      Education; Preschool Education; *Swimming
ST - Duval County School Board FL

161

These examples were printed from the last search statement. No search statement number is needed. If printing from any earlier search statement, the search statement (SS) number must be given, such as PRINT FULL SS3, that is, to instruct the system to give the first full record in search statement number 3.

Also available in the PRINT command are other options, called "tailored" prints. The user may specify for display (1) a particular number of prints; (2) certain number of prints, either consecutive or non-consecutive or both; or (3) certain fields, such as author and title. All these options can be specified in any order after the PRINT command, which must be entered first. Examples are

Certain items in title, author, and source

```
USER:
print 3-4 ti au so

PROG:

-3-
TI  - Developing More Effective Curriculum Via "Basic Stuff."
AU  - Heitmann, Helen M.
SO  - Apr 1983; 25pp

-4-
TI  - Physical Education and Sport for the Secondary School
      Student
AU  - Dougherty, Neil J., IV, Ed.
SO  - (1983); 413pp
```

Certain items in title only

```
USER:
print ti 5-6 9

PROG:

-5-
TI  - Planning Facilities
```

```
-6-
TI   - Aquatics for Disabled Persons

-9-
TI   - Drownproofing and the Water Safety Spectrum
```

Certain items in title from search statement 1

```
USER:
print ss 1 ti 1

PROG:

-1-
TI   - Physical Education Curriculum Guide. Second and
       Third Grades. 1977-78
```

Certain item (50th) in title only

```
SS 4 /C?
USER:
print ss 1 ti -50

PROG:

-50-
TI   - [Physical Education in the Out of Doors]
```

There are two methods to display a particular number of document, such as 50th document shown above. The user may use either "1 skip 49" or simply "-50" to display the 50th document only.

2. Offline printing command

The search result may be printed offline at the ORBIT site and mailed to the user. Offline printing is generally less costly for a large number of records. The PRINT OFFLINE or PRT OFF command is used to request offline printing of bibliographic citations from search results. It can be used in the same ways as the online PRT to print only certain items or to limit printing to certain fields. The PRINT OFFLINE FULL or PRT FU OFF command is used for full bibliographic records. The offline printing command defaults to printing the entire last search statement or set number unless another search statement number is specified. An option of sorting is only available in offline printing.

D. Logoff Procedure

To logoff, the user enters the STOP or LOGOFF command. After the system responds with "DONE (Y/N)," the user enters Y to disconnect. Or the user may simply enter the STOP Y or LOGOFF Y command to disconnect.

STOP Y command example

```
USER:
stop y

PRO6:
TERMINAL SESSION FINISHED 05/30/84  2:21 P.M.  (PACIFIC
TIME)
ELAPSED TIME ON INFORM: 0.09 HRS.
ELAPSED TIME THIS TERMINAL SESSION: 0.37 HOURS.
PLEASE HANG UP YOUR TELEPHONE NOW.  GOOD-BYE!
213 33 DISCONNECTED 00 00
```

E. Tutorial Commands

Tutorial commands are used to obtain online information about commands, features, and databases. The ? command can be used for the online tutorial. It displays a group of available explanations and telephone numbers of the action desk for help. There are five types of explanations: EXPLAIN, COMMANDS, PROGRAM MESSAGES, ONLINE TUTORIALS, and INFORMATION. For explanations, use the explain or EXP command.

. Command Example

USER:
?

PROG:
THE FOLLOWING GROUPS OF EXPLANATIONS ARE AVAILABLE:

EXPLAIN EXPLAIN   (COMPLETE LIST OF EXPLANATIONS)
EXPLAIN COMMANDS   (LIST OF COMMANDS AND ABBREVIATIONS)
EXPLAIN PROGRAM MESSAGES (LISTS PROGRAM MESSAGES IN SHORT AND
                           LONG MESSAGE LENGTHS)
EXPLAIN ONLINE TUTORIALS (LISTS SEARCH-RELATED EXPLANATIONS)
EXPLAIN INFORMATION   (LISTS EXPLANATIONS FOR SYSTEM INFORMATION)

IF YOU ENCOUNTER PROBLEMS, DISCONNECT PHONE FROM TERMINAL AND CALL AN ACTION
DESK FOR HELP:

SANTA MONICA, CALIFORNIA   213/453-6194
    TOLL FREE OUTSIDE CALIF.   800/421-7229 (8AM-5PM PACIFIC TIME)
    TOLL FREE IN CALIF.   800/352-6689

MCLEAN, VIRGINIA   703/790-9850
    TOLL FREE OUTSIDE VIRGINIA   800/336-3313 (8AM-5PM EASTERN TIME)

TORONTO, CANADA (INFOMART)   416/489-6640

AUSTRALIA   (008) 226-474
(SDC SEARCH SERVICE)

READING, ENGLAND   44-734-866811
(DERWENT/SDC SEARCH SERVICE)

TOKYO, JAPAN   (03)349-8520
(SDC OF JAPAN, LTD.)   (03)349-8528

EXPLAIN EXPLAIN command

SS 1 /C?
USER:
explain explain

PROG:
THE FOLLOWING ITEMS MAY BE EXPLAINED ONLINE BY ENTERING THE EXPLAIN COMMAND WITH
THE NAME OF THE ITEM TO BE EXPLAINED, E.G., EXPLAIN COMMANDS; EXPLAIN FILE.

1. COMMANDS
AUDIT, FILE, FIND, HISTORY, NEIGHBOR, PRINT, PRINT SCAN, PRINT HIT, PRINT
SELECT, PRINT SELECT NOWRAP, TFILE, STOP, BACKUP, ERASEALL, KEEP, RESTART,
SENSEARCH, STRINGSEARCH, SUBHEADINGS, SAVE, STORE, SDIPROFILE, MESSAGE LENGTH,

II. SEARCH VARIATIONS

A. Modified Searching

1. The Use of Truncation

In searching, the word can be truncated at the end, in the middle, and in some files at the beginning. The symbols # and : are used for this purpose. The symbol : is used for an unspecified number of characters or spaces. The symbol # is used for a specified number of characters or spaces. For instance

SWIM:	for any number of characters after the word SWIM
SWIM#	limited to one character or a blank after the word SWIM
SWIM####	limited to no more than four characters after the word SWIM
M#N	for one character embedded in the word M#N
COLO:R	for any number of characters embedded in any word beginning COLO and ending R feature is not available in DIALOG
COLO:R#	for any number of characters embedded in any word beginning COLO and ending R, with a space or any one character.

One of the ORBIT's features in using truncation is that the system responds with "MM," the multimeaning message, which shows variations of the word truncated in the file. The user may select the appropriate words displayed. In searching more than one truncated word, the system will respond with "MM" for each word truncated one at a time for selection. After selection of the first word displayed, the system will proceed to display the next truncated word. The search result will be given after all truncated words have been executed. Examples of using truncation in the ERIC file are given

Truncation embedded in a word

```
SS 1 /C?
USER:
colo:r

PROG:
MM (COLO:R) (7)
     1        5     COLONIZER/BI
     2     2698     COLOR/BI
     3        4     COLOREAR/BI
     4        1     COLORER/BI
     5        9     COLORIMETER/BI
     6        1     COLORIZER/BI
     7       62     COLOUR/BI
SPECIFY NUMBERS, ALL, OR NONE
```

More than one word truncated with "MM"

```
USER:
swim: and safe:

PROG:
MM (SWIM:) (9)
     1       48     SWIM/BI
     2        1     SWIMBLADDER/BI
     3        6     SWIMMER/BI
     4       33     SWIMMERS/BI
     5      423     SWIMMING/BI
     6        1     SWIMNASTICS/BI
     7        3     SWIMS/BI
     8        1     SWIMSUITS/BI
     9        1     SWIMWEAR/BI
SPECIFY NUMBERS, ALL, OR NONE
```

Words selected by number (comma optional)

```
USER:
5, 7
```

Next "MM"; result given after selection

```
PROG:
MM (SAFE:) (17)
      1     835     SAFE/BI
      2       1     SAFEBEING/BI
      3       1     SAFEGARDS/BI
      4      96     SAFEGUARD/BI
      5      12     SAFEGUARDED/BI
      6      61     SAFEGUARDING/BI
      7     241     SAFEGUARDS/BI
      8       1     SAFEKEEPING/BI
      9       1     SAFELIGHT/BI
     10     117     SAFELY/BI
     11      57     SAFER/BI
     12       1     SAFERIS/BI
     13      25     SAFEST/BI
     14    5248     SAFETY/BI
     15       1     SAFETYING/BI
     16       1     SAFEWAY/BI
     17       1     SAFEY/BI
SPECIFY NUMBERS, ALL, OR NONE

USER:
1 14

PROG:
SS 2 PSTG (75)
```

The multimeaning message can be eliminated by using the word "all" preceding the truncated word, such as

```
USER:
all colo:r

PROG:
SS 1 PSTG (2733)
```

2. The Use of Qualifiers

The searching of terms in the Basic Index can be limited to a particular field, such as title, and index terms, by using a search qualifier. A qualifier is, in general, a two-letter code preceded by a slash /. Most files have the following three qualifiers in the Basic Index:

Qualifier Field

/IT	index term
/IW	words from the index term
/TI	title

The use of /IT, for instance, will limit the search to the field of index term. The effect of /IT and /IW is comparable to that of /DF and /DE respectively in DIALOG. The search of the term SAFETY /IW, for example, will retrieve documents of any descriptors which contain the term SAFETY, such as SAFETY, SAFETY EDUCATION, and SCHOOL SAFETY. Qualifiers can be used in both the NEIGHBOR command and direct search, and more than one qualifier can be used in a single search statement. Here is an example of using qualifiers in ERIC:

```
USER:
nbr safety/ti, it

PROG:
SELECT# POSTINGS  TERM
    1        20    SAFER/TI
    2         1    SAFEST/TI
    3       969    SAFETY/TI
    4      1828    SAFETY/IT
    5         1    SAFETY CODES/IT
UP N OR DOWN N?
```

As the example indicates, since the term NEIGHBORed has a qualifier /TI, IT, only terms in the title and index term fields are shown.

In direct search, a qualifier can be entered either before or after the search terms or terms. If the qualifier is entered at the beginning of the line, the system will search all terms in the designated field only. If a qualifier is entered at the end of a term, each term must be entered with the qualifier. It may be noted that to search multiword index terms, there is no need to use the qualifier /IT; the use of qualifier IT to search multiword index terms is optional. Examples of title and index term qualifier searching are

/TI at the beginning of the line

```
SS 1 /C?
USER:
/ti swimming and safety

PROG:
SS 1 PSTG (2)
```

/TI entered after terms

```
SS 2 /C?
USER:
swimming/ti and safety/ti

PROG:
SS 2 PSTG (2)
```

SAFETY searched in title field; SWIMMING searched in Basic Index

---

```
SS 3 /C?
USER:
swimming and safety/ti

PROG:
SS 3 PSTG (11)
```

Multiword index term (the use of /IT optional)

SS 4 /C?
USER:
school community relationship

PROG:
SS 4 PSTG (6587)

SS 5 /C?
USER:
school community relationship/it

PROG:
SS 5 PSTG (6587)

3. LINK and LINK NOT

LINK and LINK NOT are two operators that have a similar but more selective function to that of AND and AND NOT in some databases in which main records and sub-records are both contained. The use of the LINK operator retrieves records where (1) all LINKed terms occur in the main record, (2) all LINKed terms are in the same sub-record, and (3) all LINKED terms are not the main and one sub-record. The use of LINK and LINK NOT enables the user to be more specific in searching than using AND and AND NOT. The difference between AND and LINK in retrieval in the ASI File is shown in the following example:

SS 1 /C?
USER:
gold and coin

PROG:
SS 1 PSTG (31)

SS 2 /C?
USER:
gold link coin

```
PROG:
SS 2 PSTG (20)

SS 3 /C?
USER:
prt fu -3

PROG:

-3-
AN  -  81-8004-2
TI  -  Statistical Appendix to Annual Report of the Secretary of the Treasury on
        the State of the Finances, FY80
SO  -  Annual. 1981. x+476 p.
AV  -  S/N 048-004-01833-1. Doc. 3282A. ASI/MF/7
IS  -  81SUPP
OS  -  Department of Treasury
SI  -  T1.1:980/app; Item 923
RS  -  17,  700,  15600
AB  -

Statistical appendix to the FY80 annual report of the Secretary of the Treasury
(for description of report volume, see above, 8004-1).
    Contents: description of statistical sources (p. vii-x); and 118 tables,
    listed below (p. 3-476).
```

-- TABLES: --
<Data shown "to date," are annual through FY80.>
--*
AN - 81-8004-2.7
ARS -   504
ATI - Account of U.S. Treasury
AAB -
53.--Assets and liabilities in the account of the U.S. Treasury, Sept. 30, 1979
and 1980. (p. 359)
54.--Location <includes mints and Fort Knox depository> of gold, coin, and
coinage metals held by the Treasury, Sept. 30, 1979 and 1980. (p. 360)
55.--Elements of changes in Federal Reserve and tax and loan note account
balances, FY66-date. (p. 361)

As shown, the terms gold and coin are contained in one of the sub-records.

4. Weighting

The use of weighting in some databases is for the purpose of limiting the search to major index terms to achieve greater relevancy. The weighted terms are generally identified by asterisks and are searchable by prefixing an asterisk * to them. Consider an example of searching the term SWIMMING weighted and the term SWIMMING in the index term field in the ERIC file to show the difference in search results.

```
PROG:

SS 1 /C?
USER:
*swimming

PROG:
SS 1 PSTG (175)

SS 2 /C?
USER:
swimming/it

PROG:
SS 2 PSTG (179)
```

5. String and Proximity Search

The STRINGSEARCH or STRS command is used to search for a string of characters, not possible through direct search of the file. Two steps are involved in the STRINGSEARCH command. Search statements with postings must be created first. Then, the terms searched are entered between two colons preceded by the STRINGSEARCH command, the number of the search statement (SS) to be stringsearched (for immediate, previous search statement, the set number is optional), and the field designated. The format is STRS n/field(s) :character string:. An example of using string search in the ERIC file is given:

First step: search statement with postings

```
SS 1 /C?
USER:
pursuit/ti and happiness/ti

PROG:
SS 1 PSTG (9)
```

Second step: terms searched between two colons

```
SS 2 /C?
USER:
strs /ti :pursuit of happiness:

PROG:
SS 2 PSTG (8)
```

To display the result

```
SS 3 /C?
USER:
print 3 ti

PROG:

-1-
TI  - The Pursuit of Happiness

-2-
TI  - Educating Our Children for Life, Liberty, and the
      Pursuit of Happiness?

-3-
TI  - Educational Purpose and the Pursuit of Happiness
```

If the number of the search statement is not given, the search will be done on the last search statement. If the field is not designated, the search in most files will be done in the field of title (/TI). A variation of STRINGSEARCH is SENSEARCH. The SENSEARCH or SENS command is used to perform the same type of search as the STRINGSEARCH command, except that the SENS command will search for a string of characters within a sentence. A sentence is defined as a string of characters that ends with a period and a space or is the end of the field.

The ORBIT system has introduced the feature of proximity search to a number of files, thus enabling the user to search directly a group of terms in these files. Like DIALOG's full-text operators mentioned in chapter nine, the following operators are used in proximity or hierarchical search:

(W) or ADJ or W/O or () or (O)	for searching terms on either side of the operator to be adjacent and in the specified order
(nW) or W/n or (n)	for searching terms with a specified distance, such as one or two intervening words between terms
(S) or W/S	for searching terms in the same sentence, in any order
(L) or LINK	for searching terms in the same sub-field or sub-record, in any order; same as LINK
(F) or W/F	for searching terms in the same field, in any order
(C) or (R) or W/R or AND	for searching terms in the same record, in any order; analogous to using AND operator

B. Other Search Strategies

1. AUDIT and AUDIT CANCEL

A similar result of DIALOG's SuperSELECT can be achieved in ORBIT by using the AUDIT command to display separate postings for each term within a search statement. The command will remain in effect until it is cancelled. AUDIT CANCEL or AUDIT OFF is used to cancel the AUDIT command. Examples of using AUDIT and AUDIT CANCEL in the ERIC file are

```
SS 3 /C?
USER:
audit


PROG:
SEARCH AUDITING IS NOW IN EFFECT.


SS 3 /C?
USER:
swimming and safety


PROG:
        OCCURS    TERM
        423       SWIMMING
        5248      SAFETY
SS 3 PSTG (72)


SS 4 /C?
USER:
audit cancel


PROG:
SEARCH AUDITING IS NO LONGER IN EFFECT.
```

2. The Saving Search

Operations from one file to another with compatible vocabularies, with the exception of the stringsearch, can be repeated by saving the search. The SAVE command saves a search strategy after it has been entered for the duration of the day. It is entered with any search name of up to twenty-six characters specified by the user. The RECALL command is used to repeat the search in other databases or later that day in the same database. To keep a search strategy indefinitely, use the STORE command and a search name after a search strategy is completed. The PURGE command is used to delete the STOREd search.

SAVE in the ERIC file

```
SS 1 /C?
USER:
(swimming or bicycling) and safety

PROG:
        OCCURS    TERM
         5248     SAFETY
          423     SWIMMING
           77     BICYCLING
SS 1 PSTG (106)

SS 2 /C?
USER:
save safe

PROG:
SAVE SAFE COMPLETED.
```

RECALL in the NTIS file

```
SS 1 /C?
USER:
recall safe

PROG:
        OCCURS    TERM
        36778     SAFETY
          337     SWIMMING
           15     BICYCLING
SS 1:  (  SWIMMING OR BICYCLING  ) AND SAFETY  (44)
```

3. Stacking Commands

Several commands can be entered in one statement with each command separated by a semicolon. The system will execute the entire sequence of operations, as in the example using stacking commands, FILE, searching, and PRINT in the ERIC file.

USER:
file eric; (swimming or bicycling) and safety; print 2 ti au

PROG:
ELAPSED TIME ON NTIS: 0.03 HRS.
YOU ARE NOW CONNECTED TO THE ERIC DATABASE.
COVERS RIE 1966 THRU APR (8404) AND CIJE 1969 THRU APR (8404)

*NOW PROXIMITY-SEARCHABLE! ENTER EX ERIC FOR SEARCHING
DETAILS!*
        OCCURS   TERM
        5248   SAFETY
        423   SWIMMING
        77   BICYCLING
SS 1 PSTG (106)

-1-
TI - Physical Education Curriculum Guide. Second and Third
      Grades. 1977-78
AU - Saul, Fran C.; Paris, Jalie

-2-
TI - Physical Education Curriculum Guide. Pre-Kindergarten,
      Kindergarten, First Grade, 1977-78

4. HISTORY

The HISTORY or HIS command functions like DIALOG's
DISPLAY SETS command. It is used to display previous search
statements in a summary format. The use of the HISTORY
command to display searches in the ERIC file in section I-B-4 is
shown as follows:

USER:
history

PROG:
SS 1: BOYS (4394)
SS 2: GIRLS (4039)
SS 3: SCHOOLING (3129)
SS 4: (1 OR 2) AND 3 (47)

5. KEEP, BACKUP, and ERASEALL

The KEEP command is used to keep specific search statements and erase all others. The BACKUP command, if not specified, is used to erase the last search statement or to erase all search statements back to and including the specified number of search statements, To erase all previous search statements, use the ERASEALL command. The user can keep a specified number of search statements or erase some or all search statements. Three examples are given: (1) To KEEP 1-5, the system begins with search statement number 6. (2) To BACKUP 3, the system begins with search statement number 3. (3) The system begins with search statement number 1, if the ERASEALL command is entered.

SS 9 /C?
USER:
keep 1-5

PROG:

SS 6 /C?
USER:
backup 3

PROG:

SS 3 /C?
USER:
eraseall

PROG:

SS 1 /C?
USER:

C. Multiple Database Subject Search

The user may use the DBI (Data Base Index) file, a master index to all ORBIT databases, to retrieve a list of databases that contains a given search term. The use of DBI consists of, in general, three steps: (1) enter the DBI file, (2) search a particular term, (3) use the PRINT RANK command to retrieve a ranked list of databases with the number of postings for the given term. If any logical operator is used in a search statement, for example, a statement with more than one term combined in logical operation, the number of postings will not be displayed.

Step 1

```
USER:
file dbi

PROG:
ELAPSED TIME ON ERIC: 0.13 HRS.
YOU ARE NOW CONNECTED TO THE DATA BASE INDEX DATABASE.
THIS IS THE MASTER INDEX TO ALL SEARCH SERVICE DATABASES.
UPDATED AS OF 6/3/83
```

Step 2

```
SS 1 /C?
USER:
swimming

PROG:
SS 1: (51) DATABASES
```

Step 3

```
SS 2 /C?
USER:
print rank 3

PROG:

-1-
DN  - SPORT
PSTG- AT LEAST 4101.
```

```
-2-
DN  - WPI
PSTG- AT LEAST 1701.

-3-
DN  - BIO7479 (PROXIMITY SEARCHABLE)
PSTG- AT LEAST 1501.
```

III. SUBJECT-IMPLICIT AND OTHER SEARCHES

A. Subject-Implicit Searches

The subject-implicit fields are not topical or subject terms but have a relationship with the subject content. These vary with databases. Check each database record description in SDC's *Quick-Reference Guide* for these fields. The subject-implicit field, designated in general by a two-character code preceded by a slash, functions as a qualifier to limit the scope of the search to a specified field or fields. Qualifiers used to restrict subject searches to title (TI), index terms, (IT), and index words (IW) have been mentioned in section I. Like subject term search qualifiers, qualifiers for the subject-implicit fields can be entered in direct search either at the beginning of the line or after the search term.

Following are selected qualifiers for subject-implicit searches.

1. Author (/AU)

Three examples show author searching in the ERIC file: (1) using indirect method by NEIGHBORing the name first with truncation, then selecting the name; (2) using indirect method by NEIGHBORing the name; and (3) direct searching.

```
SS 1 /C?
USER:
nbr li, t/au

PROG:
SELECT# POSTINGS  TERM
    1        1    LI, PEI-CHAO/AU
    2        1    LI, PETER S./AU
```

```
    3          1      LI, TING-KAI, ED./AU
    4          2      LI, TZE-CHUNG/AU
    5          2      LI, VIRGINIA C., ED./AU
UP N OR DOWN N?

USER:
sel 4
PROG:
SS 1 PSTG (2)

SS 2 /C?
USER:
li, tze-chung/au

PROG:
SS 2 PSTG (2)
```

2. Organizational Source (/OS)

The qualifier /OS is used to search author's affiliation and in some files corporate author. The example uses /OS at the beginning of the line in the ERIC file to search three terms, namely, "national," "science," and "foundation."

```
SS 4 /C?
USER:
/os national and science and foundation

PROG:
SS 4 PSTG (455)
```

3. Journal Codes, CODEN, and Names (/JC)

Journals can be searched by journal codes, CODEN's and journal names. Examples follow of using three different methods to search records on management by objectives published in the *Harvard Business Review* in ABI/INFORM and to search the journal name in ERIC.

In INFORM

```
SS 5 /C?
USER:
print 2 os

PROG:

-1-
OS  - National Science Foundation, Washington, D.C.

-2-
OS  - National Science Foundation, Washington, DC. National
      Science Board Commission on Precollege Education in
      Mathematics, Science and Technology.
```

Reproduced with permission of Data/Courier Inc.

In ERIC

```
SS 1 /C?
USER:
management by objectives and hbr/jc

PROG:
SS 1 PSTG (5)

SS 2 /C?
USER:
management by objectives and habrax/jc

PROG:
SS 2 PSTG (5)
```

B. Other Searches

Searches can be conducted in a particular database to restrict retrieval to a language, the most recent update, and/or a specified period of coverage or publication.

1. Language (/LA)

Example of limiting to Japanese language in INSPEC file

```
SS 1 /C?
USER:
paramagnetic resonance and japanese/la

PROG:
SS 1 PSTG (9)

SS 2 /C?
USER:
print 2 ti la

PROG:

-1-
TI  - A TRIP TO THE INTERDISCIPLINARY FIELD OF GEOLOGY:
      SOLID STATE PHYSICS AND GEOLOGICAL DATING
LA  - JAPANESE

-2-
TI  - DOPING AND ADSORPTION EFFECTS IN AMORPHOUS SILICON
      PREPARED BY HIGH PRESSURE RF SPUTTERING
LA  - JAPANESE
```

2. Update (/UP)

The qualifier /UP is used to restrict searches to the most recent update for a particular database. The update value is a four-digit code: the first two digits represent the year and the last two are sequential; for example in a file updated monthly these would go from 01 to 12, in a file updated quarterly from 01 to 04. Update codes do not print, but they do remain searchable on the file. The most recent update code for a file is displayed as part of the connect message.

Example of using /UP in INFORM file

```
SS 1 /C?
USER:
management by objectives and 8112/up


PROG:
SS 1 PSTG (7)


SS 2 /C?
USER:
print 1 ti so


PROG:

-1-
TI   - A Planning Program for Management
SO   - Telephone Engineer & Mgnt (TPEMAW,TEM), v85n21,
       PP.117-118, ISSN 0040-263X, Nov 1, 1981
```

Reproduced with permission by Data/Courier Inc.

3. Date Ranging

Searches can be restricted to a specified time period, usually year of publication, by using the following commands:

AND FROM year-year (or AND FROM year THRU year)

AND GREATER THAN year

AND LESS THAN year

The year is represented by four digits or two, the last two digits. Examples of data ranging are

SS 1 /C?
USER:
management by objectives and greater than 1981

PROG:
SS 1 PSTG (63)

SS 2 /C?
USER:
management by objectives and from 1980 to 1982

PROG:
SS 2 PSTG (99)

SS 3 /C?
USER:
management by objectives and 80-82

PROG:
SS 3 PSTG (99)

Reproduced with permission by Data/Courier Inc.

11

Basic BRS Searching

This chapter is prepared for 300-baud and full duplex users. For details of searching, refer to *BRS System Reference Manual*, Scotia, N.Y.: Bibliographic Retrieval Services, 1981, 160p. The *Manual*, in twenty-seven sections, details the procedure of BRS searching. There are eight appendixes: TELENET terminal model identifiers, BRS databases and search labels, stopword list, guide to descriptor searching, format guide for author searching, BRS standardized language codes, default paragraph sets (BIBL), and offline coverage of BRS databases.

For specific features of each database, refer to *BRS Database Guide* and its abbreviated version, *The BRS AidPage*. The *AidPage* is a one-sheet guide published separately for each database. It consists of general description (BRS label, scope, search aids, bibl paragraphs, producers, year of coverage, total size, updates, and so forth), record structure key (label, paragraph, function and example), and sample citations. A sample page of the *AidPage* is reproduced on the following pages.

BRS also published a pamphlet, *BRS Brief System Guide*, for quick reference to sign-on, sign-off procedures, database available from BRS, and BRS commands. A recent publication of BRS is *BRS Directory and Database Catalog*, Latham, N.Y.: Bibliographic Retrieval Services, 1983, 23p. The directory

The BRS AidPage
for the
Educational Resources Information Center

BRS Label:
ERIC

Scope:
ERIC contains over 478,000 citations covering research findings, project and technical reports, speeches, unpublished manuscripts, books, and journal articles in the field of education.

Search Aids:
Thesaurus of ERIC Descriptors.
ERIC Processing Manual.
ERIC Contract/Grant Number Index. (Annual).
ERIC Report/Project Number Index (Cumulative).
ERIC Title Index 1966–1976 (Annual cumulations with quarterly supplements, 1977 – Date).
Institutional Source Directory (Annual).

BIBL Paragraphs:
AN, AU, TI, SO, SN, IS, YR

Producer:
ERIC Processing and Reference Facility
4833 Rugby Ave. Suite 303
Bethesda, MD 20014

Contact:
Ted Brandhorst
Telephone: 301-656-9723
703–620-3660
(for search assistance)

Document Delivery
Most RIE documents are available on microfiche or in paper copy from EDRS or on microfilm from UMI:

EDRS
P.O. Box 190
Arlington, VA 22210

University Microfilms International
300 North Zeeb Rd.
Ann Arbor, MI 48106

Years of Coverage:
1966 to date

Total Size:
Over 478,000 citations;
RIE: 211,000 citations,
CIJE: 267,000 citations.

Updates:
Approximately 3,500 citations added monthly.

Print Counterparts:
Current Index to Journals in Education (CIJE).
Resources in Education (RIE).

Royalties:
None

RECORD STRUCTURE KEY

Label	Paragraph	Function	Example
AN	ERIC Accession Number	.s .l	ej266520.an. .l/1 an > ej266520
AU	Author/s	.s	jones.t$.au.
IN	Name of institution where work was performed (RIE only)	.s	education adj products adj information adj exchange.in. qpx23895.in.
TI	Title	.s	bilingual adj immersion.ti.
SO	Journal title, volume, issue, number, date, pages.	.s	journal adj child adj language with jun82.so.
*LG	Language	.s	fr.lg.
*GS	Geographic source (RIE only)	.s	ontario.gs.
SN	Sponsoring agency name and code (RIE only)	.s	cooperative adj state adj research adj service.sn. edn0001.sn.
PA	Program area code (RIE only)	.s	'08'.pa.
IS	RIE or CIJE issue number	.s	rienov81.is.
NO	Numbers: grant, contract, report, project (RIE only)	.s	dhhs-adm-80-1037.no.

Label	Paragraph	Function	Example
CH	Clearinghouse code	.s	ps.ch.
*GV	Governmental status (RIE only)	.s	state.gv.
PR	EDRS price codes (RIE only) Not available from EDRS = PR-NA	.s	pr-na.pr.
PT	Publication type code	.s	'150'.pt.
AV	Availability statement	.s	umi.av.
LV	Level of availability (RIE only)	.s	'2'.lv.
NT	Descriptive note (RIE only)	.s	kenya.nt.
YR	Year of publication or generated entry date	.s .l	81.yr. .l/1 yr > 81
MJ	Major subject descriptors	.s	liberal-arts.mj. liberal-arts.de.
MN	Minor subject descriptors	.s	cultural-background.mn. cultural-background.de.
ID	Identifiers	.s	cats.id.
AB	Abstract	.s	folk adj tale$1 with spanish.ab.

*Data elements added in 1979.

11/62

Reprinted with the permission of BRS, Bryn Mawr, Pa.

provides brief descriptions of BRS databases grouped into five broad subject areas. *BRS Bulletin* published since 1976 is important for current information, changes, and new features of the system and its databases.

For convenience of use, the basic BRS searching is preceded by contents with numbers in parentheses which refer to sections in the *BRS System Reference Manual*. This chapter also includes a section on BRS/After Dark, a new service of BRS.

Contents

*   Numbers in parentheses refer to sections in the *BRS System Reference Manual*.

I. BASIC PROCEDURE

A. Sign-on Procedure

The BRS system can be accessed through either direct dial or communication networks, such as TELENET, TYMNET, and UNINET.

TELENET, TYMNET, and UNINET Procedure

The user dials a TELENET, TYMNET, or UNINET number and obtains a high-pitched tone indicating that the system can be connected. The user then inserts the telephone handset in the acoustic coupler of the terminal.

TELENET procedure

The User Enters	The System Responds
(CR) (CR)	TELENET
	XXX XX
	Terminal =
(CR)	@
C 315 20 b (CR)	315 20 B CONNECTED
	ENTER BRS PASSWORD:
Password (CR)	

The identifier varies. On most terminals, just a carriage return without the identifier can be used.

TELENET sign-on example

```
TELENET
312 3A

TERMINAL=

@c 315 20b


315 20B CONNECTED

ENTER BRS PASSWORD
■■p■■■■■

BROADCAST MESSAGE CHANGED 05/30/84 AT 12:33:53.
ENTER 'Y' OR 'N' FOR BROADCAST MESSAGE._:
```

TYMNET procedure

The User Enters	The System Responds
	please type your terminal identifier -XXXX-XXX-
E	please log in
brs (CR)	+
(CR)	remote: call connected
	ENTER BRS PASSWORD XXXXXXXX
password (CR)	

The identifier varies. The terminal identifier E will not be shown.

TYMNET sign-on example

```
please type your terminal identifier
-3151-022-

please log in: brs
+


   remote:  call connected

ENTER BRS PASSWORD
▮▮▮▮▮▮▮▮


BROADCAST MESSAGE CHANGED 05/30/84 AT 12:33:53.
ENTER 'Y' OR 'N' FOR BROADCAST MESSAGE._:
```

UNINET procedure

The User Enters	The System Responds
	L?
(CR) . (CR)	UNINET PAD XXXX PORT XX SERVICE:
BRS; A (CR)	*XXX XXX CONNECTED TO XXXXXXX
(CR)	ENTER BRS PASSWORD XXXXXXXX
Password (CR)	

UNINET sign-on example

```
L?
uninet pad 1418 port 06
service : obrs:a

*u001 000 connected to 51800006

ENTER BRS PASSWORD
■■■■■■■■■
BROADCAST MESSAGE CHANGED 05/30/84 AT 12:33:53.
ENTER 'Y' OR 'N' FOR BROADCAST MESSAGE._:
```

An A-M-I-S password may be used as a double protection
against unauthorized use. A-M-I-S stands for Account Management of Information System. Once an A-M-I-S password is established, it must be entered in addition to the regular password for
access to BRS. The procedure of establishing an A-M-I-S
password is as follows:

Steps	The User Enters	The System Responds
		ENTER DATABASE NAME__:
1	ACCT	SIGN-ON XX.XX.XX.
		SPECIFY DATABASE NAME, TOTAL, ALL, MASTER OR PROFILE
2	PROFILE	ENTER # CORRESPONDING TO CHANGE 1: OFFLINE MAILING ADDRESS 2: PARABIBL 3: TERMINAL TYPE 4: TELE-PHONE # 5: SEARCH ANALYST 6: END PROFILE 7: PASSWORD 8: ONLINE COST
3	7	SPECIFY NEW A-M-I-S PASSWORD (MAX 6 CHRS)
4	Password	PROFILE HAS BEEN UPDATED SPECIFY DATABASE NAME, TOTAL, ALL, MASTER OR PROFILE

The procedure to change an A-M-I-S password follows the above steps through 3 and continues as follows:

Steps	The User Enters	The System Responds
		ENTER OLD A-M-I-S PASSWORD
4	Password	SPECIFY NEW A-M-I-S PASSWORD (MAX 6 CHRS)
5	Password	PROFILE HAS BEEN UPDATED SPECIFY DATABASE NAME, TOTAL, ALL, MASTER OR PROFILE

B. Search Procedure

In the BRS system, each document is divided into paragraphs. The paragraph is labeled with two alphabetical characters (see sample page). Most paragraphs are searchable and words, except stopwords, in these paragraphs can be searched. For a list of stopwords, refer to *BRS Database Guide* and appendix three of *BRS System Reference Manual.*

1. Entering Database and ..CHANGE

After signing on, the system responds with ENTER 'Y' or 'N' FOR BROADCAST MESSAGE__:. If the user keys in "n" with a carriage return, the following message will be displayed: ENTER DATA BASE NAME__:. The user simply enters the database name in a four-character code to connect with a particular database. See appendix two of *BRS System Reference Manual, AidPage,* and *BRS Directory and Database* for BRS database search labels.

The ..CHANGE or ..C command is used to change databases. After the system responds with ENTER DATA BASE NAME__:, the user then enters the database name. The user may also simplify the procedure by using stacking commands, that is, combining the ..CHANGE command and the database name with a slash / inserted between the two. See also section II-B for stacking commands. All system commands in BRS must be preceded by two decimal points.

..CHANGE command and entering database name example

         1_: ..change

*CONNECT TIME   0:01:28 HH:MM:SS   0.024 DEC HRS
  SESSION   269*

ENTER DATA BASE NAME_: eric

BRS/ERIC/1966 - MAY 1984 (BOTH)

Simplified procedure

BRS - SEARCH MODE   - ENTER QUERY
       1_: ..change/eric

*CONNECT TIME   0:00:54 HH:MM:SS   0.015 DEC HRS
  SESSION   271*

BRS/ERIC/1966 - MAY 1984 (BOTH)

When the database is changed, all previous search statements are automatically erased. The ..CHANGE command will indicate previous connect time in hours, minutes, and seconds (HH:MM:SS).

2. ROOT

In BRS, ROOT is not considered to be a command but a feature. It is used to display a list of all entries that begin with a particular "root" or stem. In each ROOT listing are given the listing number (called r number) in sequence and the postings. The ROOT numbers are usable until another ROOT is entered. In selecting ROOTed terms, r numbers may be consecutive or non-consecutive, or both, with spaces or hyphens between numbers. Hyphens are used for consecutive numbers.

Example using ROOT in the ERIC file

```
1_:     root swim

        SWIM$
R1      SWIM                           48 DOCUMENTS
R2      SWIMBLADDER                     1 DOCUMENT
R3      SWIMMER                         6 DOCUMENTS
R4      SWIMMER-GENE                    1 DOCUMENT
R5      SWIMMERS                       33 DOCUMENTS
R6      SWIMMING                      422 DOCUMENTS
R7      SWIMMING-POOLS                 81 DOCUMENTS
R8      SWIMMING/BATHING                1 DOCUMENT
R9      SWIMNASTICS                     1 DOCUMENT
R10     SWIMS                           3 DOCUMENTS
R11     SWIMSUITS                       1 DOCUMENT
R12     SWIMWEAR                        1 DOCUMENT
```

Selecting r numbers

```
1_:     r1 r3 r5-r6

RESULT       452
```

In response to ROOTing, the system will retrieve only up to 100 forms of a term. If there are over 100 terms ROOTed, the system will give the following message:

1417 MORE THAN 100 TERMS for *term$*
   LAST TERM PROCESS WAS *term*

The user may ROOT the last term processed.

One feature of the BRS system is that the term ROOTed can be restricted to a particular paragraph by entering the paragraph qualifier immediately after r numbers, such as r5.de. to confine the term "SWIMMING" to descriptor search only. Paragraph qualifiers will be mentioned in section II. Another feature is that r numbers can be used directly with other keywords in the search statement. An example is

2_: (r1 r3 r5-r6) and safety

RESULT   73

3. ..SEARCH

Similar to DIALOG's SELECT, COMBINE, or SuperSELECT commands, the ..SEARCH or ..S command is used to search free-text keywords. When a database is selected, the system will automatically put the user in the search mode:

BRS—SEARCH MODE—ENTER QUERY
1_;
There is no need to enter the ..SEARCH command. However, if for some reason during the process the system does not put the user in the search mode, it is necessary to activate it by entering the ..SEARCH command. All searchable paragraphs can be retrieved in the search mode. In searching, the system compares sets of entries and then creates a new set by using three Boolean operators: AND, OR, and NOT. AND's and NOT's are executed first, and OR's are executed last. If more than one logical operator is used, and if there is a priority in execution, nesting of the operators in parentheses for the order of execution is necessary. If no operator is inserted between two keywords, the system assumes an OR relationship, provided no other previous operator is used. If a previous operator is used, the system will assume the relationship of that operator in any spaces following it. Statement numbers can be entered in combination with search keywords.

Example of search in the ERIC file

1_: boys

RESULT   4507

```
2_:    girls

RESULT    4127

3_:    schooling

RESULT    3280
```

Set numbers combined and with term

```
4_:    (1 or 2) and 3

RESULT    51

5_:    (1 or 2) and schooling

RESULT    51
```

Since the system assumes the OR relationship if no operator is inserted between two keywords, the previous search statement can be given as follows with the same result:

```
6_:    ( 1 2) and schooling

RESULT    51
```

The use of controlled vocabularies in searching is faster, and the result is usually more relevant. In multiword search of controlled vocabularies, however, a hyphen must be used. For instance, "library science" should be entered as "library-science," and "teacher supply and demand" as "teacher-supply-and-demand." Terms separated by a comma or enclosed in parentheses should be hyphenated with the comma and parentheses removed.

4. ..COST

The ..COST or ..CO command is used to obtain an estimated searching cost during a particular search session.

..COST command example

```
7_:     ..cost
```

EST ERIC COST:	C-HRS	DB-ROY	CIT-ROY	COMM	TOTAL
	$.30	$.00	$.00	$.30	$.60

C. Result Procedure

1. ..PRINT

The ..PRINT or ..P command is used to display records online from the search result. It can be used to retrieve all paragraphs of a document or a particular paragraph of a document, or selected paragraphs of a document, and can be limited to a specific number of documents. Three options are available:

(a) Options for Paragraphs

all	all paragraphs of a document
ti	limited to title
au, ti, so	limited to the specified paragraphs of author, title, and source
bibl	limited to the predetermined set of default paragraphs or to a set of paragraphs arranged by the password holder; for predetermined set of default paragraphs, see appendix seven of *BRS System Reference Manual*
	bibl, lg, ab
bibl, lg	default paragraphs plus paragraphs of language
ab	and abstract

(b) Pre-formatted Options

The user may also use the nine pre-formatted options (see *BRS System Reference Manual*). Here are some of them:

F2   all except abstract
F3   same as the option "bibl" mentioned above
F4   title, abstract

F5   all paragraphs of a document

F6   title

F7   same as the option "bibl" plus abstract

(c) Options for the Number of Documents

doc = all   all documents of the search result

doc = 1   limited to the first document

doc = 1, 5, 12   limited to the first, fifth, and twelfth documents

doc = 1-5, 10   the first five and the tenth documents

The ..PRINT command is entered as follows: ..PRINT 5 ti, au/doc = 1-5. The system is instructed to give the first five documents in paragraphs of author and title of set number 5. Two examples of using ..PRINT in the ERIC file are given: (1) options for paragraphs and the number of documents, and (2) pre-formatted options and the number of documents. See next page for print example.

2. ..PRINTOFF

The search result may be printed offline at the system site and sent to the user. The ..PRINTOFF or ..PO command is used to request offline printing of the search result. In offline printing, there is an option of sorting; but the sorting feature is not available in online searching.

D. Sign-off Procedure

To sign-off, enter ..OFF or ..O command

TELENET sign-off example

_: ..off

*CONNECT TIME   0:02:42 HH:MM:SS   0.045 DEC HRS
SESSION   272*

*SIGN-OFF   20.22.12   05/30/84:
315 20B DISCONNECTED 00 00

e

AN EJ294194.

AU Bryant, Brenda K.

TI Context of Success, Affective Arousal, and Generosity: The Neglected Role of Negative Affect in Success Experience.

SO American Educational Research Journal; v20 n4 p553-62 Win 1983. 83.

LG EN..

IS CIJMAY84.

CH TM508622.

PT 143; 150.

AV UMI.

NT Portions of this paper were presented at the Bienial Meetings of the Society for Research in Child Development (Boston, MA, April 1981). This study was supported by the Agricultural Experiment Station, University of California, Davis, in conjunction with the W-144 regional project, Development of Social Competence in Children.

YR 83.

MJ Affective-Behavior. Locus-of-Control. Success.

MN Elementary-Education. Elementary-School-Students. Males. Prosocial-Behavior.

ID IDENTIFIERS: Generosity. Happiness.

AB Elementary Boys' generosity toward peers following a success experience varied according to resulting positive and negative affects. Role of context of success relative to affective arousal and generosity were explored. Results indicated importance of considering the context of success and relevance of negative affects induced by a success experience. (Author/DWH).

END OF DOCUMENT

If, for some reason, the user wishes to interrupt a search temporarily, the ..OFF CONT or ..O CONT command should be entered. The ..OFF CONT command enables the user to continue the search later in the day. There is no need to use a ..SAVE command to keep previous searches. When reconnected, the system asks the user to restart or not the previous database. If yes is entered, the search history in the previous database continues.

II. SEARCH VARIATIONS

A. Modified Searching

1. The Use of Truncation

In the search mode, the word can be truncated at the end, and the number of characters truncated can be specified. The symbol $ is used for truncation. Unlike the SDC or DIALOG system, the word cannot be truncated in the middle.

SWIM$ for any characters after the word SWIM

SWIM$1   limited to one character after the word SWIM

SWIM$4   limited to four characters after the word SWIM

The use of truncation in the ERIC file

```
BRS - SEARCH MODE  - ENTER QUERY
   1_:   swim$

   RESULT        459

   2_:   swim$1

   RESULT        50

   3_:   swim$4

   RESULT        455
```

2. The Use of Positional Operators

Positional operators are used to restrict free-text searching of multiwords other than the bound descriptor, that is, multiwords not recorded in the descriptor or identifier, to achieve search relevancy and precision. There are three positional operators:

same   words searched are to be in the same paragraph

with   words searched are to be in the same sentence

adj   words searched are to be right next to each other and in that order. Stopwords are not counted

Examples are

```
1_:    library same science

RESULT    2573

2_:    library with science

RESULT    2002

3_:    library adj science

RESULT    1447
```

Positional and Boolean operators can be combined in the same search statement. The order of execution of positional and Boolean operators is as follows: Operators in parentheses are executed first, followed in sequence by adj, with, same, and Boolean operators. Example

```
4_:    library adj (science or system)

RESULT    1935
```

3. The Use of Qualifiers

The search can be limited to words in a particular paragraph of a document, such as title or abstract paragraph. Each paragraph is labelled by two characters. The user may qualify the search by entering the keyword or keywords followed immediately by a paragraph label enclosed between two decimal points. More than one qualifier can be used at the same time, such as .ti,ab., which will limit the search to the title and abstract paragraphs.

Also, the keyword in a particular paragraph can be excluded by using the so-called negative paragraph qualifier, that is, using two decimal points instead of one between the label and the search word. The system will exclude the word in that particular paragraph.

Examples of using qualifiers in the ERIC file

```
5_:      library.ti. adj science.ti.

RESULT        92

6_:      library.de. and science.de.

RESULT      1357
```

The effect of using the qualifier .de. is comparable to that of /DE in DIALOG; it will retrieve documents of any descriptors, which contain the term. The use of SAFETY.de. will retrieve documents with such descriptors as SAFETY SCHOOL SAFETY, and SAFETY EDUCATION. If the search is limited to SAFETY as a major descriptor only, .mj. instead of .de. qualifier should be used.

One of the features of BRS is that qualifiers can be used with set numbers. The user need not repeat the words with qualifiers. For instance, set number 3, given above, yields 1447 documents. The user may further limit the search result to titles only by entering 3.ti.. It will achieve the same result as set number 5 also given above.

B. Other Search Strategies

1. Author

There are basically four approaches in author searching: (1) search with hyphens, such as smith-john-m; (2) search with adj, such as smith adj john adj m; (3) search with initials only, such as smith-j-m or smith adj j adj m; or (4) search with first name or initials, such as smith adj (john or j). All new databases and reloaded databases in the BRS system will have authors searchable with hyphens. Author name can be searched either directly or indirectly. By the indirect method, the user uses ROOT first then selects the r number. Or, the user may prefer searching directly for a particular name. Examples are

Indirect method in ERIC file

```
    1_:     root li-t

        LI-T$
R1      LI-TING-KAI                        1 DOCUMENT
R2      LI-TZE-CHUNG                       2 DOCUMENTS
```

Direct method

```
1_:     li-tze-chung

RESULT          2
```

2. ..SET DETAIL = ON and ..SET DETAIL = OFF

The ..SET DETAIL = ON command is used to instruct the system to give the result postings for each individual term in the search statement, in addition to the result postings for the search statement as a whole. The display of postings for each term will continue in any subsequent search statement, until the ..SET DETAIL = ON command is cancelled by entering the ..SET DETAIL = OFF command. The ..SET DETAIL = ON command will be cancelled automatically with the change of databases, except in the case of saving search.

The ..SET DETAIL = ON command for truncated terms functions like the ROOT feature. There are, however, two main differences: (1) The Root feature gives only a listing of all entries that begin with a particular "root," but no final result postings. (2) If the ..SET DETAIL = ON command is in effect, the system continues to display a list of individual postings for each term in subsequent search statements, but this will not occur in ROOT. The ROOT instruction must be given each time when the word is to be ROOTed. Shown here are examples of using the commands in the ERIC file.

..SET DETAIL = ON command

    2_: ..set detail=on

R4661 * SET-COMMAND HAS BEEN EXECUTED. RETURN TO CONTINUE.

    2_: (boys or girls) and schooling

        BOYS   4507 DOCUMENTS
        GIRLS   4127 DOCUMENTS
        SCHOOLING   3280 DOCUMENTS

    RESULT   51

..SET DETAIL = OFF command

    3_: ..set detail=off

R4661 * SET-COMMAND HAS BEEN EXECUTED. RETURN TO CONTINUE.

3. ..LIMIT

The ..LIMIT or ..L command is used to refine the search results by the "formatted field." The so-called formatted field refers generally to accession number, date, language, and publication type. It varies with databases. Check the *AidPage* for formatted fields available in each database. In many databases, formatted fields are also directly searchable.

The ..LIMIT command must consist of four parameters:

1. The number of the result statement.
2. The paragraph label of the formatted field.
3. The limit operator. The following are frequently used operators:

Operators	Meaning
eq or =	equal to
ne	not equal to
lt or <	less than
gt or >	greater than

4. The criteria, that is, the actual data to appear in a particular formatted field.

The ..LIMIT command is followed by a slash with no space and then the number of the search statement, the paragraph label, the limit operator, and the criteria. The statement, "..LIMIT/1 lg eq en," is to limit the search to documents of the set number 1 of the result statement in the English language. The use of ..LIMIT in selected fields is shown as follows:

Limiting to language (lg): The standard abbreviation for language is a two-character code, such as "en" for English. For a listing of standardized language codes, see appendix six of the *BRS System Reference Manual.*

Limiting to Japanese in the INSP file

```
BRS - SEARCH MODE  - ENTER QUERY
   1_:     magnetic-resonance

   RESULT     308

   2_:     ..limit/1 lg eq ja

   RESULT     2
```

Excluding Japanese

```
BRS - SEARCH MODE  - ENTER QUERY
   3 :     ..limit/1 lg ne ja

   RESULT     306
```

Limiting to publication date (yr): To enter "..LIMIT/1 yr gt 80" is to limit search to documents published after 1980 in set number 1 of the result statement. Only the last two digits are used for the year.

..LIMIT by date

BRS - SEARCH MODE - ENTER QUERY
    4_: ..limit/1 yr gt 80

    RESULT   113

Limiting to update (up): The command is entered as, for example, "..LIMIT/1 up gt 82$." The system is instructed to retrieve all documents added after 1982. The date in update is a four-digit code; the first two represent year and the last two represent month. For a particular year without limitation to months, use the first two digits for year plus a $ sign.

..LIMIT by update in the ERIC file

BRS - SEARCH MODE - ENTER QUERY
    5_: ..limit/1 up gt 82$

    RESULT   46

In many databases, dates of publication, language codes, publication types, and so forth are directly searchable. Here is an example to search subject, library science, in the ERIC file, but limited to CIJE articles in the English language.

Direct search not using ..LIMIT

BRS - SEARCH MODE - ENTER QUERY
    1_: library-science and 82.yr. and ej.an. and en.lg.

    RESULT   42

..PRINT for the search result

    2_: ..p 1 an,ti,lg,yr,so/doc=1

    1
AN EJ286942.
TI A Bibliometric Analysis of the Literature of Cataloguing
   and Classification.
SO Library Research; v4 n4 p355-73 Win 1982. 82.
LG EN..
YR 82.
        END OF DOCUMENT

4. ..PURGE

The ..PURGE or ..PU command is used to delete the result statements. It is also used to cancel offline printing and SDI profiles. Options in the ..PURGE command vary. The command may be used to purge all result statements or to delete selected numbers of result statements in either consecutive or non-consecutive order. Unless specifically designated, to enter simply the ..PURGE command will result in deleting the immediate, previous search statement. Examples are

..PURGE command

    7_: ..purge

I4641   QUERIES HAVE BEEN PURGED

..PURGE 1, 3, 5 command in non-consecutive order

    6_: ..purge 1, 3, 5

I4641   QUERIES HAVE BEEN PURGED

..PURGE all command

    5_: ..purge all

I4641   QUERIES HAVE BEEN PURGED

5. The Saving Search

The saving search feature enables the user to repeat operations from one database to another with compatible vocabularies. There are two procedures: permanent and temporary.

These commands are used in the permanent saving search. The user gives the ..SAVE PS command with any four characters in parentheses after a search strategy has been completed. The system will respond with acknowledgment. The user may repeat the search strategy in another database by means of the ..EXEC or ..E command with the chosen four characters. The saving search is available for use permanently, until it is cancelled. To cancel the permanent saving search, use the ..PURGE PS (four character) command.

(b) ..SAVE (four characters) and ..EXEC (four characters)

For a temporary saving search, use the ..SAVE or ..SV and ..EXEC or ..E commands. The temporary saving search will last for re-use in the same day. It can also be cancelled by using the ..PURGE four character command. Two examples are used to show the saving search in the ERIC and NTIS files: (1) ..SET DETAIL = ON, if result postings for each term are required, and ..SAVE commands; (2) change of file to NTIS and ..EXEC command.

```
1_:      ..set detail=on

R4661 * SET-COMMAND HAS BEEN EXECUTED. RETURN TO CONTINUE.


1_:      (swimming or bicycling) and safety

        SWIMMING                        422 DOCUMENTS
        BICYCLING                        77 DOCUMENTS
        SAFETY                         5371 DOCUMENTS

   RESULT      106


  2_:     ..save safe

IA681 PROFILE HAS BEEN SAVED


  2_:     ..change/ntis
```

```
*CONNECT TIME  0:06:57 HH:MM:SS    0.116 DEC HRS    SESSION  27!

BRS/NTIS/1970 - JUN 1984

BRS - SEARCH MODE  - ENTER QUERY
   1_:    ..exec safe

BRS - SEARCH MODE

00001 (SWIMMING OR BICYCLING) AND SAFETY

          SWIMMING                               601 DOCUMENTS
          BICYCLING                               25 DOCUMENTS
          SAFETY                                38190 DOCUMENTS

     RESULT        48
E1326 NO MORE QUERIES - EXECUTION ENDED.
```

6. Stacking Commands

Several commands can be combined in a single statement by using a slash to separate each command. This method is called command stacking in BRS.

Command stacking example

```
   2_:    ..c/eric/swimming and safety/..1/1/yr gt 80/..p 2
          bibl/doc=1
*CONNECT TIME  0:02:08 HH:MM:SS    0.036 DEC HRS    SESSION   276*

BRS/ERIC/1966 - MAY 1984 (BOTH)

     RESULT        72

     1
AN ED235291.
AU Saul, Fran C.; Paris, Jalie.
TI Physical Education Curriculum Guide. Second and Third Grades
   1977-78.
IS RIEFEB84.
YR 78.
          END OF DOCUMENT
```

The example of command stacking instructs the system to change the file to ERIC, search the terms "swimming and safety," limit the search to documents published after 1980, and print the first document in the format of bibl.

7. ..DISPLAY

The ..DISPLAY or ..D command instructs the system to display previous search statements. All statements or a particular result statement can be displayed. Or display can be limited to selected numbers in either consecutive or non-consecutive order of result statements. Unless otherwise designated, to enter just ..DISPLAY will result in display of the immediate, previous statement. The display also features the database masthead indicating file name and date of coverage to identify the source of the search statements and results. The following examples illustrate display of search statements from section I-B-3.

```
7_:    ..display


BRS/ERIC/1966 - MAY 1984 (BOTH) :
   6 LIBRARY.DE. AND SCIENCE.DE.
   RESULT    1357


             ****   END OF DISPLAY   ****


BRS - SEARCH MODE  - ENTER QUERY
   7_:    ..display all


BRS/ERIC/1966 - MAY 1984 (BOTH) :
   1 LIBRARY SAME SCIENCE
   RESULT    2573

   2 LIBRARY WITH SCIENCE
   RESULT    2002

   3 LIBRARY ADJ SCIENCE
   RESULT    1447
```

```
4 LIBRARY ADJ (SCIENCE OR SYSTEM)
RESULT    1935

5 LIBRARY.TI. ADJ SCIENCE.TI.
RESULT      92

6 LIBRARY.DE. AND SCIENCE.DE.
RESULT    1357

        ****    END OF DISPLAY    ****
```

C. Multiple Database Subject Search

The user may use BRS/CROS database for cross-database search to identify databases that contain numbers of records on the term(s) searched. The database consists of nine areas, namely, life sciences, medicine/pharmacology, physical/applied sciences, business, social sciences, education, reference, all databases, and user option. Three steps are involved in using BRS/CROS: (1) The user selects the database, CROS. The system will display nine areas, each identified by a number, for the user to select. (2) The user selects the area of interest by entering the number of an area. If the user selects area 9, the system will respond with ENTER DATABASE LABELS SEPARATED BY A COMMA. The user then specifies a minimum of two files. (3) The user enters the term or terms to be searched. Here is an example:

Steps 1 and 2 (number 7 is selected)

```
BRS/CROS/

1 LIFE SCIENCES          2 MEDICINE/PHARMACOLOGY
3 PHYSICAL/APPLIED SCI.  4 BUSINESS
5 SOCIAL SCIENCES        6 EDUCATION
7 REFERENCE              8 ALL DATABASES
9 USER OPTION_:    7

BRS - SEARCH MODE  - ENTER QUERY
```

Step 3

```
1_:     ESPIONAGE

AAED      28
A400     122
BBIP      90
BOOK     140
CULP       1
FILE       0
6POM      14
IRSP       0
NWSC       0
PETE       0
SOFT       0
SUPE       0
TERM       2
ULRI       0
```

If area 9 is selected, the system will ask the user to specify labels of databases. An example is given:

```
1 LIFE SCIENCES          2 MEDICINE/PHARMACOLOGY
3 PHYSICAL/APPLIED SCI.  4 BUSINESS
5 SOCIAL SCIENCES        6 EDUCATION
7 REFERENCE              8 ALL DATABASES
9 USER OPTION_:     9

ENTER DATABASE LABELS SEPARATED BY A COMMA_:
                              book,info,mgmt,ptsi

BRS - SEARCH MODE  - ENTER QUERY
    1_:     espionage

    BOOK     140
    INFO      99
    MGMT      70
    PTSI     118
```

III. BRS/AFTER DARK

The user should keep abreast of the following two publications: *BRS After Dark User's Manual*, Latham, N.Y.: Bibliographic Retrieval Services, 1983, loose-leaf. Updated by supplementary pages. *After Dark Datalines*, v. 1-, 1983-, Latham, N.Y.: Bibliographical Retrieval Services.

The *Manual* presents sign-on and search procedures and a description of databases with sample searches and citations available from BRS/After Dark. *After Dark Datalines*, a bi-monthly newsletter, provides news and views. It is also available online.

BRS/After Dark is limited to twenty or so databases. Searching capability is limited, although it retains some features of BRS, such as free-text searching, truncation, and searching qualified by fields.

A. Sign-on Procedure

BRS/After Dark can be accessed via either TELENET or UNI = NET. The procedure of connecting with BRS/After Dark via TELE-NET is shown here. Also refer to the procedure mentioned in section I-A of this chapter.

The User Enters	The System Responds
(CR) (CR)	TELENET XXX XX TERMINAL =
(CR)	@
C31520b	315 20B CONNECTED
	ENTER BRS PASSWORD
Password (CR)	ENTER A-M-I-S Password
AMIS password (Security Code)	

The identifier varies. On most terminals, just a carriage return without the terminal identifier can be used.

TELENET sign-on example

```
TELENET
312 3I

TERHINAL=

@c 315 20b


315 20B CONNECTED

ENTER BRS PASSWORD
████████████
ENTER A-M-I-S PASSWORD
████████████s


*SIGN-ON   21.11.55                    05/30/84:


WELCOME TO BRS AFTER DARK
```

After sign-on, the system asks for screen line length and the number of lines on screen so that the user may adjust them to fit the user's terminal screen. If no adjustment is needed, the user simply presses the carriage return (CR) once.

B. Search Procedure

BRS/After Dark uses both menu and free-text searching. There are six basic commands:

S   to search
P   to print items found
R   to review searches, that is, to display a list of search statements and results in a database
M   to return to master menu
D   to return to database
O   to sign off

All databases are structured by menu. After sign-on, the system displays a master menu. The master menu is further divided by menus and sub-menus. The master menu consists of seven menus, such as "search service" and "software service." In "search service," for example, all databases are classified into five broad subject categories. The user may select a category to do searching. A menu sample searching is given below:

Master menu and number 1 of the 7 categories selected

```
TONIGHT'S MENU IS:

NUMBER        ITEM
   1          LOOKING FOR INFORMATION?...SEARCH SERVICE
   2          WANT TO HEAR THE LATEST?...NEWSLETTER SERVICE
   3          NEED A PROGRAM?...SOFTWARE SERVICE
   4          KEEP IN TOUCH!...ELECTRONIC MAIL SERVICE
   5          LET'S MAKE A DEAL!...SWAP SHOP
   6          WHAT'S NEW?...NEW SYSTEM FEATURES
   7          WANT TO CHANGE YOU SECURITY PASSWORD?...
              SECURITY

TYPE IN MENU ITEM NUMBER THEN HIT ENTER KEY FOR DESIRED
    SELECTION
```

Sub-menu and number 4 of the 5 categories selected

```
YOU ARE NOW CONNECTED TO THE BRS AFTER DARK SEARCH SERVICE.
THE FOLLOWING CATEGORIES OF DATABASES ARE AVAILABLE FOR
SEARCHING.
CATEGORY      DESCRIPTION

   1          SCIENCE AND MEDICINE DATABASES
   2          BUSINESS AND FINANCIAL DATABASES
   3          REFERENCE DATABASES
   4          EDUCATION DATABASES
   5          SOCIAL SCIENCE AND HUMANITIES DATABASES

TYPE IN CATEGORY NUMBER THEN HIT ENTER KEY FOR
CATEGORY OF DATABASES DESIRED.    4
```

Sub-menu and ERIC database selected

EDUCATION DATABASES
:*:*:*:*:*:*:*:*:*:*:*:*:*:*:

DATABASE NAME   LABEL

BILINGUAL EDUCATION BIBLIOGRAPHIC   BEBA
  ABSTRACTS
EDUCATION RESOURCE INFORMATION   ERIC
  CENTER (ERIC)
EXCEPTIONAL CHILD EDUCATION RESOURCES   ECER
NATIONAL COLLEGE DATABANK   PETE
ONTARIO EDUCATION RESOURCES INFORMATION   ONED
  SYSTEM
RESOURCES IN COMPUTER EDUCATION   RICE
SCHOOL PRACTICES INFORMATION FILE   SPIF
TEXAS EDUCATION COMPUTER COOPERATIVE   TECC

TYPE IN LABEL FOR DATABASE DESIRED: eric

WOULD YOU LIKE INSTRUCTIONAL PROMPTS? PLEASE TYPE
YES OR NO: no

WOULD YOU LIKE A DESCRIPTION OF THE DATABASE?
(YES OR NO)   no

TYPE IN SEARCH TERMS
S1 -->

To change category or database, the commands M or D must be
used to return to master menu or database menu; then select the
desired item. A simplified means is to enter the M command and
number of the categories. The user will have direct access to the
category without returning to the master menu. Likewise, to
enter D with a database label will lead the user directly to the
database without returning to the database menu. An example is

D command with database label for direct access

```
ENTER COMMAND    deric

WOULD YOU LIKE A DESCRIPTION OF THE DATABASE?
(YES OR NO)    no

TYPE IN SEARCH TERMS
S1 -->    swimming

A1       422  DOCUMENTS FOUND
ENTER COMMAND
```

Also shown in the example, the user is able to use free-text searching. Some BRS searching features are available, such as logical and positional operators, combination of search statement numbers, combination of search statement numbers with terms, truncation, and search limited by fields. But features obviously lacking in BRS/After Dark include ROOT, saving search, and such commands as ..COST, ..SET DETAIL=ON, ..PURGE, and ..LIMIT. It must be noted that the user must enter S each time the system displays ENTER COMMAND to return to the search mode. Search examples are now continued from the previous one:

Free-text searching of term

```
ENTER COMMAND    s

TYPE IN SEARCH TERMS
S2 -->    safety

A2       5371  DOCUMENTS FOUND
```

Search statements 1 (swimming) and 2 (safety)

```
ENTER COMMAND    s

TYPE IN SEARCH TERMS
S3 -->    1 and 2

A3       72  DOCUMENTS FOUND
```

Search statement 3 and a term

ENTER COMMAND   s

TYPE IN SEARCH TERMS
S4 --:>   3 and children

A4   18 DOCUMENTS FOUND

Search limited by title field

ENTER COMMAND   s

TYPE IN SEARCH TERMS
S5 --:>   swimming.ti. and **safety.ti.**

A5   2 DOCUMENTS FOUND

Search term truncated

ENTER COMMAND   s

TYPE IN SEARCH TERMS
S6 --:>   swim$ and safety

A6   73 DOCUMENTS FOUND

R command for reviewing search statements

ENTER COMMAND   r

BRS/ERIC/1966 - MAY 1984 (BOTH)
1 (SWIMMING)
    RESULT   422
2 (SAFETY)
    RESULT   5371

```
3  (1 AND 2)
     RESULT        72
4  (3 AND CHILDREN)
     RESULT        18
5  (SWIMMING.TI. AND SAFETY.TI.)
     RESULT         2
6  (SWIM$ AND SAFETY)
     RESULT        73
```

The use of positional operators: adj and with

```
ENTER COMMAND    s

TYPE IN SEARCH TERMS
S1 -->    pursuit adj happiness


A1      22  DOCUMENTS FOUND
ENTER COMMAND    s

TYPE IN SEARCH TERMS
S2 -->    pursuit with happiness


A2      24  DOCUMENTS FOUND
```

C. Result Procedure

The command P is used to instruct the system to print online the search result. There are three forms of online printing: enter S for short print form, M for medium print form, and L for complete citation. Or, the user may simply hit the carriage return for complete citation. The short print form displays, in general, author, title, and source. The medium print form displays descriptors, in addition to the items in short form. The system also requests the user to specify the number of items, in either consecutive or non-consecutive order, to be printed. In the example, the user uses command P, selects the result of search number 1, that is, "pursuit of happiness," hits the carriage return for the entire citation, and selects the first item to be printed.

ENTER COMMAND   p

ENTER SEARCH QUESTION NUMBER.   1

ENTER S, M, OR RETURN

ENTER DOCUMENT NUMBER OR RANGE.   1

1
AN ED237450.
IN American Alliance for Health, Physical Education, Recreation and
   Dance, Reston, VA. National Association for Girls and Women in Sport.
   BBB20618.
TI Competitive Swimming and Diving. Official Rules, Officiating. August
   1983-August 1984. NAGWS Guide.
LG EN..
IS RIEAPR84.
NO RN: ISBN-0-88314-258-9.
PR EDRS Price - MF01 Plus Postage. PC Not Available from EDRS.
AV AAHPERD Promotion Unit, 1900 Association Drive, Reston, VA 22091
   ($3.95).
NT 99p.
YR 83.
DE Competition. Swimming. Womens-Athletics.
   Judges. Recordkeeping.
ID IDENTIFIERS: Diving. PF Project. Rules and Regulations.   TARGET
   AUDIENCE: Teachers. Community.

AB Arranged in three sections, this pamphlet details the rules,
officiating techniques, and official records for girls' and womens'
competitive swimming and diving. Section 1 lists members of the
national rules committee, major rule changes for 1983-84, and
official rules for swimming and diving competition. Section 2
contains officiating tips, swimming and diving study questions (with
an answer key for officials), and rule references. The final section
lists championship results for the 1982-83 season and current
records, and includes an application form for recording new records.
(LP).

END OF DOCUMENT. HIT ENTER TO SEE NEXT DOCUMENT, OR
TYPE ANOTHER DOCUMENT NUMBER, OR
ENTER COMMAND

D. Sign-off Procedure

To signoff, enter command O. An example is

```
ENTER COMMAND    O

TYPE S TO CONTINUE SEARCHING, P TO PRINT DOCUMENTS FOUND,
R TO REVIEW SEARCH QUESTIONS, M TO RETURN TO MASTER
MENU, D TO RETURN TO DATABASE MENU, OR O TO SIGN OFF.
```

12

CompuServe, The Source, and Dow Jones Searching

CompuServe, The Source and Dow Jones use basically the menu or code search. All databases in the systems, except one in Dow Jones, are structured in menus. The user must follow the displayed menu instructions and search information step by step. It is very easy to use. There is, however, one drawback—the user must select pre-formatted options one at a time; therefore, the method lacks the flexibility of free-text searching in which any term contained in the text can be searched.

COMPUSERVE

The user who purchases a kit is entitled to five hours' free use of CompuServe during standard service hours and then may decide whether to subscribe as a permanent customer. The kit, a loose-leaf binder publication entitled *CompuServe Information Service Starter Kit*, consists of questions and answers about the service, access numbers, logon procedures, password, rates, data dictionary, user's guide, and supplements. A CompuServe subscriber also receives update sheets about the service and a monthly newsletter, *CompuServe Update*. Two sheets are particularly important: (1) subject index, a listing of over 700 subjects with direct command to provide quick access to a particular database; and (2) access numbers, giving local access telephone numbers of networks for each location, including CompuServe's own numbers.

Radio Shack has been marketing its Videotex Plus communication software for its TRS-80 Models I and III. The owner of Videotex Plus is entitled to one hour of free use of both CompuServe and Dow Jones and a loose-leaf binder, which consists of (1) *Videotex Plus User's Guide*, (2) *CompuServe Information Service User's Guide*, and (3) *Dow Jones Information Service User's Guide*.

Logon Procedure

The user dials a local CompuServe telephone number, or a TYMNET or TELENET number if the local CompuServe number is not available, to obtain a high-pitched tone and then inserts the telephone handset into the acoustic coupler of the terminal. The CompuServe logon procedure is used as an illustration.

The User Enters	The System Responds
Control C	$^\wedge$C
	User ID:
User ID (CR)	Password:
Password (CR)	COMPUSERVE INFORMATION SERVICE
	XXXX XX XXXXXXXX XX-XXX-XX

The user may press carriage return once instead of using Control C. The system will respond with "HOST NAME:." The user then enters CIS for CompuServe Information Service, presses a carriage return, and follows the same procedure as shown earlier after "USER ID:" is displayed.

CompuServe logon example

U8C6Q
Host Name: CIS

User ID: 70156,507
Password:

COMPUSERVE INFORMATION SERVICE

11:07 CST   SATURDAY   26-NOV-83

Search and Result Procedure

CompuServe uses menu or code search. The menu is structured by top menu, menu for the top menu, sub-menu, and item numbers. There are ten basic commands:

T	top menu page, returns to the main menu
M	previous menu, returns to previous menu
F	moves forward one page within the current series of pages
B	moves back one page within the current series of pages
H	help, displays information about the area being used
R	re-sends a page
S	scroll, displays pages
S n	scroll from item number
G n	go directly to page number
N	displays next menu item

In menu search, more than one menu has to be used to locate a particular item of information. The top menu consists of six categories, namely, Home Services, Business and Financial, Personal Computing, Services for Professionals, User Information, and Index.

All other menus are structured under the six categories. The user enters commands when the system displays a prompt sign !. The ! display indicates that the system is ready to accept commands. There are navigational prompts that suggest the next step for the user. They are all self-explanatory. Examples are

LAST MENU PAGE. KEY DIGIT OR M FOR PREVIOUS MENU.

ENTER YOUR SELECTION NUMBER OR H FOR MORE INFOR-
MATION.

After sign-on, the system displays the top menu. The user then
follows displayed instructions to do further searching. Searching
examples are

Top menu

```
COMPUSERVE              PAGE CIS-1

COMPUSERVE INFORMATION SERVICE

1 HOME SERVICES
2 BUSINESS & FINANCIAL
3 PERSONAL COMPUTING
4 SERVICES FOR PROFESSIONALS

5 USER INFORMATION
6 INDEX

ENTER YOUR SELECTION NUMBER,
OR H FOR MORE INFORMATION.
```
Top menu 1
  selected

```
COMPUSERVE              PAGE HOM-1

HOME SERVICES

  1 NEWS/WEATHER/SPORTS
  2 REFERENCE LIBRARY
  3 COMMUNICATIONS
  4 HOME SHOPPING/BANKING
  5 DISCUSSION FORUMS
  6 GAMES
  7 EDUCATION
  8 HOME MANAGEMENT
  9 TRAVEL
 10 ENTERTAINMENT

LAST MENU PAGE. KEY DIGIT
OR M FOR PREVIOUS MENU.
```

Previous menu 2
  selected
12

```
COMPUSERVE            PAGE HOM-20

     REFERENCE LIBRARY

$ 1 ACADEMIC AMER. ENCYCLOPEDIA
  2 INFORMATION ON DEMAND
  3 U.S. GOVERNMENT PUBLICATIONS
  4 BIBLIOGRAPHIC SERVICES
  5 FAMILY        6 FASHION
  7 GARDENING     8 GOLF
  9 DEVELOPMENT  10 SCIENCE
 11 SATIRE       12 SEXUALITY
 13 WINE

LAST MENU PAGE. KEY DIGIT
OR M FOR PREVIOUS MENU.
```

Previous menu 4
  selected
14

```
5TH AVENUE SHOPPER    PAGE FTH-53

  ---------------------------------
          THE BOOK LOOP
  ---------------------------------
  1 ABOUT THE BOOK LOOP
  2 USING THE BOOK LOOP
  3 BOOK SELECTIONS
  4 BOOK REQUESTS
  5 BIBLIOGRAPHIC SERVICES
  6 HOW TO ORDER
  7 PLACE AN ORDER

LAST MENU PAGE. KEY DIGIT
OR M FOR PREVIOUS MENU.
```

T for top menu

1T

```
COMPUSERVE               PAGE CIS-1
COMPUSERVE INFORMATION SERVICE
```

```
1 HOME SERVICES
2 BUSINESS & FINANCIAL
3 PERSONAL COMPUTING
4 SERVICES FOR PROFESSIONALS

5 USER INFORMATION
6 INDEX

ENTER YOUR SELECTION NUMBER,
OR H FOR MORE INFORMATION.
```

The user may also use commands to have direct access to a particular database and page number without returning to the step-by-step menu search. The subject index mentioned earlier provides a listing of quick access codes for each subject for direct approach. The user may change from direct approach to menu search or vice versa. An example of using direct command follows:

GO TCB-13 command – directly to Continuing Education File

```
!GO TCB-13


REQUEST RECORDED,
ONE MOMENT, PLEASE

THANK YOU FOR WAITING


COMPUSERVE            PAGE TCB-13

        ADULT EDUCATION

1. GOING BACK TO SCHOOL
2. LEARNING OPPORTUNITIES
3. YOU'RE NOT TOO OLD TO LEARN

LAST MENU PAGE. KEY DIGIT
OR M FOR PREVIOUS MENU.
```

Item 3 selected

!3

COMPUSERVE   PAGE TCB-30

 YOU'RE NOT TOO OLD TO LEARN
==================================

A DISCUSSION OF THE 10 MOST
FREQUENTLY EXPRESSED FEARS OF
ADULTS CONSIDERING A RETURN
TO EDUCATION.

KEY S OR <ENTER> TO CONTINUE

Logoff Procedure

The command OFF is used to disconnect the system.

OFF command example

!OFF

OFF AT 11:26 CST   26-NOV-83
CONNECT TIME =   0:20

HOST NAME:

THE SOURCE

Two publications are basic references for using The Source: *The Source User's Manual*, McLean, Va.: Source Telecomputing Corp., 1983, 277p. *The Source Command Guide*, McLean, Va.: Source Telecomputing Corp., 1983, 25 p.

The *Manual* is a guide to The Source services and programs. It describes logon and logoff procedures and services and programs, with step-by-step illustrations for using the system. The Guide lists over 500 commands under 8 broad headings and many sub-headings. The commands are used to connect directly to many databases. The Source also publishes the *Sourceworld,* a monthly newsletter providing current information on The Source services.

Logon Procedure

The Source can be accessed either directly or via communication networks, such as TELENET, TYMNET, and UNINET. The following is an example of using TELENET to connect The Source:

The User Enters	The System Responds
(CR) (CR)	TELENET
	XXX XX
	TERMINAL=
(CR)	@
C 30138 (CR)	301 38 CONNECTED
	CONNECTED TO THE SOURCE
ID (CR)	PASSWORD?
Password (CR)	XXXXXX (user XX) logged in . .

The terminal identifier varies. On most terminals, a carriage return without the terminal identifier can be used. 30138 is a code number corresponding to the user's system in TELENET to connect with The Source. There are currently six systems. See *The Source User's Manual* for corresponding codes.

TELENET logon example

```
TELENET
312 3B

TERMINAL=

@c 30138


301 38 CONNECTED
Connected to THE SOURCE
> id ti4969
Connected to THE SOURCE
> Password?
TI4969 (user 22) logged in Wednesday, 30 May 84 21:50:56.
Welcome, you are connected to THE SOURCE.
Last login Thursday, 19 Apr 84 21:48:36.
```

(C) COPYRIGHT SOURCE TELECOMPUTING CORPORATION 1984.

Search and Result Procedure

The Source is structured in a menu format. Its main menu consists of eight categories, namely, News and Reference Resources, Business/Financial Markets, Catalogue Shopping, Home and Leisure, Education and Career, Mail and Communications, Creating and Computing, and Source*Plus.

Each category is further divided into sub-menus. For instance, the main menu, News and Reference Resources, has five sub-menus: News and Sports, Travel and Dining, Government and Politics, Consumer Information, and Bylines News Features. Again, the sub-menu Government and Politics, contains four more menus: President's Schedule (Daily), Senate Committee, House Committee, and Political Commentary.

Commands basic to searching are

HELP   to request instructions, entered at either command
                        level or "-more-" or "-end-" prompts, HELP plus

	a program name to explain the program's operation
MENU or M	to access the first page of The Source main menu
PLAY	preceding the name of a game to activate the game
P	to return to the next previous menu
QUIT	at most prompts to return to command level

The method of control with other keys, that is, depressing the control key and typing another character key, is used to perform certain functions. In searching, the following three methods are particularly important:

CONTROL S	to stop the display
CONTROL Q	to continue the display
CONTROL P	to interrupt the program to return to the primary prompt or to command level

Commands are entered when the system displays a prompt sign→or ?>. The display of a prompt indicates that the system is ready to accept commands. Two other prompts may be mentioned:

| —more = | to press carriage return (CR) to continue the display or to enter acceptable command depending on databases |
| —end = | to press carriage return (CR) to return to primary menu or command level |

There are also navigational prompts used to give suggestions to the next steps; all are self-explanatory, such as

ENTER THE NUMBER OF HELP
ENTER OPTION DESIRED OR QUIT

All databases in The Source can be accessed by using either MENU command or direct command to a particular database and its contents. The *Guide* is a handy reference for direct commands. To access The Source menu, enter the MENU command. To leave the menu, enter QUIT at any menu prompt. It must be noted that the direct command is used to expedite access to a particular database and its contents. Once the database is accessed, however, its operation will be the same in spite of the method of access, menu or direct. Examples of using two methods are given here.

Menu search

```
                              WELCOME TO THE SOURCE


                              1. OVERVIEW OF THE SOURCE
                              2. INSTRUCTIONS
                              3. THE SOURCE MENU
                              4. COMMAND LEVEL
                              5. TODAY
                              6. TEXNET


                              Enter item number or HELP   3
```

Select 3 for
  The Source
  Main Menu

```
                              THE SOURCE MAIN MENU

                              1   NEWS AND REFERENCE RESOURCES
                              2   BUSINESS/FINANCIAL MARKETS
                              3   CATALOGUE SHOPPING
                              4   HOME AND LEISURE
                              5   EDUCATION AND CAREER
                              6   MAIL AND COMMUNICATIONS
                              7   PERSONAL COMPUTING
                              8   SOURCE*PLUS

                              Enter item number or HELP  1
```

Select 1 for
  News and Reference
  Resources

```
NEWS & REFERENCE RESOURCES

I   NEWS AND SPORTS
2   GOVERNMENT AND POLITICS
3   BYLINES  NEWS FEATURES

Enter item number or HELP 2
```

Select 2 for
  Government
  and Politics

```
GOVERNMENT AND POLITICS

1   PRESIDENT'S SCHEDULE (DAILY)
2   SENATE COMMITTEE
3   HOUSE COMMITTEE
4   POLITICAL COMMENTARY

Enter item number or HELP
```

Direct search

Direct access to
  Domestic Air
  Schedules

```
      -> airsched-d
```

```
Domestic Air Schedules (USA, CAN, MEX,)

-C- Copyright 1982 Dittler Brothers Inc.,  Atlanta, Ga.
All Flight Information cannot be reproduced in whole or
in part without written permission of Dittler Bros. Inc.

Enter Departure City / Destination City in the format
CITY, STate / CITY, STate  TIME(s)   (Times Optional)
EXAMPLE:   Chicago, Il / New york, Ny    0900A-0200P .
```

Entering Chicago
to D.C.

chicago,il/washington,dc

FROM: CHICAGO, IL
TO: WASHINGTON, DC

DEPART	APT	ARRIVE	APT	FLIGHT	CLASS	DAYS	MEALS	PLANE	STOPS
06:45A	0	09:23A	N	UA 0800	FYBQM	1234567	B B	72S	0
		EFFECTIVE 06/01/84							
07:00A	0	09:38A	N	UA 0800	FYBQM	1234567	B B	72S	0
				DISCONTINUE 05/31/84					
07:10A	0	09:48A	N	AA 0246	FYMBQ	1234567	B B	727	0
				DISCONTINUE 05/31/84					
07:10A	0	09:48A	D	UA 0840	FYBQM	1234567	B B	73S	0
		EFFECTIVE 06/01/84							
07:10A	0	09:51A	N	AA 0246	FYMBQ	1234567	B B	727	0
		EFFECTIVE 06/01/84							
07:15A	0	09:53A	D	UA 0840	FYBQM	1234567	B B	73S	0
				DISCONTINUE 05/26/84					
07:15A	0	09:53A	D	UA 0840	FYBQM	1234567	B B	73S	0
		EFFECTIVE 05/28/84							
07:44A	0	10:22A	N	UA 0802	FYBQM	1234567	B B	72S	0
		EFFECTIVE 06/01/84							
07:45A	0	10:23A	N	UA 0802	FYBQM	1234567	B B	72S	0
				DISCONTINUE 05/31/84					
08:10A	0	12:45P	N	RC 0546	CY	123456	S S	D9S	2
		EFFECTIVE 06/01/84							

---MORE----

Logoff Procedure

To log off, the user enters OFF and presses the carriage return.

OFF example

```
-> off
TI4969 (user 15) logged out Wednesday, 30 May 84 22:08:40.
Time used: 00h 07m connect.

Wait...
Bye


Disconnected from SYS13

301 38 DISCONNECTED 00 00

@
```

DOW JONES NEWS/RETRIEVAL

These publications should be consulted for Dow Jones service: *The Dow Jones News/Retrieval Fact Finder,* Princeton, N.J.: Dow Jones News/Retrieval, *Dow Jones Text-Search Services User's Guide,* 1982, 198p. *The Dow Jones News/Retrieval Fact Finder: Supplement* Princeton, N.J.: Dow Jones News/Retrieval [n.d], 23p. Princeton, N.J.: Dow Jones News/Retrieval, [1984], 18p.

The *Fact Finder* is an introduction to the use of communication networks and menu or code search and is a directory of symbols, which represent stocks, options, mutual funds, corporate bonds, companies, news categories, and industry groups. The *Supplement* adds new databases with revised symbols for new categories and shows changes in communication networks. The *Guide* is a concise aid to basic free-text searching. The user may also find useful *Dowline: The Magazine of Dow Jones News/Retrieval,* a quarterly journal containing Dow Jones news, news features, software, databases, customer's questions and answers, and News/Retrieval guide. Also noted earlier, *Dow*

Jones Information Service User's Guide, a part of the package deal of Videotex Plus marketed by Radio Shack, is a handy reference for menu searching.

Logon Procedure

The Dow Jones can be accessed through direct dial over standard telephone lines or communication networks, such as TELENET, TYMNET, and UNINET. The TELENET procedure is given as an example:

The User Enters	The System Responds
(CR) (CR)	TELENET
	XXX XX
	Terminal =
(CR)	@
C 60942 (CR)	609 42 CONNECTED
	WHAT SERVICE PLEASE????
(CR)	ENTER PASSWORD
Password (CR)	DOW JONES NEWS/RETRIEVAL . . .

The terminal identifier varies. On most terminals, just a carriage return without the terminal identifier can be used.

TELENET logon example

```
TELENET
312 3B

TERMINAL=

@c 60942

609 42 CONNECTED

WHAT SERVICE PLEASE????
```

ENTER PASSWORD
██ ██ ██ ██ ██ ██ ██ ██ ██
     DOW JONES NEWS/RETRIEVAL
        COPYRIGHT (C) 1984
     DOW JONES & COMPANY, INC.
       ALL RIGHTS RESERVED.

Search and Result Procedure

Dow Jones is using basically the menu search. Free-text searching is available only in its Dow Jones News database. In the menu search, codes, symbols, characters and/or numbers must be used to search subject, company, date, page, and so forth. In the Dow Jones News database, AT&T is represented by T and XON is used for EXXON. T and XON are two company codes. In the Current Quotes database, the symbols /, +, −, and # are used to represent corporate and foreign bonds, mutual funds, options, and U.S. Treasury issues, respectively. Also, numbers are used for the four exchanges, for example, 1 for New York, and 2 for American. In the Weekly Economic Survey database, three characters are used: A for commentary and analysis, B for median forecasts of monetary and economic indicators, and C for charts showing distribution of forecasts.

To begin a database, use two slashes // and the code for the database; for instance, enter //INTRO to begin the Introduction database for up-to-date information on Dow Jones databases and for customer's information. For a listing of databases available from Dow Jones, enter //MENU.

Menu Search

Here are some examples of using menu search:

Begin menu database; display of categories

//menu
        Master Menu
     Copyright (C) 1984
 Dow Jones & Company, Inc.

PRESS   FOR

```
A    Dow Jones Business And
        Economic News Services
B    Dow Jones Quotes
C    Dow Jones Text-Search
        Services
D    Financial And Investment
        Services
E    General News And
        Information Services
F    Mail Service and
        Free Customer Newsletter
```

Category A selected

```
a
        Dow Jones Business
    And Economic News Services

 For help, type code and HELP.
    (Example: //DJNEWS HELP)

    TYPE      FOR

//DJNEWS   90-Day News From The
           Broadtape, Selections
           From Barron's And The
           Wall Street Journal

    -PRESS RETURN FOR MORE-
```

Begin Historical Quotes database

```
    //hq
HISTORICAL QUOTES  BEING ACCESSED
```

Enter 1T P1 (1, New York Exchange; T, company code for AT&T; P1, the twelve most recent trading days)

ENTER QUERY
    1t p1

DOW JONES HISTORICAL
STOCK QUOTE REPORTER SERVICE

STOCK 1T

DATE	HIGH	LOW	CLOSE	VOL(100/S)
05/11/84	15 7/8	15 5/8	15 3/4	9662
05/14/84	15 7/8	15 5/8	15 5/8	8230
05/15/84	15 7/8	15 5/8	15 3/4	7826
05/16/84	16	15 3/4	15 3/4	8812
05/17/84	15 7/8	15 5/8	15 3/4	6061
05/18/84	15 7/8	15 5/8	15 7/8	6810
05/21/84	16	15 3/4	15 3/4	7248
05/22/84	15 7/8	15 5/8	15 5/8	6452
05/23/84	15 7/8	15 5/8	15 5/8	7228
05/24/84	15 3/4	15 1/2	15 1/2	9861
05/25/84	15 3/4	15 1/2	15 1/2	8758
05/29/84	15 5/8	15 3/8	15 1/2	5777

Reproduced with permission by Dow Jones News/Retrieval®

Free-Text Search

The user may also use free-text searching in the Dow Jones News database. Dow Jones and BRS have similar capability, and, in essence, the protocol and commands of Dow Jones are based on the software of BRS. From 1981 to 1983, Dow Jones offered its News Retrieval Service through BRS. Since March 1, 1983, Dow Jones has marketed its service solely on its own system. But the search features remain basically the same as BRS. Like BRS databases, a unit record is divided into different fields. The Dow Jones unit record consists of eight fields as follows:

AN   accession number

HL   story headline

DD   display date or date article appeared

SD   source
CO   company code

IN   industry category and code

CV   government category and code

TX   story text

To begin free-text searching, the user enters &FTS. The system will display two files for choosing: The *Wall Street Journal* and Dow Jones News. The example here is to select Dow Jones News for free text searching.

&FTS and free-text searching

```
    &fts

        DOW JONES TEXT-SEARCH SERVICES
             COPYRIGHT (C) 1984
        DOW JONES & COMPANY, INC.

PRESS     FOR

   1      THE WALL STREET JOURNAL:
             FULL-TEXT VERSION
             FROM JANUARY 1984
          * * A NEW SERVICE * *

   2      DOW JONES NEWS:
             BROADTAPE, AND SELECTED
             STORIES FROM BARRON'S AND
             THE WALL STREET JOURNAL
             FROM JUNE 1979
      2
DJ/NRS  - SEARCH MODE - ENTER QUERY
    1_:       korean adj airliner and Soviet adj union
RESULT        12 DOCUMENTS
```

..PRINT for headlines of document

```
2 :      ..print hl/doc=5

          DOCUMENT=        5 OF     12    PAGE =     1 OF

     CANADA SEEKS COMPENSATION FOR KOREAN AIR CRASH VICTIMS  1

        END OF DOCUMENT
```

Reproduced with permission by Dow Jones News/Retrieval®

..PRINT complete record of sixth document

```
..print all/doc=6

          DOCUMENT=        6 OF     12    PAGE =     1 OF       4
AN  110909-0268.
HL  SHULTZ DENOUNCES SOVIET STANCE ON KOREAN JET ATTACK
DD  09/08/83
SO  WALL STREET JOURNAL AND DOW JONES NEWS WIRE (W)
CO  FREST
IN  AIRLINES (AIR)
GV  EXECUTIVE (EXE)
TX      MADRID -AP- DECLARING 'THIS IS NOT THE END OF THE MATTER
     SECRETARY OF STATE GEORGE SHULTZ SAID HE RECEIVED ANOTHER
                          - MORE -
```

Reproduced with permission by Dow Jones News/Retrieval®

Logoff Procedure

To disconnect, enter DISC followed by a carriage return. The system will display the logon, logoff, time, date, and disconnect message. To logoff from the free-text searching mode, the user must first enter &OFF to disconnect the free-text search database, then enter the DISC command to disconnect the system. An example is

&off

TEXT-SEARCH SIGNOFF COMPLETE

disc
LOG ON: 12 19 LOG OFF: 12 22 EASTERN TIME MAY 31, 1984
609 42 DISCONNECTED 00 00

@

Reproduced with permission by Dow Jones News/Retrieval®

13

Microcomputer Searching and Downloading

Many microcomputers can be used to connect with online searching systems. They can also be used to store information retrieved from the system and have the information later printed in an original or edited format. Because of the sharp reduction of microcomputer cost, more use of microcomputers is anticipated. It is estimated that 50 to 80 million people will purchase home computers this decade.[1] CompuServe, The Source, Dow Jones, Knowledge Index, and BRS/After Dark all aim primarily to serve the market of microcomputer users. Both CompuServe and Dow Jones, for example, provide their services through Radio Shack's software, Videotex Plus, for TRS-80 Models I and III.

Microcomputers provide a variety of functions; they are not just a substitute for terminals. They can be used for database management, accounting, statistics, programming, and word processing; and in online searching, the microcomputer's capability for downloading, that is, capturing the information and storing it on a disk, is highly useful.[2] Pemberton compared the cost of terminals and microcomputers in 1981—from $4,000 for a high-speed terminal and a printer to $8,200 for a 64K microcomputer with a letter-grade printer, auxiliaries, and software—and concluded that microcomputers should be seriously considered as an alternative to plain terminals because of their enormous capabilities, even though the cost is higher than that of a terminal.[3] The reduced cost of microcomputers in recent years is a more persuasive reason to purchase a microcomputer than a single-purpose terminal.

Using microcomputers for online searching requires a telephone, a modem, a communication interface, all mentioned in chapter six, and, in addition, communication software. The communication software allows the microcomputer to operate as a terminal.The software must have the ASCII code (American Standard Code for Information Interchange) and be compatible in transmission speed and able to set the telecommunication protocols used by the host systems.[4] It is highly desirable that the software have the interrupt or break function. For downloading, the software should have the capability of storing, deleting, and editing the data and having it printed in a hard copy.

To ensure proper access to the host system, the equipment must have the following settings:[5]

transmission	asynchronous mode
telecommunications protocols	1 start bit, 7 data bits, 1 parity bit, 1 stop bit for a total of 10 bits
baud (transmission rate)	300 or 1200 baud
parity	none
XON/XOFF	on

Some microcomputers cannot display up to 80 characters in line width on the screen, thus wrapping lines around. In DIALOG and SDC, the number of characters can be specified to fit the line size. DIALOG can also adjust the number of lines. In DIALOG, the SET H command plus the number of characters and the SET V command plus the number of lines are used to adjust, respectively, line size and the number of lines. SDC has the capability of adjusting only the line size. The term LS command plus the number of characters is used for specifying the number of line characters. The adjustment of line size and the number of lines is also available in BRS/After Dark mentioned in chapter one.

The following is an example of adjusting the size in DIALOG:

SET H command

? set h 40
Horizontal line length changed from 75 to 40
Vertical line count remains 24

Display in line size of 40

? t 1/5/2
1/5/2
ED181889   IR007957
    A   Selective   Bibliography   on   Asian
Americans.
    Li. Tze-chung
    1979   18p.;   Prepared for   the   Asian
American   Ethnic   Resources   Institute
(River Forest, IL, October 19-20, 1979)
    EDRS Price - MF01/PC01 Plus Postage.
    Language: English
    Document Type: BIBLIOGRAPHY (131)
    Geographic Source: U.S.; Illinois
    Journal Announcement: RIEJUN80
    This bibliography is divided into five
parts: (1) reference sources, including
bibliographies,   guides,   directories,
biographies,   statistical   sources,
handbooks,   and   chronologies;   (2)
monographs   concerned   with   Asian
Americans, Chinese Americans, Japanese
Americans, and Korean Americans;   (3)
documents; (4) doctoral dissertations on
Asian Americans, Chinese Americans, and
Japanese Americans; and (5) periodicals.
(JD)
    Descriptors: *Asian   Americans;
Bibliographies;   *Books;   *Doctoral
Dissertations; *Government Publications;
*Periodicals; *Reference Materials

For searching and downloading with microcomputers, some users have developed their own software. It was reported that the University of Strathelyde used its own software capable of downloading from the host computer and storing on floppy disk for later processing and printing.[6] There is, however, a variety of commercially available software at an affordable price. Zeck presented seven pieces of communication software from very basic to sophisticated, such as CROSSTALK and MICROTERM.[7] *Online Micro-Software Guide and Directory, 1983-84,*[8] though far from complete, is a recent guide to software. It consists of feature articles, charts for comparison of selected software, bibliography, glossary, and indexes. Over forty software items, each for communication and word or text processing, are given.

Apple IIe microcomputer with a micromodem II, produced by Hayes Microcomputer Products, Inc., and the communication software, Hayes Terminal program, is capable of connecting over telephone lines with the host system for searching and downloading. Stored data can be later processed and printed in a chosen format by using Apple II Writer word processing software. A less expensive communication software for Apple IIe is the NETWORKER direct-connect modem and the communication software, NETMASTER. Radio Shack's Videotex Plus, communication software for microcomputer users, is much easier to use than Radio Shack's other version, Communications Package.[9]

The Institute for Scientific Information has developed the Sci-Mate software. It consists of Sci-Mate Universal Online Searcher and Sci-Mate Personal Data Manager. Sci-Mate Universal Online Searcher enables the user to search DIALOG, BRS, MEDLINE, SDC, or ISI in one language. The search can be conducted with ISI's menu-driven language. The user may also use the original language of the system. The software is capable of downloading. Sci-Mate Personal Data Manager is capable of creating one's own text file and storing, editing, deleting, and formatting the text downloaded in Sci-Mate Universal Online Searcher. The list price for the two software items is over $800.

The procedure of microcomputer searching and downloading is a simple one. As an illustration, a TRS-80 Model III two-drive microcomputer with Telephone Interface II modem, Videotex

Plus and SuperScripsit software is used for searching and downloading.

I. VIDEOTEX PLUS FOR SEARCHING[10]

Connection with a host system by using Videotex Plus, communication software, involves the following steps:

1. Turn on the printer power first, if the printer is used, then the microcomputer and modem power.
2. Insert the Videotex Plus diskette into drive 0 and press the orange reset button.
3. When the computer displays ENTER DATE (MM/DD/YY)? type two digits each for the month, day, and year. Press ENTER.
4. The computer will respond with ENTER TIME (HH:MM:SS)?, either type two digits each for the hour, minute, and second and press ENTER or simply press ENTER.
5. When the prompt, TRSDOC READY, appears, type VIDTEX and press ENTER.
6. The computer displays **DATA CARRIER LOST!**. The user dials a telephone number and places the telephone handset into the acoustic coupler to connect with the host system. Once connected, the computer displays **DATA CARRIER RESTORED**. The user then begins a particular host system's logon procedure.

II. VIDEOTEX PLUS FOR DOWNLOADING

To download retrieved information requires two steps. First, the RAM Buffer is used to store information captured. The user types — O and presses ENTER. The computer will respond with BUFFER OPENED. From this point on, the information appearing on the screen will be saved in the memory until the RAM Buffer is closed. To close the RAM Buffer, type — C and press ENTER.

Second, to save the information stored in the RAM Buffer to TRSDOC compatible ASCII format, the command —S is used to save the information in the RAM Buffer onto the diskette in unedited ASCII format. The computer responds with ENTER THE FILE NAME. The user must give a file name and press

ENTER. The information will be saved in the assigned file name. As an example, the name SAVE is assigned as the file name. The use of —X command is to exit VIDTEX to TRSDOC and quit. Remove the Videotex Plus diskette from drive 0.

The information now saved in the SAVE file (the name just assigned) can be edited and printed in a chosen format by using SuperScripsit, word processing software. To do this requires conversion from ASCII format to word processing format.

III.   SUPERSCRIPT FOR RE-FORMATTING AND PRINTING[11]

A few comments should be made about the use of SuperScripsit. There are three basic steps in using the word processing software. First, the user must open a document and assign it a unique file name. Second, the user sets the format, such as margin and tabs. Third, the user inputs the information and may edit, delete, or revise it and have the edited version printed. A step-by-step procedure using SuperScripsit is given:

1. Insert the SuperScripsit diskette in drive O and press RESET.
2. The computer will ask the user to type in MM/DD/YY and HH:MM:SS format, one at a time. To enter the time is optional. Press ENTER.
3. When the computer displays TRSDOC READY, type SCRIPSIT and press ENTER. The computer will respond with the following selection menu. Now the user is in the word processing mode.

```
* * * * * * * * * SCRIPSIT WORD PROCESSING  * * * * * * * *
                  <O>   Open a document
                  <D>   Display disk directory
                  <S>   System setup utility
                  <P>   Proofread a document
                  <C>   Compress a document
                  <A>   ASCII text conversion utility
                  <E>   Exit to TRSDOS

                  What is your selection?
```

Reproduced with permission by Radio Shack

4. Type O to open a document and to assign the document a file name. The procedure is necessary for identifying, tracing, editing, and retrieving the document. The computer will display SCRIPSIT— open document options, as shown:

```
* * * * * * SCRIPSIT – OPEN DOCUMENT OPTIONS * * * * * * *
               Document name:    - - - - - - - - - - - - - - - - - - - - - - -
                      Author:    - - - - - - - - - - - - - - - - - - - - - - - - - - - -
                    Operator:    - - - - - - - - - - - - - - - - - - - - - - - - - - - -
                    Comments:    - - - - - - - - - - - - - - - - - - - - - - - - - - - -
                Printer type:    DW2- - - - -
               Lines per page:   54        (4-99)
                       Pitch:    P-        (1-20 or P)
   Line spacing (to 3 + , " + " = 1/2):   1-
         1st page to include header:   1- -      (1-999)
         1st page to include footer:   1- -      (1-999)
```

5. Type a document name (let's assign the name FILE as an example) and then move the cursor by pressing the arrow keys (don't press ENTER) to the appropriate space to type author, operator, and comments, all of which are optional, and to change the printer type, the lines per page, pitch, line spacing and others, if necessary. Press ENTER. The system displays a screen page as follows:

Ghost cursor

Tab line (- - - I- 2 - - - + - - - - -3 - - - - + - - - - -4 - - - - + - - - - -5 - - - - + - - - - -)

Status   FILE   Pg:1   Ln:1   Pos:1.8   Pitch:PS LS:1
line

6. Depress the control key @ and type T for adjusting tab line. A ghost cursor will be shown with a ? question mark. As the previous example show, the status line indicates FILE as the document name just assigned, page number 1, line number 1, ghost cursor position at 1.8, pitch proportional, and 1 line space. To adjust tab line, move the cursor to the position and type (for left margin,) for right mar-

gin, + for tab line, and I for indention. After the tab is adjusted, press ENTER to return. Depress the control key and type Q to quit the document, ready for conversion.

It must be noted that the information saved in the SAVE file (assigned name) in the Videotex Plus diskette is in ASCII format, which must be converted to the Scripsit format in order to edit and re-format the information for printing. Steps of the converting process are as follows:

1. Insert the Videotex Plus diskette where the SAVE file is stored in drive 1.

2. Insert the SuperScripsit diskette where the document is assigned. File as its name in drive 0.

3. Use procedure III, steps 2 and 3, mentioned before to be in word processing mode.

4. The computer displays SCRIPSIT word processing as shown in procedure III.

    Type A for ASCII text conversion utility.

5. The computer will display FROM WHICH FORMAT DO YOU WISH TO CONVERT (SCRIPSIT/ASCII)? Type A to convert a file from ASCII to SCRIPSIT.

6. The computer will respond with NAME OF SCRIPSIT FILE. Type FILE as the file name just assigned and press ENTER.

7. The computer displays NAME OF ASCII FILE. Type SAVE:1 (the file name assigned to the Videotex Plus diskette; the use of :1 indicates that the SAVE file is in drive 1). Press ENTER.

The program performs the conversion and creates the SCRIPTSIT document file named FILE. The user may then edit, re-format, and print it in the SCRIPSIT word processing format.

For printing the document, depress the control key and type P. The computer will display

```
* * * * * * * * SCRIPSIT – PRINT TEXT OPTIONS * * * * * * *
```

Document name:	- - - - - - - - - - - - - - - - - - -	
Paper size:	66	(1-99)
Pause between pages:	Y	(Yes/No)
Begin numbering as page:	1- - -	(1-9999)
Method of justification:	P	(Proportional//Mono/None)
Number of copies:	1-	(1-99)
Display codes:	N	(Yes/No)
Suppress widow lines:	N	(Yes/No)
Column to start printing:	1- -	(1-132)

Reproduced with permission by Radio Shack

If no change in text options is made, simply press ENTER to print the document. After printing is completed, the computer returns to display the text. The user may quit the word processing mode by depressing the control key and typing Q. The computer responds with TRSDOC READY. The user may remove diskettes from the drives and turn off the power.

NOTES

1. 15 *Information Hotline* (1983) 19.

2. Susan Casbon, "Online Searching with a Microcomputer—Getting Started," 7 *Online* (1983) 42-43.

3. Jeffery K. Pemberton, "Should Next Terminal Be a Computer?" in *Online Terminal/Microcomputer Guide and Directory, 1982-83* (Weston, Conn.: Online, 1982) p. 29.

4. Greg Zeck, "Communication Software," 1 *Linkup* (1983) 28-29.

5. Ron Kaminecki, "Online Searching and the Microcomputer" paper presented at the 1983 Minnesota Online User Group Conference, April 15, 1983, p. 9. *See also Making the DIALOG Connection with a Personal Computer* (1983, a DIALOG flyer) and *Stepping Up to a Micro* (1983, a SDC flyer).

6. D. M. Nicholson and J. H. Petrie, "Using a General Purpose Microcomputer for Online Searching," 36 *Aslib Proceedings* (1983) 254-57.

7. Greg Zeck, "Communication Software."

8. Weston, Conn.: Online, 1983, 346p. and addendum. Updated by supplements in 1983 and 1984.

9. Fort Worth, Tx.: Tandy Corp., 1981.

10. *Videotex Plus User's Guide*, Fort Worth, Tx.: Tandy Corp., 1983. A part of Videotex Plus Communication Software for Information Services and Computer Systems.

11. *SuperScripsit Reference Manual*, Fort Worth, Tx.: Tandy Corp., 1982, 144p.; *SuperScriptsit Figures Book*, Fort Worth, Tx.: Tandy Corp., 1982, loose-leaf.

14

Standardization of Searching Diversities

The three major online services, DIALOG, SDC's ORBIT, and BRS, do not differ in the concept of searching and the basic searching features. Online searching is characterized by free-text and multifaceted other-than-subject searching. In DIALOG and ORBIT, the former refers to the Basic Index searching and the latter to the Additional Index searching. BRS does not make such a distinction, but the two methods of searching are available. The basic searching operation in all three systems is easy to grasp. The use of free-text subject searching is particularly simple. Yet, in operation details, each system differs from the other in access, protocol, command language, output, and format. For search system comparisons, reference may be made to a recent bibliography compiled by Pugh and John.[1] Some diversities in both commands and operations are worth noting.

DIVERSITIES

Different Procedure for Access

Each system uses its own procedure for connection, called "logon" in DIALOG, "login" in ORBIT, and "sign-in" in BRS. ORBIT features a special security code that is required for login as a double protection against unauthorized use. After logoff from DIALOG, ORBIT, and BRS, the terminal can be connected via telecommunication to another system with no need to dial again. But, the access procedure differs as mentioned in chapter eight.

Different Commands with the Same Results

This can be found in the logoff and search procedures.

Systems Commands	DIALOG	ORBIT	BRS
Logoff	LOGOFF	STOP Y or LOGOFF Y	..OFF
Search	SELECT	FIND (optional)	..SEARCH (optional; if not in a search mode)
	SuperSELECT	AUDIT*	..SET DE-TAIL = ON*

*Has to be cancelled if not needed.

All three systems use logical operators: AND, OR, and NOT. If a search statement consists of more than one kind of logical operator, the sequence of execution in DIALOG is this: NOT's are executed first followed by AND, and OR's are executed last. In ORBIT and BRS, AND's and NOT's are executed according to their order, and OR's are executed last. An XOR operator is available in BRS. The XOR is used to instruct the system to search documents with either A or B present, but not both. The same result can be achieved by using (OR) NOT (AND) operators, called the NAND strategy in ORBIT.

In DIALOG, ORBIT, and BRS, documents in either consecutive or non-consecutive order, or both, can be displayed online. For instance, all systems can be instructed to retrieve documents 1-3, 5, and 9-10 from the search results. It appears that ORBIT offers the most varied options of display. Numbers of items to be displayed can be entered before or after field(s), and field displays can be requested in any order.

Similar Features with No Compatible Results

One example is the display of alphabetically related search terms. In DIALOG, the EXPAND command will display up to 50. In ORBIT, the use of the NEIGHBOR command will display up to 30 terms. BRS will respond to ROOT by displaying up to 100 terms. One important feature of ORBIT's NEIGHBOR command is that each term is indicated by a qualifier. Both DIALOG and ORBIT can limit their display of terms to a specified field.

Although DIALOG and ORBIT can both truncate characters within a word, there is a difference. In ORBIT, the number of characters truncated within a word can be either specified or unspecified. The number of characters to be truncated within a word must be specified in DIALOG.

Different Features with Compatible Results

The following chart indicates the different features with compatible results.

Systems Features	DIALOG	ORBIT	BRS
Full-text searching	(W) For searching terms in either side of the operator to be adjacent and in the specified order	String Search (W) or ADJ or W/O or (O)	ADJ
	(nW) For terms with a specified distance, such as one or two intervening words	(nW) or W/n or (n)	
	(F) For terms to be within the same field, in any order	(F) or W/F	SAME
	(C) For terms in the same document or AND	(C) or (R) or W/R or AND	AND
	(L)	Index term searching SENSEARCH For terms in the same sentence (S) or W/S	Descriptor searching WITH

Systems Features	DIALOG	ORBIT	BRS
Erasing search retrieval restriction	BEGIN	ERASEALL BACKUP n	..PURGE ..PURGE n
Date ranging	SELECT PY = or DT = L n/ PY = year:Py = year	AND FROM year-year AND GREATER THAN year AND LESS THAN year	..LIMIT /n yr gt year ..LIMIT/n yr lt year ..LIMIT/n eq year (also directly searchable)
Update	SELECT or LIMITn/ UD = year UD = year:UD = year	AND year/up	..LIMIT/n up gt (code) ..LIMIT/n up lt (code) ..LIMIT/n up eq (code)
Language	SELECT or LIMIT n/ (language)	AND (Language)/ LA	..L/n lg eq ..L/n lg ne (also directly searchable)
Restriction before search	LIMITALL LIMITALL/ALL (for cancellation)	SUBHEADING SUBHEADING CANCEL/ (for cancelation)	
Display of terms	PAGE	DOWN	
result	ORBIT	Tailored print (to print fields specified)	Tailored print (to print paragraph specified)

Features Not Common to All Systems

Each system has its own unique features, some of which are presented as follows:

Systems Features (Y/N)	DIALOG	ORBIT	BRS
Online thesaurus	Y	N	N
SELECT STEPS search	Y	N	N
Field search (qualifier before the word/term)	N	Y	N
Field search (qualifiers used with set numbers)	N	N	Y
Negative qualifier operator	N	N	Y
LINK and LINK NOT	N	Y	N
Left side truncation	N	Y	)N
Select after each word/term expanded required	Y	N	Y
Display of terms UP	N	Y	N
Erase of search (number specified)	N	Y	Y
Online sorting	Y	N	N
Print trial	N	Y	N
Print scan	N	Y	N

Although free-text and controlled vocabulary search are provided by all three systems, the availability of controlled vocabulary search varies. Using NTIS is an example, mutiword controlled vocabulary can be directly searched in both DIALOG and BRS. In ORBIT, however, to search controlled vocabulary terms in the NTIS database, one must use /IT qualifier; direct search of multiword as controlled vocabulary is not currently available.

In the system itself, operation discrepancies and lack of uniformity are also common. As mentioned in chapter eight, each document contained in the file is divided into a number of fields or paragraphs. In the Basic Index searching, search of words can be limited by the field, such as the field of title, abstract, or index terms. A user may also acquire the search result by using the Additional Index. The Additional Index refers to all searchable fields that are not part of the Basic Index. Though no distinction is made between the Basic and Additional Indexes in BRS mentioned earlier, most of the fragments of a document, that is, paragraphs, are searchable. There is, however, no consistency in the availability and the value of fields. For instance, the saving search cannot be used indiscriminately to repeat a completed search from one file to another, if field or paragraph qualifiers have been applied. The saving search with a field limitation must be used in files in which the same field is available. Variations in the availability and value of fields exist in each system.

FIELD VARIATIONS

Fields in DIALOG

In DIALOG, File 222 (CLAIMS/CITATIONS) does not provide free-text searching features. Free-text searching is available in File 43 (ADTRACK), yet no fields in the Basic Index are provided. The number of fields varies in each file from one field in File 105 (Foreign Traders Index) to as many as 7 in File 100 (Disclosure II). An examination of 144 files (excluding the ontap files for training and File 411, a master index which does not specify files) reveals that there are 67 fields in the Basic Index. Of the 67 fields, the two fields, /DE and /TI, are provided in most files. Following is a listing of fields in the Basic Index available in most files.

All fields are represented by a two-character code preceded by a slash /. Occasionally, the same code is used to designate different fields. For instance, the code /GS represents four different fields: (1) auxiliary descriptor, (2) genus species, (3) geographic descriptor/name, and (4) tag. The code /NA is also used for four different fields: (1) named person, (2) officer

Suffix	Field Name	Number of Files	Percentage
/DE	Descriptor	113	79.8
/TI	Title	107	74.3
/AB	Abstract	85	59.0
/DF	Descriptor full	79	54.8
/ID	Identifier	49	34.0
/IF	Identifier full	31	21.5
/CS	Corporate source	23	15.9

names, (3) school name, and (4) sub-file name.

Of the 144 files examined, there are over 400 fields in the Additional Index. All fields in the Additional Index are represented by a two-character code followed by an equal sign =. Here are fields in the Additional Index available in a number of files.

Prefix	Field Name	Number of Files	Percentage
UD =	Update	107	73.2
AU =	Author	97	66.4
PY =	Publication year	74	50.6
JN =	Journal name	69	47.2
LA =	Language	56	38.3
DT =	Document type	55	37.6
CS =	Corporate source	41	28.0
JA =	Journal announcement	35	23.9
CO =	CODEN	32	21.9
PU =	Publisher	31	21.2
PN =	Patent number	26	17.8
SH =	Section heading code	22	15.0
AN =	Accession number	21	14.3
BN =	ISBN	10	13.6

The same two-character code may designate different fields. The code CC= designates eleven fileds, CN= ten different fields, and AC= six different fields. Fields available in each file vary, ranging from six fields in File 113 (Standards and Specifications) to eighty-nine fields in File 100.

Fields in ORBIT

The situation in ORBIT is more complicated. In the first place, each field in the Basix Index and in the Additional Index is represented by a code preceded by a slash /. The code /IT for an index term is used in the Basic Index and in the Additional Index as well. Second, the number of characters used for the field code varies from one to four characters and includes character and number combinations. Third, the same code is used to designate different fields. Last but not least, the same file uses different codes to designate the same field. File NUC/CODES uses codes, /AN, and /AV, for availability (accession number).

In ORBIT 72 files were examined excluding the special files developed by ORBIT, such as ORBCHEM; 9 files do not specify the fields of the Basic Index. They are AGRICOLA, BIOSIS, CIN, CRECORD, ENERGYLINE, GRANTS, NTIS, APPERCHEM, and USCLASS. No basic index is available in six files: CHEMDEX, CRDS, PESTDOC, RINGDOC, VETDOC, and WPI/WPIL. The remaining 57 files give a total of 44 fields. The fields of title, index terms, and index words are provided by most files as shown:

Qualifier	Field	Number of Files	Percentage
/TI	Title	50	87.7
/IT	Index term	47	82.5
/IW	Words from index terms	43	75.4

ORBIT's Additional Index has 156 fields in the 72 files that were examined. The following are fields in the Additional Index available in many files.

Qualifier	Field Name	Number of Files	Percentage
/AN	Accession number	63	87.5
/UP	Update	50	69.4
/AU	Author	44	61.1
/OS	Organizational source	38	52.7
/CC	Category codes	34	47.2
/DT	Document type	30	44.4
/LA	Language	27	37.5
/FS	File segment	18	25.0
/JC	Journal CODEN/code	16	22.2
/JC	Journal citation name	12	16.6
/PN	Patent/priority number	10	13.8

Quite a few files have only one field. Searching by fields in those files is extremely limited.

Fields in BRS

In BRS, 47 files examined excluding 4 BRS-generated files, provide a total of 208 fields. One field, .IN., has ten different values, ranging from author affiliation to work location. Different values are also found in many other fields: .PD. has four and .SO. has five. Below are the fields available in a number of files.

Qualifier	Field Name	Number of Files	Percentage
.AN.	Accession number	39	83
.TI.	Title	36	77
.AU.	Author	32	68
.AB.	Abstract	31	66
.DE.	Descriptor	24	51
.YR.	Publication year	19	40
.SO.	Source	18	38

Formats in Three Systems

There is not much discrepancy in format, though the number of formats available and format content differ with databases. Taking DIALOG for example, there are nine formats. Not all databases have the nine formats, nor is the record content of each format standardized. Formats 2, 3, 4, 6, 7, and 8 all contain bibliographic citations. Title is found in formats 2, 3, 4, and 7. Formats 3, 4, 6, 8, and 9 give the full record; but the content of the full record varies. Format 1 is an exception; it refers exclusively to the DIALOG accession number. It must be noted, however, that other formats also contain the DIALOG accession number, such as formats 4, 6, and 9.

The record content of each format varies. The format and its availability in a number of files are listed:

Format	Number of Files
1	all
2	37
3	20
4	24
5	4
6	23
7	14
8	19
9	4

Format 2 has the most variations, ranging from "basic company information," "class code, level, and subclass title," to "topic and codes."

STANDARDIZATION OF DIVERSITIES

For ease of use of different systems and a quick look at the varying operations, in 1979 the University of Pittsburgh's On-Line Bibliographic and Information Systems Training Center published a legal-size sheet comparing twenty-eight functions of the three systems.[2] In 1980, the California Library Authority for Systems and Services (CLASS) released reference charts of the most heavily used databases, mentioned earlier in chapter two. Conger also prepared a chart, a summary of commands and other features in forty-one categories of seven systems, including DIALOG, ORBIT, NLM, and BRS.[3]

All these publications are designed to compare the features of different systems, not to solve the problem of diversity. Efforts have been made to set standards. Atherton suggested three steps to reduce variety and diversity: (1) standards for the technical terms and symbols used in the functional areas of interactive retrieval systems; identified four functional areas: search/query negotiation, instructional/tutorial, output, and supervisory/operational control; (2) standards for a code of practice for access, message transmission, and mode switching; and (3) dimensional standards for interchangeability among systems.[4] In Clayton's view, an intermediary to perform the translation and merging function is a true standardization.[5] Williams also suggested the development of more user-oriented transparent systems, that is, a system containing the necessary converters or transistors to help the user understand the difference.[6]

In 1980, Subcommittee Z-39 G (Standard Terms, Abbreviations, and Symbols for Use in Interactive Information Retrieval) of the American National Standard Committee X-39 was formed for the purpose of reducing existing diversity in the command languages presently in use.[7] At the same time, an ISO Technical Committee 46/Sub-Committee 4/Working Group 5 was created for the same purpose.[8] The Z-39G Subcommittee consists of representatives of the major vendors, a representative from database suppliers, a researcher in online retrieval, and users-trainers in this area. Four functional areas are categorized: (1) operation control, (2) search formulation control (and access points), (3) output control, and (4) user assistance: information and instruction.[9]

Diversity in operations, in many instances, serves no meaningful purpose. There is no reason why, for instance, the operation of logon and logoff cannot be standardized. Klugman has questioned the validity of having different commands for logoff, varied symbols for truncation, and the inconsistent format in citation.[10] The lack of consistency and standardization not only among the systems but also within the system itself is one area that most users consider an inconvenience. A user must remember different commands and features in switching from one system to another.

Standardization can only be achieved by voluntary co-operation and constant improvement among the systems. There has been, however, noticeable progress in this direction. The ORBIT system has improved its service and reduced diversities by introducing proximity searching, LOGOFF as an alternative to STOP, and the AUDIT command, comparable to DIALOG's SuperSELECT; BRS has taken a significant step to standardize its author searching. For ease of use, these are good but not good enough. Though complete standardization of searching operations remains a major task to accomplish, the following should be given high priority as a first step to overcoming diversity:

1. Standardization of logon and logoff commands
2. Standardization of the keyboard functions of the terminal
3. Standardization of the break function
4. Standardization of controlled vocabulary searching.
5. Consistency of field or paragraph content and designation in each system
6. Consistency of full-text operator searching
7. Standardization of truncation and its symbols
8. Standardization of alphabetical listing of terms in a dictionary order
9. Consistency of citation format
10. Standardization of author search
11. Uniformity of printing request in consecutive and non-consecutive order
12. Availability of tailored display in all systems

NOTES

1. Jean W. Pugh and Stephanie C. John, "A Bibliography of Database and Search System Comparisons," 6 *Online* (1982) 42-54.

2. Sharon Cline Farmer, *Quick Reference Guide to DIALOG, ORBIT, and BRS* (1979).

3. Lucinda D. Conger, *Online Command Chart*, 2d ed. (Weston, Conn.: Online, 1982) 19p.

4. Pauline Atherton, "Standards for a User-System Interface Language in On-line Retrieval Systems," 2 *Online Review* (1978) 60.

5. Audrey Clayton, "Factors Affecting Future Online Services," 5 *Online Review* (1981) 296.

6. Martha E. Williams, "Online Retrieval—Today and Tomorrow," 2 *Online Review* (1978) 360-61.

7. Pauline A. Cochrane, "Can a Standard for an Online Command Language Be Developed?" 7 *Online* (1983) 36.

8. Ibid.

9. Ibid.

10. Simone Klugman, "Online Information Retrieval Interface with Traditional Reference Services," 4 *Online Review* (1980) 271.

Bibliography

MONOGRAPHS

Atherton, P. and Christian, R. W. *Libraries and Online Services.* White Plains, N.Y.: Knowledge Industry, 1977.

Bringing Information to People, Dublin, Ohio: OCLC, 1981.

BRS Directory and Database Catalog. Latham, N.Y.: Bibliographic Retrieval Services, 1983.

BRS System Reference Manual. Scotia, N.Y.: Bibliographic Retrieval Services, 1981.

Byerly, G. *Online Searching: A Dictionary and Bibliographic Guide.* Littleton, Colo.: Libraries Unlimited, 1983.

Chen, C. and Schweizer, S. *Online Bibliographic Searching: A Learning Manual.* New York: Neal-Schuman, 1981.

Chicago Online Users Introductory Guide. Chicago: COLUG, 1978.

Christian, R. W. *The Electronic Library: Bibliographic Data Bases, 1975 1976.* White Plains, N.Y.: Knowledge Industry, 1975.

Conger, L. D. *Online Command Chart.* 2d ed. Weston, Conn: Online, 1982.

CompuServe Information Service User's Guide. Fort Worth, Tex., Tandy Corp. 1983.

CompuServe Starter Kit. Columbus, Ohio: CompuServe, 1982.

DIALOG Database Catalog. Palo Alto, Calif.: DIALOG Information Services, July 1983.

Directory and Database Catalog. Latham, N.Y.: BRS, 1983.

Directory of On-line Information Resources. 10th ed. Rockville, MD.: CKS Press, 1982.

Dow Jones Information Service User's Guide. Fort Worth, Tex.: Tandy Corp. 1983.

The Dow Jones News/Retrieval Fact Finder. Princeton, N.J.: Dow Jones News/Retrieval, 1982.

The Dow Jones News/Retrieval Fact Finder: Supplement. Princeton, N.J.: Dow Jones News/Retrieval, [n.d.]

Dow Jones Text-Search Services User's Guide. Princeton, N.J.: Dow Jones News/Retrieval, [1984]

Encyclopedia of Library and Information Science. New York: Marcel Dekker, 1968-1983.

Farmer, S. C. *Quick-Search: Cross-System Database Search Guides.* San Jose, Calif.: California Library Authority for Systems and Services, 1980.

Fenichel, C. H., and Harter, S. P. *Survey of Online Searching Instruction in Schools of Library and Information Science.* Dublin, Ohio: OCLC, 1981.

Fenichel, C. H., and Hogan, T. H. *Online Searching: A Primer.* Marlton, N.J.: Learned Information, 1981.

Financial and Economic Data Bases Reference Guide. Toronto, Canada: I. P. Sharp, 1983.

Foskett, A. C. *The Subject Approach to Information.* 4th ed. Hamden, Conn.: Shoe String, 1982.

Gerrie, B. *Online Information Systems: Use and Operating Characteristics, Limitations.* Arlington, Va.: Information Resources Press, 1983.

Gorman, M., and Winkler, P. W., *Anglo-American Cataloging Rules.* 2d ed. Chicago: American Library Association, 1978.

Guide to DIALOG Searching. Palo Alto, Calif.: DIALOG Information Retrieval Services, 1979.

A Guide to SEC Corporate Filings. Bethesda, Md.: Disclosure, 1982.

Hall, J. L. *On-line Information Retrieval, 1965-1976.* London: Aslib, 1977.

On-line Information Retrieval Sourcebook. London: Aslib, 1977.

Hall, J. L., and Brown, M. J. *Online Bibliographic Databases: An International Directory.* 2d ed. London: Aslib, 1981.

Hall, J. L., and Dewe, A. *Online Information Retrieval, 1976-1979: An International Bibliography.* London: Aslib, 1980.

Hawkins, D. T., *Online Information Retrieval Bibliography, 1964-1979.* New York: Learned Information, 1980.

Henry, W. M., et al. *Online Searching: An Introduction.* Boston: Butterworths, 1980.

Hoover, R. E. *The Library and Information Manager's Guide to Online Services.* White Plains, N.Y.: Knowledge Industry, 1980.

_____.*Online Search Strategies.* White Plains, N.Y.: Knowledge Industry, 1982.

Houghton, B., and Convey, J. *On-line Information Retrieval Systems.* Hamden, Conn.: Linnet Books, 1977.

Information Industry Market Place: An International Directory of Information Products and Services. New York: Bowker, 1981.

Katz, B., and Clifford, A. *Reference and Online Service Handbook: Guidelines, Policies, and Procedures for Libraries.* New York: Neal-Schuman, 1982.

Kent, A., and Garvin, T. J. *The On-line Revolution in Libraries.* New York: Marcel Dekker, 1978.

Kruzas, A. T., and Schmittroth, J. *Encyclopedia of Information Systems and Services.* 4th ed. Detroit: Gale Research, 1981.

Lockheed Missiles and Space Company. *Subject Guide to DIALOG Databases.* Palo Alto, Calif., Oct. 1978 and April 1979.

Lynch, M. J. *Financing Online Search Services in Publicly Supported Libraries.* Chicago: American Library Association, 1981.

MAGIC User's Manual. Toronto, Ontario, Canada: I. P. Sharp, 1980.

Malony, J. J.. ed. *Online Searching Technique and Management.* Chicago: American Library Association, 1983.

Management Contents Data Base Thesaurus. Northbrook, Ill.: Management Contents, 1980.

Mathies, L. M., and Watson, P. G. *Computer-Based Reference Service.* Chicago: American Library Association, 1973.

Max, D. M. *On-line Bibliographic Search Services.* Washington, D. C.: Association of Research Libraries, 1976.

Meadow, C. T., and Cochrane, P. A. *Basics of Online Searching.* New York: John Wiley, 1981.

Online Micro-Software Guide and Directory, 1983-84. Weston, Conn.: Online, 1982.

Online Terminal/Microcomputer Guide and Directory, 1982-83. 3rd ed. Weston, Conn.: Online, 1982.

ORBIT Database. Santa Monica, Calif.: System Development Corporation, May 1983.

ORBIT User Manual. Rev. ed. Santa Monica, Calif.: System Development Corp., 1982.

Palmer, R. C. *Online Reference and Information Retrieval.* Littleton, Colo.: Libraries Unlimited, 1983.

Predicasts Terminal System User Manual. Cleveland, Ohio: Predicasts, 1980.

Quick Reference Guide. Santa Monica, Calif.: System Development Corp., [n.d]

Schmittroth, J., and Maxfield, D. M. eds. *Online Database Search Service Directory.* 1st ed. Detroit: Gale Research, 1983.

Schneider, J. H., et al. *Survey of Commercially Available Computer-Readable Bibliographic Data Bases.* Washington, D. C. : American Society for Information Science, 1973.

Simonton, W., ed. *Information Retrieval Today*. Minneapolis, Minn.: University of Minnesota, 1963.

The Source User's Manual. McLean, Virg.: Source Telecomputing Corp., 1983.

SuperScripsit Figures Book. Fort Worth, Tx.: Tandy Corp., 1982.

SuperScripsit Reference Manual. Fort Worth, Tx.: Tandy Corp., 1982.

Tauber, M., and Associates. *Studies in Coordinate Indexing Documentation*. Washington, D. C.: Documentation, Inc., 1953.

Telecommunications and Libraries: A Primer for Librarians and Information Managers. White Plains, N.Y.: Knowledge Industry, 1981.

Thesaurus of ERIC Descriptors. Rev. ed. Phoenix, Ariz.: Oryx Press, 1980.

Thurman, K. K. *Self-Instructional Workbook*. Santa Monica, Calif.: System Development Corp., 1982.

U. S. Department of Health, Education, and Welfare. Public Health Service. National Institute of Health. *National Library of Medicine Guide to MEDLARS Service*. Washington, D. C.: Superintendent of Documents, 1970.

U. S. Library of Congress. Subject Cataloging Division. *Library of Congress Subject Headings*. 9th ed. Washington, D. C.: Library of Congress, 1980.

Videotex Plus User's Guide. Fort Worth, Tex.: Tandy Corp., 1983.

Wanger, J., et al. *Impact of on-line Retrieval Services: A Survey of Users, 1974-1975*. Santa Monica, Calif.: System Development Corporation, 1976.

Wessel, A. E. *Computer-Aided Information Retrieval*. Los Angeles, Calif.: Melville, 1975.

Westley, B. M. *Sears List of Subject Headings*. 12th ed. New York: H. W. Wilson, 1982.

Williams, M. E. *Computer Readable Data Bases: A Directory and Data Sourcebook*. White Plains, N.Y.: Knowledge Industry, 1982.

SERIALS

Advanced Technology Libraries
Advances in Librarianship
American Libraries
American Society for Informtion Science. *Bulletin*
American Society for Information Science. *Journal*
American Society for Information Science *Proceedings*
Annual Review of Library and Information Science
Aslib Proceedings

BRS Bulletin
Business Publications Index and Abstracts
Cataloging and Classification Quarterly
Chronolog
College and Research Libraries
CompuServe Update
Database Alert
Database; The Magazine of Database and Review
Database Update
Datamation
Directory of Online Databases
Dowline: The Magazine of Dow Jones News/Retrieval
Information Hotline
Information Today; The Newspaper for Users and Producers of Electronic Information Services
Information Reports and Bibliographies
Information Technology and Libraries
Journal of Education for Librarianship
Journal of Library Automation
Journal of Library and Information Science
Legal Economics
Library Journal
Library Systems Network
Linkup
Medical Library Association. *Bulletin*
Online; The Management of Online Information Systems
Online Review; The International Journal of Online Information Systems
Perspectives in Computing
Reference Service Review
RQ
Searchlight
Source World
Special Libraries
Today; The Videotex/Computer Magazine
Wilson Library Bulletin

Index

About the Author

TZE-CHUNG LI is Dean and Professor at Rosary College Graduate School of Library and Information Science. He is the author of *Social Science Reference Sources: A Practical Guide* (Greenwood Press, 1980), *A Manual for Basic DIALOG Searching*, and numerous articles dealing with librarianship and information science.